Perspectives on the Information Society

Edited by Jonathan Bishop – Foreworded by Piet Kommers

Editor: Jonathan Bishop
Foreword: Piet Kommers
Afterword: Jonathan Bishop
Reviewers: Jason W. Barratt, Jonathan Bishop, Ashu M. G. Solo
Contributors: Fancis Iloani Arinze, Jonathan Bishop, Ashu M.G. Solo, Nuhu Gapsiso, Ivan Mugabi, Sabiiti Mulema, Hirwa Ramadhan, Anna Y Ni, Samuel Sudhakar, Shefali Virkar, Joseph Wilson, Jake Zhu

Published in Great Britain and Ireland by The Crocels Press Limited of Ty Morgannwg, PO Box 674, Swansea, Glamorganshire, SA1 9NN, Wales.

ISBN: 9781785180071

Contents

Foreword

Piet Kommers

In the book before you, you will get absorbed in the thematic in how far what cloud services need to be adopted for corporate functions. Its thematic exemplars are:

- The intriguing processes of trolling and lulz for creating well-organized chaos by hacktivists and cyber-protestors in hyper-networked modern-day civil societies.

- The question in how far bio-tracking like chipping animals is still compatible with the growing awareness of animal rights and animal privacy.

- Retaliatory feedback as a major problem due to the ability to post content to the Internet without being caught.

- The counter side of increasing abuse that gave force to the Government's attempts at censoring social media and its desire for regulation of social media through a specific legislation rather than censorships.

- Citizens' journalism via the web and its credibility.

Additionally, you will find the chapters on electronic banking, fighting online defamation, doxing, and impersonation, and finally the evaluation of two successful and two failed multi-organisation e-learning software development projects using service-orientated approaches.

They have in common that new ICT functionalities proliferate far beyond the scope of its initial functionality and in fact needs a secondary design in order to embed its social and societal ethical application. This holds for instance for new electronic banking protocols but also for preventing running out of hand social arousal, scapegoating, etc. Finally, in Jonathan Bishop's chapter, the focus is on the need to take into account the organisational culture, including organisational architecture, of all organisations participating in a project, even where a common project management methodology is used.

The landscape of new web-based bottom-up citizen actions triggers a clearer awareness on ethics and jurisprudence. It also opens the question in how far our shared sense of common reality awareness is suffering from media-affordances and the trend to personalise world views and disentangle fake news.

Researchers lately report that truth is key to normal human interactions and consider how society might be losing its sense of shared reality. How social media and the overall envelope of social constructivism may hamper this consensus is the main topic in the book before you.

May it help to convert hesitance and doubt into critical confidence in your professional and private networks.

Dr Piet Kommers

University of Twente

Information Society Services

Moving to the Cloud: A Case of Migrating Information Systems in a Public University

Samuel Sudhakar, Anna Y Ni, Jake Zhu

Abstract

Cloud computing, being simple, cheap, and scalable, is a groundbreaking technology that has transformed the deployment of information systems. This manuscript describes the rationale, process, and impact of a public university's cloud migration experience. The case study indicates the cloud is a feasible alternative for public institutions and provides lessons for similar organizations seeking for best practices. The manuscript recommends that future studies in cloud migration may explore mechanisms to quantify such costs to enable a more comprehensive economic impact examination. Although the manuscript highlighted many important issues that arise when dealing with cloud migration, many issues remain open for future research.

Introduction

Cloud technologies have matured significantly over the past decade, giving consumers and organizations confidence in pursuing them as viable alternatives to on-premise systems. According to a 2013 study by Gartner, information technology (IT) executives from around the world ranked cloud computing among the top technologies in 2013 (McDonald & Aron 2013). Public institutions of higher education have openly embraced and adopted cloud technologies over the past five years as a way of enhancing the services they provide to their students, faculty, and staff while reducing fixed operating expenses.

Although there are a handful of studies that investigate the migration of existing information systems to the cloud (e.g., Babar and Chauhan 2011; Khajeh-Hosseini, Greenwood, and Sommerville 2016; Sriam and Khajeh-Hosseini 2010), few of them examine the issue in the public sector institutional environment. In addition, little has been empirically learned about the implications of cloud computing from an economic or organizational standpoint.

Adopting the lens of economic impact theorists, this study identifies the potential of cloud services to reduce fixed operating expenses at public four-year educational institutions for systems they maintain on premises and examines California State University San Bernardino's rationale, as well as the economic and organizational impacts of migrating its existing information systems from an in-house data center to the cloud. The main focus of this case study was on the financial, technical, and organizational issues that decision makers should consider in the process of cloud migration.

In the following section, the paper introduces cloud computing and its potential benefits and risks. The discussion of theoretical framework lays the rationale for the study. The research method section describes the approach used to collect and analyze data. The case description traces the migration of three systems to the cloud and is followed by the analysis of organizational impacts. Practical lessons are offered to institutions who are considering migration. The paper concludes by discussing the contributions of the case study and looking at future work.

Cloud Computing

Cloud computing refers to the use of the Internet to access data and programs from servers maintained by various service providers across the globe that are connected to the Internet (Rajaram 2014). Generally, there are three main categories of cloud services:

- Software as a Service (SaaS): where providers offer the point of access, usually via web browsers, to software running on servers. Compared to traditional in-house software management, SaaS reduces the cost of software ownership, such as the cost of software licenses as well as payroll to technical staff for software installation, upgrade, and maintenance.

- Infrastructure as a Service (IaaS): where providers give their clients direct access to their cloud servers, storage, and other associated resources via dashboard and/or Application Program Interface (API). Users of IaaS gain access to a much higher level of scalability as well as similar technologies and capabilities of a traditional data center without investing in the physical infrastructure or the management and maintenance of it.

- Platform as a Service (PaaS): where providers provide a platform, or a set of tools and service, on which software can be developed and deployed. It allows users to focus on the application development of their product or service, leaving management of the server-client environment, including the operating system, server software, supporting server hardware, and network infrastructure, to the providers.

Of these three cloud service categories, SaaS has gained the most adoption, particularly SaaS hosted on the public cloud. Gartner predicts that public cloud services will grow 17 percent worldwide. Infrastructure as a Service (IaaS) will grow by 42.8 percent, followed by SaaS at 21.7 percent (Spadafora 2016).

The primary advantage of cloud computing is that resources available on the Internet can be accessed from anywhere, at any time, through any device or platform. Cloud computing offers enterprises access to a multitude of services at very little upfront cost (Lee & Mautz 2012). Organizations can be proactive in delivering value to their customers by launching new initiatives via the cloud much faster than they can on-premise. A software download service, for example, can be implemented via the cloud in less than two weeks while it may take several months to purchase and implement the solution in-house. While this makes organizations agile in delivering products and services to their customers, there are inherent risks involved as well. According to Newman (2014), despite the wide use of cloud services by organizations, the expectations of trustworthiness placed on providers may be unrealistic.

The proliferation of mobile smart devices over the past five years has created an expectation among consumers for all services to be available to them on their mobile devices in the form of an app or, at the very least, mobile compatible. According to Pew Research, 68% of US adults have a smart phone, up from 35% just four years ago (Anderson 2015). Most cloud services are mobile-enabled which allows organizations to make their services available on mobile devices with fewer steps. The rise of mobile devices has contributed significantly to the rise of cloud computing adoption across industry spectrums (Ratten 2015).

Cloud computing has fundamentally changed the way organizations look at providing solutions to their stakeholders. In higher education, cloud computing not only allows institutions to bring services online at a faster pace, it also helps students, faculty, and staff acquire skills needed in the global marketplace (Isaila 2014). By bringing services to constituents at a faster pace and making them available anywhere, anytime, on any platform, creates the flexibility campus constituents need to work efficiently and productively. Cloud computing is an extension of how the Internet revolutionized the way we now work, play, and learn.

Cloud computing allows institutions of higher education to deliver services to their campus community at a lower cost and a faster pace than traditional methods. In addition, the cloud offers mobility, storage, and efficiency (Pardeshi 2014). An assessment of current and future trends and anticipated demands will allow institutions to strategically plan for the deployment of cloud services. Cloud computing as an added service will not necessarily reduce costs or add value to an institution. Cloud usage should be a part of an overall strategy that enhances the value IT organization provide to the campus while reducing fixed long-term operating expenses.

Higher education in the US is at the crossroads of disruption. The traditional higher education model is being challenged by the public, industry, and the government. Rising student debt, precipitated by the rising costs of higher education, has put public and private institutions of higher learning in the spotlight of public debate (Thelin 2015). Institutions need to find more efficient and cost-effective ways to deliver education or face extinction. Information technology can be used effectively by institutions of higher education to control costs (Kim 2012). The right kind of technology implemented for the right reason can reduce the costs of higher education and at the same time enhance student learning and success.

Given the inherent risks associated with using cloud services, especially when it involves storing and transacting with personal identification information (PII) such as social security numbers, date of births, credit card numbers, etc., one has to carefully evaluate the security and privacy of data they store on the cloud. Newman (2014) warns that many cloud providers don't take security risks seriously. It is up to the organization contracting with a provider to vet the cloud storage and transaction systems of that provider.

Providers of cloud services, such as Microsoft and Google, do so at no cost to educational institutions, thus making them attractive, as such organizations often strapped for budgets and human resources to maintain systems on premise. Higher education institutions look at clouds as a way to rationalize the way they steward their resources (Sultan 2010). Over the past decade, public cloud services such as Google for Education which offers a variety of services including e-mail, storage, synchronous communication platforms, and productivity applications, and Office 365 from Microsoft which has similar offerings at no cost, have been widely adopted by higher education institutions.

Economic Impact of IT investment

To examine the effect of cloud computing in public higher education, we investigate a specific public institution's rationale, process, and outcome of cloud migration, adopting the lens of economic impact theorists (Pleeter 1980). Economic impact theory studies the possible effects of an economic investment, estimating the possible returns to a business or community (Pleeter 1980). A number of authors have used economic impact theory in various fields, such as to evaluate the economic impact of tourism industry (Tyrrell & Johnston 2008), to examine the potential effects of lack of governmental investments in infrastructure (Sporri, Borsuk, Peters, & Reichert 2007), and to assess the effects of increased spending in higher education (Archibald & Feldman 2006). However, no prior studies have been identified for which the focus was on investing in IT infrastructure to improve operational efficiency and, therefore, cost control. To address this gap, economic impact theory was used in the study to inform the problem and interpret the results of the study in order to examine if the use of cloud technologies in higher education can lead to significant efficiency improvements and therefore, cost control. We also look beyond the economic impact to examine some of the organizational implications of cloud migration.

Research Methodology

This case study involves fieldwork of one of the authors who managed cloud migration at California State University San Bernardino between 2013 and 2016. All documents of the three systems under investigation were collected and analyzed. The analysis involves the following three phases:

Phase one: Identify the projects and trace the migration between systems.

Phase Two: Analyze the economic impact of the migration by calculating their infrastructure costs and comparing them with the costs of in-house hosting.

Phase Three: Investigate the broader implications for the organization by reviewing documents, identifying stakeholders, and interviewing related parties.

The Case of CSUSB

California State University San Bernardino (CSUSB) is one of 23 campuses among the largest public higher education system—California State University (CSU)—in the United States. Whereas the Governor of California appoints trustees who administer the 23-campus system, each campus governs its own policies within the statewide framework. As a center of intellectual and cultural activity in Inland Southern California, CSUSB opened its doors in 1965 to service a financially distressed region of California. The university serves more than 20,000 students each year and graduates about 4,000 students annually.

Akin to other CSU campuses, CSUSB enjoys a healthy technology budget. The central IT technology budget is around eight percent of the overall operating budget of the University. However, there is increasing pressure to optimize operations and reduce fixed operating expenses due to declining state support for the University budget and the constant expansion of student enrollment. Overall pressures facing the state such as declining revenues, increasing healthcare costs, and increasing cost of operations are impacting the CSU budget and, subsequently, the CSUSB budget.

The structure of decentralized IT units at the University, combined with redundant systems and software campus-wide, is contributing to the overall technology spend at the University. The University's central Information Technology Service (ITS) unit oversees a large number of decentralized IT units. Over the past three years, the central ITS unit has worked collaboratively with the decentralized units through a mechanism called the Technology Advisory Group (TAG) to standardize commodity computing systems and software and centralize college/departmental servers to the Data Center. However, there are still significant savings that can be realized by centralizing IT units across campus. The goal is to reduce the ITS budget overall by about 10% in the next two to three years.

The technology infrastructure at CSUSB is traditional and similar to most public institutions of higher learning in the United States. There is a central fiber network backbone that connects the different buildings and end user computers to the data center for access to premise-hosted applications and storage. The edge router, situated behind a firewall, connects the campus network to resources on the Internet. There are distributed server rooms across the campus in different college buildings that house discipline-specific applications and resources.

CSUSB, as compared with other CSU campuses (e.g., San Diego, Channel Islands, and Dominguez Hills), was slower in the adoption of cloud technologies. However, with new leadership provided by the CIO, CSUSB has become one of the leading adopters of cloud technologies in the state. One reason other state university are lagging behind in cloud adoption is a mindset among leadership and staff of IT organizations that the value they create for the university is based on the systems and software they maintain and optimize on premise for the campus community. They are concerned that once the software/system moves to the cloud, they would have no control over performance or security.

However, these fears are mitigated by the fact that cloud vendors and technologies have improved significantly over the past five years and, in many cases, maintaining certain mission critical systems are better on the cloud than on premise (Riahi 2015). Cloud vendors have invested heavily in performance and security technologies to become more marketable and relevant to the industry. Guleria, Sharma, and Arora (2012) argue the economies of scale that cloud technologies provide are not only significant but also optimal for institutions to pursue.

However, starting in 2013 with the new leadership and information technology services team, CSUSB has moved several of its services to the cloud, enhancing availability and stability of the systems, while at the same time reducing fixed operating costs. The leadership transition at CSUSB occurred at an optimal time. The CSU system was coming out of a significant recession during which the overall CSU budget declined by one third. Every organizational unit within CSUSB experienced funding cuts, and ITS did its best to keep systems operational for the campus community. Moreover, the ITS leadership team was quite settled in, with its leaders having spent at least two decades in the ITS organizational unit at CSUSB.

When the recession started impacting the CSUSB ITS budget in 2009, departments within ITS started competing with each other for funding and became siloed. Cloud technologies were not mature enough, nor did the campus community yet have confidence in the leadership of the ITS team to safely migrate applications to the cloud. When new leadership arrived and a new three-year technology plan was developed, the existing senior leadership took the opportunity to exercise their option for retirement. This gave the new CIO a chance to restructure the ITS Division (formerly IRT Division) repositioning it to provide the best possible class technology support services to students, faculty, and staff, to support faculty driven innovation and research, and to improve operational efficiency through business intelligence and analytics.

A new leadership team was brought on board to provide guidance and coordination for the newly formed departments focused on serving the campus community. The other significant change that occurred was a transitioning of academic technologies from under the leadership of the Associate Provost for Academic Affairs to the ITS Division.

Once the new leadership team was in place, they started working with the staff to build credibility and trust regarding the new direction of ITS. Assurances had to be given that if the staff retrained themselves on the new cloud technologies, their services would continue to remain valuable to the University.

Table 1. Systems Hosted In-House vs Over the Cloud

In-House Systems	Systems that are Considering the Cloud	Systems Over the Cloud
OnBase (Enterprise Workflow Management System) Medicat (Medical Management System) Help Desk Software	Active Directory Infrastructure Authentication Servers Help Desk Software	Office 365 Blackboard Web content Student Information System Human Resources Recruiting System (NeoGov)

The reasons for CSUSB to move applications to the cloud were multi-faceted. Below we describe the rationale and process of cloud migration by using three of the major applications the University moved to the cloud between 2013 and 2016.

Email system: Office 365

CSUSB's e-mail system has evolved over the years, from a Sun Microsystems-based system to a Microsoft Exchange environment.

The in-house maintained email system was facing service challenges. First, the cost and manpower required to maintain the existing system was continually rising with the volume of e-mails going through the system daily, a number which was approximately 77,500. Second, the lack of parameters governing the use of the existing e-mail system had caused the volume of e-mails and size of attachments to grow exponentially higher and higher.

Two options were considered to address these challenges. First, the University could continue to maintain the Exchange Server in-house and incur the cost of software licensing, hardware maintenance, and personnel costs, a figure now hovering around $50,000 a year. Second, the University could migrate to Microsoft-hosted Office 365, which, in addition to offering free hosting of e-mails, also offered a large range of other services, such as the Online Microsoft Office Suite, 1 TB of cloud-based storage, Sharepoint Online Collaboration, and video conferencing.

The second option was apparently more attractive. The University implemented a two-stage migration: 1) a migration of student accounts to Google in 2012 and 2) a migration of faculty and staff mailboxes, completed at the end of 2016.

Migration of mailboxes to Office 365 was pursued in stages with the consensus of the IT Governance Executive Committee and the campus community. The ITS Team worked with the O365 team to create a hybrid environment whereby users could be migrated in batches without any downtime. The ITS team then worked with college and departmental technicians to communicate with groups of faculty and staff by department and college. The entire migration process took ninety days and was completed with minimal disruption to campus operations. The background work that was done by the ITS team in collaboration with Microsoft lead to the smooth transition.

The migration significantly reduced cost as measured by total Information Technology Service (ITS) spending in the University (see Table 2). The new email system, featuring more user-friendly interface as well as enhanced tools for collaboration, also garnered much faculty and staff satisfaction. Office 365 has allowed the campus community to take advantage of the entire suite of tools that are available, including OneDrive, Skype for Business, and Yammer. Moreover, the migration gave the campus community an opportunity to manage their mailboxes better since Microsoft limited the mailbox size to 50GB per user. When Microsoft Exchange was hosted on premise, there was no mailbox quota which resulted in mailbox storage having to be managed and optimized every week. A technician spent 30 hours a week just managing the Exchange environment. Today, it takes roughly 5 hours to maintain the system.

Instructional Platform: Blackboard Hosting

The second system targeted for migration was the Blackboard Learning Management System, which has been a resource for faculty and students as CSUSB since 2001. About 70% of the faculty use Blackboard for either fully online course delivery, hybrid courses, or as supplements to their face-to-face class. The adoption and use of Blackboard have been growing as a student engagement and resource tool as faculty focus on student learning and success at CSUSB.

The in-house Blackboard (BB) system was facing several challenges. Firstly, whilst resource allocation for Blackboard has been increased and it has been upgraded since the unplanned downtime in spring 2013, there is a growing need to allocate more resources in personnel and hardware to continue to support BB usage and growth. Second, there was a lack of redundancy in support personnel who were experts in Blackboard system administration. Third, the University was facing a growing need for Enterprise Applications Support for the campus community, as more faculty were encouraged to develop online or hybrid instruction. Subsequently, there had been a growing demand for performance of timely upgrades of the system for continued system stability and new features.

It was possible that the University could continue maintenance of Blackboard in-house, but it needed to train other staff within ITS to support Blackboard administration and to purchase new hardware to support the growing needs of the Blackboard user community. If it did so, the system would be more likely to lag behind in patches as enterprise system administration staff are challenged to support other enterprise systems. Meanwhile, it also meant a lower level of service to campus units that require support of other enterprise applications. Because of various competing demands, the service level for Blackboard could continuously going down.

ITS explored the alterative to host Blackboard on the Blackboard Cloud with the Blackboard Managed Hosting Service. This service would cost the University $64,000 a year, yet it would largely free up ITS technicians to meet other competing demands. In addition, given that Blackboard is a valuable student success and faculty resource on campus, ITS was determined to make sure that BB would run optimally with the most updated version and always be available for campus use. Once the IT Governance Executive Committee approved the migration of Blackboard to the hosted solution, the Academic Technologies and Innovation team started working with the faculty community to develop a schedule for the migration to take place. The schedule took into account the academic calendar as a primary factor in deciding the appropriate time. The team wanted to make sure there was minimal disruption to faculty and students who rely on Blackboard for their coursework.

A time was chosen after the summer session and agreed upon by the faculty community. The ITS team then worked with the managed hosting team at Blackboard to work out the logistics. There were several activities that could be pursued without interrupting the production system. All operations were done first on the staging system and then the production system. Courses that were inactive and archived were moved to the new instances of BB on the cloud with no interruption to the production system. After the inactive courses were moved, faculty and instructional designers validated the integrity of the courses moved and performed several tests to make sure all operations within each course were functional and optimal.

The final stage of the move consisted of courses that were currently active. Courses that were active were archived to hard drives on a Friday evening and shipped overnight to the BB managed hosting center. As soon as the hosting center received the hard drives, they started reloading the courses into the staging and production systems. Once tests were completed and validated, DNS entries were modified at the campus level to redirect the BB link on the portal to the new instance of BB on the cloud. Except for a few minor issues that were fixed immediately, the migration was very successful.

The migration largely improved the system performance of Blackboard and all features of the instructional tools have been kept up-to-date. Blackboard used to experience an unscheduled outage at least once a month when it was hosted on campus. After it was moved to the cloud, the campus has not had a single unscheduled outage. Moreover, since Internet connectivity was upgraded from a 1GB link to a 10 GB link, faculty and students experienced an improvement in the performance and responsiveness of Blackboard. It also gets timely upgrades from the service provider as well as rapid response from the Enterprise Applications Team.

Web Content Management System

The CSUSB web presence has grown steadily from when it was first introduced in 1996 as a collection of web pages managed and maintained by several departments on a variety of hardware platforms to 2013 when it underwent the changes discussed here. Although the csusb.edu website represented the University, the subpages and sub domains under csusb.edu didn't follow University branding and web standards on a variety of fronts. Due to the fact that sub domain web pages were maintained by various departments and colleges, there was no central content management system, agreed design standard, or any unified disaster recovery protocols. The staff responsible for maintaining the systems also lacked standardized training across the campus. As a result, the website had encountered serious accessibility and security issues.

ITS was facing the challenge of whether to continue to maintain the 60,000 plus web pages and establish standards for branding, design, accessibility, and security or to implement a university- wide content management system that would enable the web development team to establish standards across the University.

The University was at a point in its web presence maturity cycle that it needed a unified web content management system which could consistently tell its story and provide relevant information to a variety of audiences. The csusb.edu website should primarily be focused on external audiences such as prospective students, parents, and community while the internal facing resources need to be moved behind the MyCoyote portal.

ITS decided to host the content management system needs on the cloud to allow for better performance, less maintenance, and disaster recovery. The recommendation was to implement Drupal CMS hosted on the Pantheon ONE cloud and work with the campus community to migrate current content into Drupal, as a central management system would allow the University to provide consistent branding and web standards to a University web presence across all divisions, departments, and colleges.

The University formed an institution-wide web migration committee with representatives from all departments and colleges in the University. The committee spent the greater part of a year discussing and building consensus on design of the new website, its access controls, and tentative timeline for mass migration. It was agreed that any colleges and departments that had their web content ready would be moved ahead of the published schedule.

When content was proofed for accuracy and ready for migration, it would take the Drupal web team a day or two to transfer an entire website of about thirty to forty pages. Previously it took more than a week to accomplish such a task. Moreover, since there was now a strict level of consistency across all colleges and departments, the web development team did not have to deal with customized web designs or templates for each website.

With the standardization of web pages, rather than having to run accessibility and security compliance tests on every single web page, this step needed to be done only on the templates. As long as the templates were not modified or updated, the content of the websites was assured of being compliant and secure. When templates were updated, accessibility and security tests were run again to ensure adherence to the same level of compliance.

The migration led to better content management as measured by the accuracy and timeliness of web content. The accessibility and security audit reports also indicated improved accessibility and security.

Organisational Impact of Migration

The above three-system migration presents an opportunity to substantively cut the direct operating costs of a data center (see Table 2). Roughly speaking, hosting the three systems over the cloud costs slightly more than half the annual operating expense of hosting them in the University Data Center.

Indirectly, such solutions facilitate easy cash-flow management for finance staffers as there is only a small upfront cost followed by recurrent monthly billing. In addition, by using an external provider, the University also benefits from lower energy costs as a result of the providers' wholesale energy prices. Subsequently, the University has been considering the migration of more systems to the cloud (see Table 1).

In addition to the economic impact, there are also considerable organizational implications to the University.

Initially when migration was discussed, staff were nervous about their job duties. However, moving to the cloud was presented in the overall context of reinventing the ITS organization as an agile, routinely proactive, and innovative organization with a commitment to retraining its members on emerging technologies. This commitment was followed by several professional development and technical training workshops for staff members, resulting in development of a team which is confident of new and emerging technologies. Staff members who were working on the above three systems on premise were reassigned to other managing-the-cloud based applications. Their system management duties were replaced with other systems on premise in anticipation of an eventual move to the cloud.

The administration kept up with its commitment of retraining and providing professional development opportunities for staff. Many staff members took this as an opportunity to train in emerging technology areas in which they were interested. Even staff who were skeptical about the move to the cloud started embracing the new technology as an opportunity to advance their careers.

Table 2. Comparison of System Costs between Cloud and CSUSB's Data Center

Period	Over the Cloud Cost ($)			Data Center Cost ($) Three Systems
	Office 365	*Blackboard*	Web Content	
1 Month	0	7,916	2,500	19,898
1 Year	0	95,000	30,000	238,776
5 Years	0	475,000	150,000	1,193,880

Feedback from stakeholders has been very positive, in particular because moving critical systems to the cloud brought stability and optimal performance to systems that were unstable and unreliable. Staff technicians, freed up from their once day-to-day operations of maintaining server hardware and software, are now available to assist faculty and staff in providing solutions and becoming true information technology consultants.

Lessons Learned

In an Information Technology organizational unit, people, process, and technology are the primary elements to serving its customers. Of these three key elements, people are the most important and valuable asset to the unit. Given the trend in technology and automation of replacing people and jobs, there is a justifiable nervousness among employees when new leaders come on board or new technologies are introduced. The success of an IT organizational unit in continuing to stay relevant and creating value to the mission of the organization depends on how leadership is able to introduce and manage change. The first step towards introducing and managing change is to earn the trust of the leadership team and staff. Barsh and Lavoie (2015) declare that "If we want to inspire trust, we must learn what others value." Once people identify with the vision of the organizational unit and align themselves to value creation, innovation starts occurring.

The experience of cloud migration at CSUSB points to several lessons for public practitioners:

First, not all projects should be considered to be moved to the cloud.

As Pardeshi (2014) recommends, each application not only needs to be carefully considered for cloud worthiness, but that it also complements existing IT infrastructure. Some services are too expensive to move to the cloud. Applications with very high storage requirements might be too costly to be moved since storage can be purchased inexpensively in-house. Also, applications that require high throughput and fast response times may not tolerate the latency that comes with cloud hosting.

In selecting applications to be moved to the cloud at CSUSB, a careful analysis was done on which applications are to be moved and why. The management action plan (MAP) document outlines the challenges the organization faced with applications that were on premise, and their stability. The rationale describes why the ITS team at CSUSB chose to move that particular application to the cloud.

Second, it is critical to help associated personnel adjust to the change.

Moving applications to the cloud presents a new paradigm for a team used to managing servers and applications in-house. It takes some time for staff to grasp the fact that they will not have physical access to the servers they manage. The ITS leadership team has intentionally worked with the staff on this transition, assuring them along the way that they will receive all the support they will need both during and after the transition. As Wang, Wood, Abdul-Rahman, and Lee (2016) point out, stakeholder expectations and their relationships as well as social and cultural factors related to the change need to be carefully mapped out and addressed. It is inevitable that some team members will not buy into the transition and will leave the team, choosing a different career path. It is, however, the responsibility of leadership to provide opportunities and training for existing staff to learn emerging technologies.

Third, building stakeholder consensus is the key.

Moving to the cloud not only represents change for the technology staff but also for the organization as a whole. Stakeholders across the organization might have concerns about the security and privacy of data stored on the cloud, connectivity and bandwidth considerations, and the ability to customize software according to organizational needs. Consultation, collaboration, and communication are three important elements when it comes to managing organizational change. The more consensus is built around the benefits of the cloud and risk mitigation measures are put in place, the more stakeholders will feel confident (Howell, 2015). As with any organizational change, there will be a transitional period during which time users will grow to feel comfortable with the new paradigm of cloud computing.

Conclusion

Cloud computing, being simple, cheap, and scalable, is a groundbreaking technology that has transformed the deployment of information systems. When faced with public sector "doing more with less" challenges, cloud-computing services provide potentially viable solutions. This manuscript describes the rationale, process, and impact of a public university's cloud migration experience. The University was motivated by its computing challenges and by the need to keep their information service up-to-date to meet increased demands. The case presented herein demonstrates how cloud computing has enabled CSUSB to address various technical challenges, meet increased service demands, and cut costs, all while addressing the many organizational issues that need to be accommodated. In summary, this case study indicates the cloud is a feasible alternative for public institutions and provides lessons for similar organizations seeking for best practices.

We admit that an unneglectable limitation of this study is that the economic impact analysis solely focused on the system infrastructure and maintenance costs, not accounting the transaction costs, such as cost for the migration process, cost of training and reassigning support IT staff, cost of maintaining and monitoring the cloud contract, as well as the cost of end user adjustment to cloud environment. Instead of quantifying such costs, we addressed them qualitatively in the discussion of organizational implications. Future studies in cloud migration may explore mechanisms to quantify such costs to enable a more comprehensive economic impact examination.

Although we have highlighted many important issues that arise when dealing with cloud migration, many issues remain open for future research. For example, our study was solely based on the experience of a public university, could other public institutions (e.g., government agencies) with different information systems tell a different story about cloud migration? A multi-case study with various types of organization may delineate and differentiate the factors that are critical to the success of cloud migration.

References

Anderson, M. (2015). *Technology Device Ownership: 2015*. Pew Research Center: Washington DC.

Archibald, R., & Feldman, D. (2006). Explaining increases in higher education costs. *IDEAS Working Paper Series from RePEc*.

Babar, M. A, & Chauhan, M. A. (2011) Migrating Service-Oriented System to Cloud Computing: An Experience Report. 2013 IEEE Sixth International Conference on Cloud Computing, vol. 00, no., pp. 404-411.

Guleria, P., Sharma, V., & Arora, M. (2012). Development and usage of software as a service for a cloud and non-cloud-based environment- an empirical study. *International Journal of Cloud Computing and Services Science (IJ-CLOSER)*, *2*(1), 50-58.

Howell, J. (2015). Moving to the cloud: Cloud technology may be the latest "new thing" to change business, but the issues involved with its adoption should feel very familiar. *Strategic Finance*, *96*(12), 30.

Isaila, N. (2014). Cloud Computing in Education. *Knowledge Horizons. Economics, 6*(2), 100-103.

Khajeh-hosseini, A., Greenwood, D., Smith, J., & Sommerville, I. (2012). The cloud adoption toolkit: Supporting cloud adoption decisions in the enterprise. *Software: Practice and Experience, 42*(4), 447-465.

Lee, L., & Mautz, R. (2012). Using cloud computing to manage costs. *The Journal of Corporate Accounting & Finance, 23*(3), 11-15.

McDonald MP, Aron D (2013) Research presentation for 'hunting and harvesting in a digital world: the 2013 CIO agenda'.

Neuman, P. (2014). Risks and myths of cloud computing and cloud storage. *Communications of the ACM, 57*(10), 25.

Pardeshi, V. (2014). Cloud computing for higher education institutes: Architecture, strategy and recommendations for effective adaptation. *Procedia Economics and Finance,* 11, 589-599.

Pleeter, S. (1980*). Economic impact analysis: Methodology and applications.* The Netherlands: Martinus Nijhoff Publishing.

Rajaraman, V. (2014). Cloud computing. *Resonance, 19*(3), 242-258.

Ratten, V. (2015). Factors influencing consumer purchase intention of cloud computing in the united states and turkey. *EuroMed Journal of Business, 10*(1), 80-97.

Riahi, G. (2015). E-learning systems based on cloud computing: A review. *Procedia Computer Science, 62,* 352-359.

Sporri, C., Borsuk, M., Peters, I., & Reichert, P. (2007). The economic impacts of river rehabilitation: A regional input-output analysis. *Ecological Economics, 62*(2), 341-351.

Sriram, I. and Khajeh-Hosseini, A. (2010). Research Agenda in Cloud Technologies, Submitted to 1st ACM Symposium on Cloud Computing (SOCC 2010).

Sultan, N. (2010). Cloud computing for education: A new dawn? *International Journal of Information Management*, *30*(2), 109-116.

Thelin, J. (2015). Why did college cost so little? affordability and higher education a century ago. *Society*, *52*(6), 585-589.

Tyrrell, T., Tyrrell, & Johnston, R. (2008). Tourism sustainability, resiliency and dynamics: Towards a more comprehensive perspective. *Tourism & Hospitality Research*, *8*(1), 14.

Wang, C., Wood, L., Abdul-Rahman, H., & Lee, Y. (2016). When traditional information technology project managers encounter the cloud: Opportunities and dilemmas in the transition to cloud services. *International Journal of Project Management*, *34*(3), 371-388.

Documentation

Kim, J (2012). 4 ways technology can reduce the higher ed costs. Retrieved June 10th, 2016 from https://www.insidehighered.com/blogs/technology-and-learning/4-ways-technology-can-reduce-higher-ed-costs.

Spadafora, A. (2016). Gartner projects worldwide public cloud services will grow by 17 per cent in 2016. Retrieved June 10th, 2016 from

http://www.itproportal.com/news/gartner-projects-worldwide-public-

cloud-services-will-grow-by-17-per-cent-in-2016/.

The Influence of Electronic Banking on Performance of Ecobank Burundi: A Case Study of Ecobank Main Branch Bujumbura

Sabiiti Mulema, Hirwa Ramadhan

Abstract

The purpose of the study was to examine the impact of electronic Banking on performance of Eco Banks in Burundi using the main branch as a case study. The objectives of the study were to: assess the Ecobank performance strategy; evaluate the relationship between electronic banking and performance of Ecobank; examine the relationship between services profile and performance of Ecobank and to study the factor structure between electronic banking, services profile and performance of Ecobank.

The research design used both descriptive and analytical Research Designs. The study population for the study was 61 staff and a sample size of 53 was used. Stratified and purposive samplings were used to select respondents. The data collected was analyzed using SPSS version 22.0. Pearson correlation was used to test the relationship between the study variables, while regression analysis was used to test the effect between the variables of the study. Furthermore, factor analysis was employed to determine contribution of independent attributes to Electronic banking, services profile and performance in EcoBank.

The result indicated that there is a positive relationship between Electronic Banking in Ecobank (r = 0.511, P-value < 0.01). There is a positive relationship between Services profile and Bank performance (r = 0.339, P-value < 0.01). The variables explained 72% of the variance of Bank performance (R Square =.720). The most influential predictor of Bank performance was Services profile (β = .427, Sig .142) followed by Electronic Banking (β = .388, Sig .308) which is less likely to influence Bank performance since it portrays a low value of significance in the model.

The study recommends that there is need to create a secure, stable electronic banking platform especially the online banking applications, that quality improvement and assurance is also necessary especially the quality of existing services, need to create awareness about the Bank's services, how they work and how they can be accessed and the need to enlighten its staff on the need for timely service of customers and enrol them on how to use new banking platforms. The study further recommended that the Bank aligns electronic banking platforms like ATMs, debit cards and mobile banking with the needs of the customers, among others.

Introduction

The study sets out to examine how electronic banking has affected the performance of Eco Banks in Burundi taking main branch as a case study.

Electronic banking is the use of computers and telecommunications to enable banking transactions to be done by telephone or computer rather than through human interaction. Its features include electronic funds transfer for retail purchases, automatic teller machines (ATMs), and automatic payroll deposits and bill payments. Some banks offer home banking, whereby a person with a personal computer can make transactions, either via a direct connection or by accessing a web site. Electronic banking has vastly reduced the physical transfer of paper money and coinage from one place to another or even from one person to another (Kraiwanit, Panpon & Thimthong, 2019).

Commercial Banking is a heart of every robust economy, if it collapses so will the economy and it is absolutely evident from current recession in UK, and in turn, Information Technology has become the heart of banking sector. Investment and reliance in e-banking innovation by its providers to offer their services makes it essential to understand how various aspects of consumer behavior affect the innovation and respond to service quality. Increased adoption of internet as a delivery channel contributes a gradual reduction in overhead expenses (White, Afolayan & Plant, 2014).

The world of banking and financial services is in the midst of dramatic change, moving away from traditional "brick and mortar" branches and focusing on new delivery channels, to improve customer service and give 24-hours-a-day access to information and transactions (Durkin, 2007).

Internet technology holds the potential to fundamentally change banks and the banking industry. An extreme view speculates that the internet will destroy old models of how bank services are developed and delivered due to its competitive advantage (Noh & Lee, 2016).

Electronic banking in Kenya has emerged a strategic resource for achieving higher efficiency, control of operations and reduction of costs by replacing paper based and intensive methods with automated processes thus leading to higher productivity and profitability (Gikandi & Bloor, 2010).

Ecobank Transnational Incorporated (ETI), a public limited liability company, was established as a bank holding company in 1985 under a private sector initiative spearheaded by the Federation of West African Chambers of Commerce and Industry with the support of the Economic Community of West African States (ECOWAS).

It has been argued that the challenges that financial institutions are facing these days – and with the memories of the recession still painfully fresh in their minds – it's no wonder that a growing number of banking executives are focusing intently on cutting costs, trimming payrolls, and "right-sizing" their operations, especially in Kenya (Mathuva, 2009). However, a relentless focus on cost-cutting alone is not a formula for long-term success. What's needed is a more balanced approach – one that enables an institution not only to improve operating efficiency but also to upgrade its capabilities to respond to market needs and prepare for the future.

Theoretical review

The theory postulates that the intention to use a certain technology is influenced by attitude, subjective norm and perceived behavior control. Some of the influencing factors are; trust and security, culture, time, cost and accessibility (Johnson & Nino-Zarazua, 2011).

Innovation diffusion theory (IDT)

The theory explains individuals` intention to adopt a technology as a modality to perform a traditional activity. In terms of banking, the theory identifies critical factors that determine the adoption of an innovation at the general level; relative advantage, compatibility, complexity, trial ability and observability (Nor & Pearson, 2015).

Empirical review

Technology is evolving faster than ever, and as banking and money management becomes increasingly electronic, it's important to understand new capabilities – not only for convenience, but also for security. Electronic banking, which is also known as electronic fund transfer (EFT), refers to the transfer of funds from one account to another through electronic methods. A 2015 study by the Federal Reserve found that 22 percent of mobile phone owners use mobile payments. As electronic banking becomes increasingly widespread, you will likely encounter instances where it's preferable to make payments or transfer money electronically.

Understanding how electronic banking can be used will benefit you and your finances. Using it to your advantage not only will improve convenience, but can also help you track your transfers and payments. There are three key aspects of electronic banking: automated teller machines (ATMs), direct deposits and debit card purchases (Hopkins, 1986; Snee, Goode & Moutinho, 2000).

Performance of the Bank

A strong banking sector is important to every country to stimulate economic growth and to maintain financial stability for the whole financial system. Hence, information and technological revolution motivated banks to spend more on technology to maximize return and attracting more customers who are not willing to take the risk of using less than above-average services (Cockrill, Goode & Beetles, 2009).

In addition, banks have changed to keep up with the information technology and communication developments. This change includes using the technology of computer and communications to replace manual and paper operations to electronic operations; electronic banking (e-banking) or internet banking is the commonly method adopted by banks (Abaenewe, Ogbulu & Ndugbu, 2013).

Electronic banking has a significant negative impact on banks' performance. Electronic banking has not improved the performance of these banks. Banks' customers in Jordan depend as much on traditional channels to carry out their banking operations (Al-Smadi & Al-Wabel, 1970). As a result, costs associated with adopting electronic banking are still higher than revenues from provision electronic services (*ibid*).

Internet technology has brought about a paradigm shift in banking operations to the extent that banks embrace internet technology to enhance effective and extensive delivery of wide range of value added products and services. However, the fact that e-banking is fast gaining acceptance in Nigerian banking sector does not assuredly signify improved bank performance nor would conspicuous use of internet as a delivery channels make it economically viable, productive or profitable. Whether progression is made in the use of internet technology (e-banking) or not, there should be parameter to empirically assess its impact over specified period of adoption (Beynon, Goode, Moutinho & Snee, 2005).

Research Gap

On the basis of literature above, there is enough literature on the relationship between E-banking and Commercial banks' performance. However, most of those studies done have been in various sector and the researcher didn't come across one study done on the influence of Electronic Banking on Performance of commercial banks in Burundi and specifically on Ecobank. There is therefore a need to conduct such studies within the Burundian context, to assess the kind of relationship existing between Electronic Banking and the Performance of Commercial Banks. Also, there is no statistical evidence among the relationship between those variables. So, it will be the contribution of researcher's work. In conclusion, the literature review has showed that, although empirical evidence appears to be limited, the Electronic banking accelerates the performance of Commercial banks.

Research methodology methods

This section sets out the research design, sampling procedure, source of data, data collection tools and techniques and validity and reliability of instruments.

Research Design

The study was carried out using both descriptive and analytical Research Designs. This design was preferred because the study intended to rely on the views of the respondents only during the Study.

Study Area

The study area was Ecobank main branch on plot No. 06, Rue de la science in Bujumbura the capital city of Burundi.

Sampling Method

The researcher used both probability and non-probability sampling methods so as to be exhaustive in the research findings. Purposive sampling technique was used to select the respondents from senior managers of Ecobank. Stratified sampling was used to select junior employees of Ecobank. The study population of **61** had a sample size of **53**. This followed a confidence level of 95 per cent which gives a margin of error of 5 per cent. Purposive sampling technique was also used to select the respondents from operations, retail, retail Sales and Marketing of Ecobank. Stratified sampling was used to select employees of human resource department.

Sample Size

The sample size was computed based on Slovin's formula (1960) and this gave a practical ratio according to the population size. The study population of **61** had a sample size of **53.** This followed a confidence level of 95% which gave a margin of error of 5%. This was determined using Slovin's formula as shown below in Equation 1 and Calculation 1.

$$n = \frac{N}{1 + Ne^2}$$

Equation 1. Slovin's formula

where n = Number of samples, N = Total population and e = Error tolerance.

$$n = \frac{61}{1 + 61x0.05^2}$$

n=53

Calculation 1. Implementation of the Slovin's formula

Source of Data

This researcher used both primary and secondary source of data as is described below.

Primary data

The researcher gathered this data from the field through questionnaires from the various respondents selected from the employees of Ecobank. Interview guide was used on the managers of the bank.

Secondary data

The researcher collected the data from printed materials such as books, reports and government journals from reliable sources which were used to further justify and confirm data that was gathered from the field.

Data Collection Techniques and Tools

This study used interviews as data collection method while questionnaires and interview guides served as data collection tools. The researcher used closed questionnaires as a data collection instrument to obtain information from the Ecobank employees. The questionnaire was designed according to the objectives of the research. They contained close-ended questions. The close ended questions were based on the 5- point Likert Scale format.

Validity and Reliability of Instruments

To ensure the validity and reliability of the instrument, the researcher employed expert judgment method. After constructing the questionnaire, the researcher contacted experts in this area to go through it to ensure that the instrument was clear, relevant, specific and logically arranged. Also a pre-test was conducted in order to test and improve on the reliability and validity of the instrument. Cronbach's Alpha test was employed to measure the reliability. Content validity index (CVI) was used to establish the validity of the questionnaire. CVI of 0.7 and above was considered as acceptable.

Data processing

The data collected from the field was coded, edited, processed and analyzed using descriptive analysis options of SPSS version (22.0). The data was then presented using Pearson's correlation to test the relationship between variables of study and regression analysis was used to test the potential predictors of the dependent variable.

Data Analysis and Presentation

The descriptive statistics in Table 1, below, included in the output are the number of respondents (N), the Minimum (lowest) response in the select variable and the Maximum(highest) possible response, the Mean (or average), for each variable, the standard deviation), and the Skewness statistic as well as the Std. Error of the skewness. Note, from the bottom line of the outputs, that the Valid N (list wise) is 50, which is the number of participants in the data file. There were no respondents with missing data on any variable requested in the output.

Table 1 Descriptives for the Ordinal Variables

Factor						Skewness	
	N	Min	Max	Mean	SD	Statistic	Std. Error
Gender	50	1.00	2.00	3.52	.822	-1.910	.277
Employment terms	50	1.00	2.00	2.67	.794	.533	.281
Age	50	1.00	4.00	2.84	.897	.923	.277
Department	50	2.00	4.00	2.82	.922	.422	.279
Education level	50	2.00	3.00	2.16	.906	-.579	.279
Duration in Service	50	1.00	5.00	1.61	.971	1.581	.277

Source: Primary data computed

Relationship between Study Variables

The relationship between electronic banking and service profile was investigated. Pearson correlation coefficient was used to determine the degree of relationship between the study variables as shown in the Table 2 below.

Table 2 Pearson's zero order correlation matrix

Factor	1	2	3
Electronic Banking (1)	1		
Services profile (2)	.432**	1	
Bank performance (3)	.511**	.339**	1

** Correlation is significant at the .01 level (2-tailed).

Source: Primary data computed

The results in Table 2 above indicate a positive relationship between Electronic Banking and service profile (r = 0.432, P-value < 0.01). Table 2 above also indicates a positive relationship between Services profile and Bank performance (r = 0.339, P-value < 0.01).

Regression analysis

Regression analysis was used to examine the Electronic Banking, Services profile and Bank performance in Ecobank. Table 3 presents the results of the regression modelling. Results in Table 3 above show (R= 0.772) a combination of Electronic Banking and Services profile in assessing the level to which they influence Bank performance in Ecobank. These variables explained 72% of the variance of Bank performance (R Square =.720). The most influential predictor of Bank performance was Services profile (β = .427, Sig .142) followed by Electronic Banking (β = .388, Sig .308) which is less likely to influence Bank performance since it portrays a low value of significance in the model.

Table 3 below shows the regression model for Electronic Banking, Services profile and Bank performance in Ecobank

Model	Un-standardized coefficients		Standardized coefficients		
	B	Std. Error	Beta	T	Sig
(Constant)	11.33 1	37.055		.322	.580
Electronic Banking	.463	.418	.388	1.05 2	.308
Services profile	.551	.503	.427	2.10 1	.142
R= .772; R- Square =0.720, Adjusted R- square = 0.588, F= 3.054, Sig = 0.812					

Source: Primary data computed

This research used factor loading in order to check how much a variable loads into its corresponding factor. To understand how each item is loaded into its relevant principal component we use table 4.10-12 for the factor loading of each item. The value of each item in factor loading should be at least 0.50 into its relative principal component. The factor loadings of Electronic Banking, Services profile and Bank performance in Ecobank are in Table 4.

Factor Analysis of Electronic Banking

Table 4 Factor Analysis of Electronic Banking

Variables	ATMs	Mobile banking	EFT	Debit cards
The bank`s ATMS are operational all the time	0.954			
Most customers know how to use ATM	0.932			
Customers don`t complain about ATM	0.918			
Customers like mobile banking		0.892		
Most customers have signed up for mobile banking		0.870		
Customers know how to use mobile banking		0.855		
EFT is preferred by many customers			0.865	

EFT contribute a bigger share on bank`s revenue			0.843	
Bank customers understand how EFT works			0.801	
Bank has given out Debit cards to most customers				0.788
Most customers are using Debit cards to transact				0.718
Electronic banking has generated more revenue for the bank				0.706
Eigen Value	1.385	1.249	0.867	0.499
Variance %	34.623	31.223	21.679	12.466
Cumulative	34.623	65.846	87.525	100

Source: Primary data computed

The results in table 4.10 above show the factor analysis results of Electronic Banking, four factors were extracted and the first component (ATMs) explained Electronic Banking better with 34.6%, the second component (Mobile banking) also explained more of Electronic Banking with 31.2%,followed by EFT with 21.6% and lastly Debit cards which least explained Electronic Banking with 12.4%. The results in Table 5 below show the factor analysis results of Services profile, four factors were extracted and the first component (Awareness) explained Services profile better with 43.6%, the second component

(Accessibility) also explained more of Services profile with 26.1%, followed by Quality with 21.6% and lastly Efficiency which least explained Services profile with 8.6%.

Table 5 Factor Analysis of Services profile

Variables	Awareness	Accessibility	Quality	Efficiency
Ecobank`s ATMs operate 24/7	0.944			
Customers prefer ATM services to counter service	0.923			
E-banking has saved a lot of money due to e-banking	0.909			
Many customers have joined Ecobank due to e-banking		0.931		
E-banking has increased number of transactions per day		0.911		
Customers can view their accounts in real time		0.890		

Customers complaints have reduced drastically			0.922	
Customers' queries are always handled with care			0.903	
Bank staff are well trained on E-Banking			0.885	
Management ensures that goals of the bank are made known to all its employees				0.910
Ecobank staff strive to be efficient at customer handling				0.892
There are strict deadlines for giving customer feedback				0.854
Eigen Value	1.748	1.042	0.867	0.343
Variance %	43.694	26.060	21.667	8.579
Cumulative	43.694	69.754	91.421	100

Source: Primary data computed

Factor Analysis of Bank performance

The results in Table 6 show the factor analysis results of Bank performance, four factors were extracted and the first component (Profitability) explained Bank performance better with 46.3%, the second component (Customer satisfaction) also explained more of Bank performance with 34.3%, followed by Sales growth with 15.3% and lastly Timeliness which least explained Bank performance with 3.9%.

Table 6 Factor Analysis of Bank performance

Variables	Profitability	Customer satisfaction	Sales growth	Timeliness
Ecobank`s profitability is increasing every year	0.953			
Active accounts have grown in number	0.920			
Customer referrals has grown the number of customers	0.892			
Customer benefits are now much better		0.934		
Most customers are happy with the bank service		0.905		
There is timely feedback to customers		0.876		
Customer recruitment rate has gone high			0.890	

Customer deposits have gone high in the bank			0.863	
Operational costs of the bank have reduced			0.839	
Customers are attended to on time in the banking hall				0.862
There is timely feedback to customers				0.796
Customers get online services in real time				0.771
Eigen Value	1.853	1.374	0.615	0.158
Variance %	46.324	34.345	15.381	3.950
Cumulative	46.324	80.669	96.050	100

Source: Primary data computed

Analysis of Variance for the independent and dependent variables

This research used analysis of variance in order to check for variations amongst groups/ categories of respondents' opinions. Klaus, (2013) suggests that the Sigma value of each item in analysis of variance should be between 0.1 and 1.0 in its relative principal group for it to be deemed of significance (Negative or positive).

ANOVA for Electronic Banking

Table 7 below represents the ANOVA of Electronic Banking. It indicates a statistically significant difference between gender groups and how such groups would influence Electronic Banking for better Bank performance with result (.234); it also indicates a statistically significant difference and how employment terms would influence Electronic Banking for better Bank performance with result of (.348).

Table 7 Showing the ANOVA of Electronic Banking

Electronic Banking		Sum of Squares	Df	Mean Square	F	Sig.
Gender	Between Groups	676.500	8	84.563	10.570	.234
	Within Groups	8.000	1	8.000		
	Total	684.500	9			
Employ ment terms	Between Groups	825.600	8	228.200	4.564	.348
	Within Groups	50.000	1	50.000		

	Total	875.600	9			
Age	Between Groups	1182.400	8	272.800	6.736	.290
	Within Groups	40.500	1	40.500		
	Total	1222.900	9			
Department deployed	Between Groups	1274.400	8	39.200	.710	.494
	Within Groups	110.500	1	55.250		
	Total	1384.00	9			
Level of Education	Between Groups	1315.600	8	16.514	.777	.505
	Within Groups	42.500	1	21.250		
	Total	1358.100	9			

	Between Groups	1484.900	8	26.414	1.057	.488
Years in Service	Within Groups	50.000	1	25.000		
	Total	1534.900	9			

Source: Primary data computed

Table 7 further indicates a statistically significant difference between the age categories of respondents and how such categories would influence Electronic Banking for better Bank performance at (.290) as well as (.494) for variations in department of deployment. Levels of education of the respondents had a statistical significant difference on how such differences would influence Electronic Banking for better Bank performance at (.505).Lastly the Years in service classes had a statistical significant difference amongst the respondents and how such classes would influence Electronic Banking for better Bank performance at (.488).

ANOVA for Services profile

Table 8 below represents the ANOVA of Services profile. It indicates a statistically significant difference between gender groups and how such groups would influence Services profile for better Bank performance with result (.209); it also indicates a statistically significant difference and how employment terms would influence Services profile for better Bank performance with result of (.136). It further indicates a statistically significant difference between the age categories of respondents and how such categories would influence Services profile for better Bank performance at (.461) as well as (.522) for variations in department of deployment. Levels of education of the respondents had a statistical significant difference on how such differences would influence Services profile for better Bank performance at (.464). Lastly the Years in service classes had a statistical significant difference amongst the respondents and how such classes would influence Services profile for better Bank performance at (.337).

Table 8 ANOVA of Services profile

Services profile		Sum of Squares	Df	Mean Square	F	Sig.
Gender	Between Groups	331.900	8	41.488	13.370	.209
	Within Groups	40.500	1	10.500		
	Total	372.400	9			
Employment	Between Groups	214.400	8	40.800	3.144	.136

terms	Within Groups	12.500	1	9.500		
	Total	226.900	9			
Age	Between Groups	198.900	8	28.414	.789	.461
	Within Groups	72.000	1	6.000		
	Total	270.900	9			
Department deployed	Between Groups	174.400	8	39.200	.710	.522
	Within Groups	110.500	1	5.250		
	Total	284.900	9			
Level of Education	Between Groups	215.600	8	16.514	.777	.464
	Within Groups	42.500	1	2.250		
	Total	257.100	9			
Years in Service	Between Groups	284.900	8	26.414	1.057	.337
	Within Groups	50.000	1	2.000		
	Total	334.900	9			

Source: Primary data computed

ANOVA for Bank performance

Table 9 below represents the ANOVA of Bank performance. The result in Table 9 above indicates a statistically significant difference between gender groups and how variations in such groups would influence the Bank's strategies for better Bank performance (Sig=0.366). It also indicates a statistically significant difference between employment terms and how variations in such groups would influence the Bank's strategies for better Bank performance (Sig=0.401). Table 9 further indicates a statistically significant difference between the age categories of respondents and how variations in such groups would influence the Bank's strategies for better Bank performance (Sig=0.262, Sig=0.394) for variations in department of deployment.

Table 9 Showing the ANOVA for Bank performance

Bank performance		Sum of Squares	Df	Mean Square	F	Sig.
Gender	Between Groups	628.900	8	23.613	4.072	.366
	Within Groups	50.000	1	5.000		
	Total	678.900	9			
Employment terms	Between Groups	178.400	8	14.800	3.328	.401
	Within Groups	40.500	1	4.500		

	Total	218.900	9			
Age	Between Groups	198.900	8	8.414	.789	.262
	Within Groups	72.000	1	3.000		
	Total	270.900	9			
Department deployed	Between Groups	274.400	8	7.200	.710	.394
	Within Groups	110.500	1	2.250		
	Total	384.900	9			
Level of Education	Between Groups	315.600	8	6.514	.777	.415
	Within Groups	42.500	1	1.250		
	Total	358.100	9			
Years in Service	Between Groups	384.900	8	2.414	1.057	.333
	Within Groups	50.000	1	1.000		
	Total	434.900	9			

Source: Primary data computed

As can be seen from Table 9, levels of education of the respondents had a statistically significant difference on how variations in such groups would influence the Bank's strategies for better Bank performance (Sig=0.415). Lastly the Years in service classes had a statistically significant difference amongst the respondents and how variations in such groups would influence the Bank's strategies for better Bank performance (Sig=0.333).

Discussion of the findings

The results indicated a positive relationship between Electronic Banking and Bank performance in Ecobank (r=0.511, p=<0.01) which implied that Electronic Banking is crucial for proper Bank performance. This is because Electronic Banking extends Automated Teller Machines, Electronic fund transfer services and eases transactions with Debit cards. The results are in line with Dilley (2015) who said that understanding how electronic banking can be used will benefit you and your finances. Using it to your advantage not only will improve convenience, but can also help you track your transfers and payments. There are three key aspects of electronic banking affecting customer satisfaction, including automated teller machines (ATMs), direct deposits and debit card purchases (Goode, Moutinho, Chien, 1996; Hopkins, 1986).

The results indicated a positive relationship between Services profile and Bank performance (r=0.339, p=<0.01) which implied that healthy Services profile is key recipe for Bank performance in any country since it facilitates service accessibility, usability and efficiency.

The regression for Electronic Banking, Services profile and Bank performance in Ecobank

Results indicated (r= 0.772) a combination of Electronic Banking and Services profile in assessing the level to which they influence Bank performance in Ecobank. These variables explained 72% of the variance of Bank performance (R Square =.720). The most influential predictor of Bank performance was Services profile (β=.427, Sig=0.142) followed by Electronic Banking (β=0.388, Sig=0.308) which is less likely to influence Bank performance since it portrays a low value of significance in the model. All the factors showed a positive relationship in influencing the level of Bank performance, such that if Electronic Banking is well phased in and incorporated into the existing Services profile then there will be better Bank performance.

The results suggest that information and technological revolution motivated banks who spend more on technology are more likely to maximize return and attract more customers who will not accept less than above-average services. In addition, banks have changed to keep up with the information technology and communication developments. This change includes using the technology of computer and communications to replace manual and paper operations to electronic operations; electronic banking (e-banking) or internet banking is the commonly method adopted by banks.

Factor loadings for the study variables

The factor analysis supported the importance of perceived risk and trust in customer satisfaction with banking, including automated teller machines (Cockrill, Goode & Beetles, 2009). The factor analysis results of electronic banking under ATMs attribute were explained that; The bank`s ATMS are operational all the time 95%, Most customers know how to use ATM 93% and that Customers don`t complain about ATM 92%.

Under Mobile banking attribute, they were explained that; Customers like mobile banking 89%, Most customers have signed up for mobile banking 87% and that Customers know how to use mobile banking86%. Under EFT attribute, they were explained that; EFT is preferred by many customers 87%, EFT contribute a bigger share on bank`s revenue 84% and that Bank customers understand how EFT works80%. The factor analysis results of Services profile under Awareness attribute were explained that; Ecobank`s ATMs operate 24/7 94%, Customers prefer ATM services to counter service 92% and that E-banking has saved a lot of money due to e-banking 91%.

Under Accessibility attribute, they were explained that; Many customers have joined Ecobank due to e-banking 93%, E-banking has increased number of transactions per day 91% and that Customers can view their accounts in real time 89%.

Under Quality attribute, they were explained that; Customers complaints have reduced drastically 92%, Customers' queries are always handled with care 90% and that Bank staff are well trained on E-Banking86%.

The factor analysis results of Bank performance under Profitability attribute were explained that; Ecobank`s profitability is increasing every year 95%, Active accounts have grown in number 92% and that Customer referrals has grown the number of customers 89%.

With Customer satisfaction attribute, results were explained that; Customer benefits are now much better 93%, most customers are happy with the bank service 91% and that There is timely feedback to customers 88%.

Under Sales growth attribute, they were explained that; Customer recruitment rate has gone high 89%, Customer deposits have gone high in the bank 86% and that Operational costs of the bank have reduced84%.

Conclusion

The study established that generally, electronic banking is a very important element in modern banking and is therefore very important for any bank that seeks to appeal to the modern customer and a key driver of performance in any Bank. ATM use, internet banking and mobile banking were found to be the in-thing when it comes to banking, multitudes of customers take long without visiting banking halls because of the ease of access provided by these alternative platforms and therefore, installation and implementation of these platforms should be the primary target of every 21st century bank.

However, more effort will be required to create awareness towards Electronic Banking as it proved to be a less popular concept especially among the traditional bank customers and the unbanked population. It is heaped with praises in environments with youthful and tech-savvy population but has a bad reputation among people with a high liquidity preference who are convinced that electronic cash is many times unreliable and most times insecure. These have a preference for armed guards protecting liquid cash as more secure over a PIN-protected electronic account which, they believe, can be logged into with just a single click or a guessed password. Banks have invested heavily in electronic account security with PINs, key cards and multi-level encryption and it a great milestone but there is still one big challenge, convincing the masses that their money is secure, available whenever needed and that the systems are efficient. This should be top priority for every bank operating in this error especially in 3rd world countries.

The study also discovered that ensuring a quality service profile is vital since services profile is the glue that holds the entire Bank's services and products together without which the Bank just has beautiful empty banking halls. The quality, security, availability of banking services needs to be on a growth trend every single day.

Recommendations

The results indicated a positive relationship between Electronic Banking and Bank performance in Ecobank (r=0.511, p=< 0.01) which implied that Electronic Banking is a vital ingredient for betterBank performance, the study therefore recommends;

1. Electronic banking is premised on the existence of ATMs, Debit cards and other electronic banking platforms but Ecobank still has a bit of insufficiency, the study therefore recommends that the bank acquires new electronic banking resources in order to widen the scope of usability.

2. There is also need to create a secure, stable electronic banking platform especially the online banking applications. Electronic banking platforms enable easy, efficient real time access to account details, status and all issues pertaining to credit and savings and these will improve Ecobank's performance while at the same time increasing its chances to compete fairly in Burundi's banking sector.

3. The results indicated a significant positive relationship between Services profile and Bank performance (r=0.339, p=0.01) which implied that a quality comprehensive Services profile is an important driver for better performance in a Bank. The study recommends;

4. Quality improvement and assurance is also necessary especially the quality of existing services. Better service quality will increase the number of bank customers while at the same time setting the Bank's brand apart and this will also influence performance levels. This can be done through sharing the Bank's objectives with workers at all levels and motivating them to continuously motivating and empowering them to meet these objectives.

5. There is need to create awareness about the Bank's services, how they work and how they can be accessed. It was discovered that there are some customers who would be interested in using the Bank's services and resources like cheques, ATMs and debit cards but they do not know how to acquire them while others had acquired them but did not know how to use them and feared they could lose their money.

Results indicated (R= 0.772) a combination of Electronic Banking and Services profile in assessing the level to which they influence Bank performance in Ecobank implying that is easily accessible, secure and user-friendly. Electronic Banking greatly aids the effectiveness of a Bank's entire services profile platforms and both, if well integrated, contribute to better Bank performance. The study therefore recommends;

6. Ecobank ought to enlighten its staff on the need for timely service of customers and enrol them on how to use new banking platforms/ systems and electronic access to services such that they serve customers

quickly and diligently. This will increase their confidence and also improve customer trust in the workers which will eventually lead to better performance in Ecobank.

7. There is need to align electronic banking platforms like ATMs, debit cards and mobile banking with the needs of the customers while concurrently streamlining the services profile to ensure all these services are secure, accessible, efficient and of the highest possible quality. Proper alignment of all these features will lead to more profitability, sales growth and a bigger market share all of which are key highlights of better performance.

Implications and directions for future resources

This study identified the need to investigate the factors hindering the introduction and mass usage of internet banking services in Burundi as this was found to be a key area that needs attention if the banking sector in Burundi is to grow.

References

Abaenewe, Z. C., Ogbulu, O. M., & Ndugbu, M. O. (2013). Electronic banking and bank performance in Nigeria. West African journal of industrial and academic research, 6(1), 171-187.

Beynon, M., Goode, M. M., Moutinho, L. A., & Snee, H. R. (2005). Modelling satisfaction with automated banking channels: Using variable precision rough set theory. Services Marketing Quarterly, 26(4), 77-94.

Cockrill, A., Goode, M. M., & Beetles, A. (2009). The critical role of perceived risk and trust in determining customer satisfaction with automated banking channels. Services Marketing Quarterly, 30(2), 174-193.

Durkin, M. (2007). Understanding registration influences for electronic banking. International Review of Retail, Distribution and Consumer Research, 17(3), 219-231.

Gikandi, J. W., & Bloor, C. (2010). Adoption and effectiveness of electronic banking in Kenya. Electronic commerce research and applications, 9(4), 277-282.

Goode, M. M., Moutinho, L. A., & Chien, C. (1996). Structural equation modelling of overall satisfaction and full use of services for ATMs. International Journal of Bank Marketing, 14(7), 4-11.

Hopkins, D. A. (1986). Factors affecting adoption of automated teller machines, direct deposit of paychecks and partial direct deposit to savings where available (Doctoral dissertation, The Ohio State University).

Kraiwanit, T., Panpon, P., & Thimthong, S. (2019). Cashless Society in Thailand. Cashless Society in Thailand. Review of Integrative Business and Economics Research (2019), 8, s4.

Mathuva, D. M. (2009). Capital adequacy, cost income ratio and the performance of commercial banks: The Kenyan Scenario. The International Journal of Applied Economics and Finance, 3(2), 35-47.

Noh, M. J., & Lee, K. T. (2016). An analysis of the relationship between quality and user acceptance in smartphone apps. Information Systems and e-Business Management, 14(2), 273-291.

Nor, K. M., & Pearson, J. M. (2015). The influence of trust on internet banking acceptance. The Journal of Internet Banking and Commerce.

Snee, H. R., Goode, M. M., & Moutinho, L. A. (2000). Predicting customer satisfaction from ATMs: A cross country study. Journal of Professional Services Marketing, 20(2), 133-149.Johnson, S., & Nino-Zarazua, M. (2011). Financial access and exclusion in Kenya and Uganda. The Journal of Development Studies, 47(3), 475-496.

White, G. R., Afolayan, A., & Plant, E. (2014). Challenges to the adoption of e-commerce technology for supply chain management in a developing economy: a focus on Nigerian SMEs. In E-commerce Platform Acceptance (pp. 23-39). Springer, Cham.

Documentation

Ecobank (2016). Annual Consumer Report.

Ecobank (2017). Annual Report.

Essays UK (2013). Importance of and benefits of E-banking. Retrieved from

https://intsearch.myway.com/search/GGmain.jhtml?

Federal Reserve (2015). Consumers and Mobile Financial Services. Retrieved

from: http://www.federalreserve.gov/econresdata/consumers-and-

mobile-financial-services-report-201503.pdf

Information Management and Data Misuse

Prevention of Disinformation Society: Fighting Online Defamation, Doxing, and Impersonation

Ashu M. G. Solo

Abstract

Online defamation, doxing, and impersonation are three of the major problems of the Internet age. As technology advances, defamation, doxing, and impersonation become greater problems. Online defamation, doxing, and impersonation can cause serious damages to victims. The laws badly need to be updated to deal with defamation, doxing, and impersonation in the information age. This research paper makes 12 recommendations to effectively combat online defamation, doxing, and impersonation in different countries.

Introduction

This research paper focuses on combating online defamation, doxing, and impersonation (Collins, 2011; Cox, 2014; Koch, 2016; Reznik, 2013). Defamation against an individual involves the communication of false statements that harm the individual's reputation. Doxing of an individual involves the publication of an individual's private information such as his home address or family members.

People can be impersonated for many purposes such as to harm their reputations, to gain personal information on them, to cause them to lose business, to cause them to lose friends, to write exams for them, to vote for them, to spread false information about them, etc.

In the old days, it was hard to spread false information or private information about people. It had to be done by telling people face to face or handing out flyers or something. Only the mainstream media had the means to reach a lot of people. The mainstream media is generally more careful in what it says, although it has crossed the line into defamation many times too, but not anywhere near the extent that people can on the world wide web. Now false information or private information about people can just be posted on the web using a fake name for the world to see (Banerjee & Chua, 2019; Chiluwa, 2019; Pal & Banerjee, 2019; Reynard, 2019; Solo, 2019a, 2019b, 2019c). Defamation, doxing, and impersonation on the web are three of the major new problems of the information age.

Social networks like Facebook and Twitter are frequently used to spread defamatory information. Fake news, which is used to spread disinformation or defamatory information, is a growing problem (Adikpo, 2019; Assay, 2019; Bradshaw & Howard, 2019; Dale, 2019; Grazulis & Rogers, 2019; Guadagno & Guttieri, 2019; Mach, 2019; Stengel, 2019; Watts, 2018). Fake news and defamation on the web are frequently used to attack politicians, an unethical type of network politics (Solo & Bishop, 2011, 2014, 2016, 2017). *Deepfakes* are videos featuring humans manipulated by computational intelligence. Deepfakes can be used to impersonate individuals while conveying disinformation or defamatory information. The use of deepfakes to impersonate politicians while conveying misinformation is an unethical form of political engineering or computational politics (Solo, 2011, 2014, 2017, 2019d). As technology advances, more sophisticated means can be used to fool people with defamation and impersonation. The laws need to be updated as recommended in this research paper to stop the spread of defamatory information using social networks, fake news, and deepfakes too.

Internet defamation, inter alia, severely harms people's reputations; prevents them from getting gainful employment; ruins romantic relationships; causes depression, anxiety, and distress; causes mental health problems, etc. Internet doxing, inter alia, endangers people; causes depression, anxiety, and distress; causes mental health problems; etc. Internet impersonation, inter alia, severely harms people's reputations; prevents them from getting gainful employment; ruins romantic relationships; causes depression, anxiety, and distress; causes mental health problems, etc.

Most private employers these days do web searches on prospective employees to see what turns up. If they have a bunch of people applying for one position, as is usually the case, they aren't going to risk selecting the candidate with a bunch of injurious claims about him on the world wide web whether or not they can determine if it's true.

Humans have a hard time distinguishing between true and false information (Kaufman, 2018; Marsh, Cantor, & Brashier, 2016; Vosoughi, Roy, & Aral, 2018). Andrew Butler, an associate professor of psychological and brain sciences at Washington University in St. Louis, said, "Even when people have knowledge that directly contradicts false information, they fail to detect that it is false information (Kaufman, 2018)." Furthermore, humans are predisposed to believing false information. Butler said, "People have a bias to assume truth (Kaufman, 2018)." A research study found that Twitter users are twice as likely to repost fake news as they are to repost real news (Kaufman, 2018; Vosoughi et al., 2018).

The civil remedies for dealing with defamation or doxing are extremely inadequate. Lawyer fees for a defamation or doxing claim are typically in the range of $30,000 USD or more. The vast majority of defamation or doxing victims can't afford the legal costs. A civil lawyer with expertise in defamation law said that he got inquiries from a bunch of people defamed on an online hate group, but none could afford to retain him. Most lawyers charge more than this lawyer who has been practicing for a few years. When someone is defamed or doxing on the world wide web, the defamation or doxing typically remains on the Internet until a civil court judgment is obtained and this usually takes years. In the mean time, the victim continues to accumulate all kinds of damages. The author of this research paper has seen people being defamed and doxed on the world wide web contemplate criminal violence as the only means they have to get the defamation and doxing removed.

Freedom of speech was never meant to protect defamation and has never protected defamation. We don't have the right to go around falsely claiming someone is a prostitute or pedophile, but those are the kinds of false statements you regularly see on online hate groups primarily against members of minority groups.

Case studies on online defamation and impersonation

Bhanu Prasad, an associate professor in the Department of Computer and Information Sciences at Florida A&M University, was found liable by a court for a defamation campaign using numerous fake names to defame research conferences in computer engineering and applied computing as well as an individual involved in organizing the conferences. Also, Prasad was found liable for impersonating an individual involved in the conferences to falsely claim that the conferences had been cancelled. Prasad was incarcerated for not removing libelous posts from the Internet. Prasad was an organizer of rival research conferences in computer engineering and applied computing.

Joshua Conner Moon operates a neo-Nazi white supremacist hate group and cyberbullying website that targets disabled people, especially people with autism, Jews, Muslims, black people, Hispanics, transgendered, vulnerable people, highly accomplished people, and other minorities. Kiwi Farms has ruined the lives of countless people with defamation and cyberbullying. Five victims of Kiwi Farms have committed suicide after being cyberbullied.

Victims of Kiwi Farms found it infeasible to sue Moon because of the high legal costs, because of their lack of legal knowledge, and because that would make them a primary target for cyberbullying and defamation by thousands of Moon's followers on Kiwi Farms. Victims of Kiwi Farms fought back by anonymously getting Moon's mother terminated from being a real estate agent for Keller Williams Realty because she housed and financially supported Moon while he ran a cyberbullying website. Also, the group of victims of Kiwi Farms fought back by anonymously defaming and telling the awful truth about Moon and his family all over the web to give Moon a taste of his own medicine. They set up two web forums to give Moon and his family a taste of Moon's medicine. Furthermore, victims of Kiwi Farms got most of Moon's funding sources cut off. After being contacted by victims of Kiwi Farms, Mastercard, Visa, PayPal, Uphold, Authorize.Net, Patreon, and Hatreon banned Kiwi Farms from using their services for donations; RedBubble banned Kiwi Farms from selling merchandise on the RedBubble website; and Google Adsense banned Kiwi Farms from using its banner ads service.

Recommendations to effectively fight online defamation, doxing, and impersonation

For the reasons above, the laws need to be updated to deal with online defamation, doxing, and impersonation in the information age. Following are 12 recommendations for public policies to effectively combat online defamation, doxing, and impersonation:

1. Criminal laws for defamation need to be enforced. These laws are rarely enforced in the U.S. and Canada.

2. Defamation should be a criminal offense in every country.

3. Impersonation should be a criminal offense in every country.

4. Online posting of a person's home address without permission should be a crime. This leads people with adversaries to fear for the safety of themselves and their families and their property.

5. Small claims courts must be equipped to deal with defamation, doxing, and impersonation lawsuits and must be able to order preliminary and permanent injunctions. Most victims do not have the expertise for pro se legal representation in higher courts and can't afford the costs of lawyers to represent them in higher courts.

6. Every website owner should be required to record the IP addresses of its website users for five years. For each post made on an online forum, the website owner should be required to record the IP address of the

individual who made the post and should be required to store this information for five years. This information may be required by law enforcement or people suing for defamation, doxing, or impersonation and must be turned over with search warrants or subpoenas.

7. No website owner should be able to hide her identity in a domain name registration. Every website owner should be required to provide an address in a domain name registration where he can be served with civil claims, subpoenas, search warrants, etc. for content on the website.

8. A website owner should be liable for defamation, doxing, or impersonation by a website user if the website owner doesn't delete the defamation, doxing, or impersonation after it's complained about by the subject of the defamation, doxing, or impersonation. In the United Kingdom, under the Defamation Act 2013, a website owner can be liable for defamation by a website user if it isn't deleted after being complained about.

9. Search engines should be stopped from indexing and displaying hyperlinks to websites notorious for defamation or doxing. There should also be public pressure on search engine companies to stop indexing and displaying hyperlinks to websites notorious for defamation or doxing.

10. Archiving websites including Google should be stopped from caching or archiving websites notorious for defamation or doxing. There should

also be public pressure on archiving website companies to stop caching or archiving websites notorious for defamation or doxing.

11. Search engines should be required to follow injunctions to remove hyperlinks to defamation, doxing, or impersonation on third party websites as well snippets of defamation, doxing, or impersonation on third party websites from search engine return pages.

12. Foreign defamation, doxing, or impersonation judgments must be enforceable in the U.S. It would be impossible for a middle class or poor person in a developing country who is being defamed, doxed, or impersonated on an American website to afford a lawyer in the U.S. to handle a civil claim. People should be able to sue for defamation, doxing, or impersonation in their own countries and get defamation, doxing, or impersonation judgments enforced in the U.S.

Conclusion

Online defamation, doxing, and impersonation are three of the major problems of the computer age. The laws desperately need to be updated and enforced to deal with these problems using the recommendations in this research paper.

Online hate groups use defamation and doxing as a weapon to cyberbully disabled people, particularly people with autism, Muslims, Jews, black people, Hispanics and Latinos, transgendered people, vulnerable people, highly accomplished people, and other minorities. If the laws are updated to prevent online defamation and doxing, online hate groups will no longer be nearly as effective in cyberbullying individuals in minority groups.

References

Adikpo, J. A. (2019). Fake Online News: Rethinking News Credibility for the Changing Media Environment. In I. E. Chiluwa & S. A. Samoilenko (Eds.), *Handbook of Research on Deception, Fake News, and Misinformation Online* (pp. 152-166). Hershey, PA: IGI Global.

Assay, B. E. (2019). Social Media and the Challenges of Curtailing the Spread of Fake News in Nigeria. In I. E. Chiluwa & S. A. Samoilenko (Eds.), *Handbook of Research on Deception, Fake News, and Misinformation Online* (pp. 226-263). Hershey, PA: IGI Global.

Banerjee, S., & Chua, A. Y. K. (2019). Toward a Theoretical Model of Authentic and Fake User-Generated Online Reviews. In I. E. Chiluwa & S. A. Samoilenko (Eds.), *Handbook of Research on Deception, Fake News, and Misinformation Online* (pp. 104-120). Hershey, PA: IGI Global.

Bradshaw, S., & Howard, P. N. (2019). *The Global Disinformation Order: 2019 Global Inventory of Organised Social Media Manipulation.* Computational Propaganda Research Project. Oxford, GB: Oxford Internet Institute, University of Oxford. URL:

https://comprop.oii.ox.ac.uk/wp-

content/uploads/sites/93/2019/09/CyberTroop-Report19.pdf

Chiluwa, I. E., & Samoilenko, S. A. (Eds.). (2019). *Handbook of Research on

Deception, Fake News, and Misinformation Online*. Hershey, PA: IGI

Global.

Collins, M. (2011). *The Law of Defamation and the Internet, Third Edition.*

Oxford, GB: Oxford University Press.

Cox, C. (2014). Protecting Victims of Cyberstalking, Cyberharassment, and

Online Impersonation through Prosecutions and Effective Laws.

Jurimetrics, 54(3), 277-302.

Vosoughi, S., Roy, D., & Aral, S. (2018). The spread of true and false news

online. *Science, 359*(6380), 1146-1151.

Dale, T. (2019). The Fundamental Roles of Technology in the Spread of Fake

News. In I. E. Chiluwa & S. A. Samoilenko (Eds.), *Handbook of

Research on Deception, Fake News, and Misinformation Online* (pp.

122-137). Hershey, PA: IGI Global.

Grazulis, A., & Rogers, R. (2019). Ridiculous and Untrue—FAKE NEWS!":

The Impact of Labeling Fake News. In I. E. Chiluwa & S. A.

Samoilenko (Eds.), *Handbook of Research on Deception, Fake News,

and Misinformation Online* (pp. 138-151). Hershey, PA: IGI Global.

Guadagno, R. E., & Guttieri, K. (2019). Fake News and Information Warfare:

An Examination of the Political and Psychological Processes from the

Digital Sphere to the Real World. In I. E. Chiluwa & S. A. Samoilenko (Eds.), *Handbook of Research on Deception, Fake News, and Misinformation Online* (pp. 167-191). Hershey, PA: IGI Global.

Kaufman, M. (2018, March 8). Twitter users are twice as likely to retweet fake news stories than authentic ones. *Mashable.*

Koch, C. M. (2016). To Catch a Catfish: A Statutory Solution for Victims of Online Impersonation. *University of Colorado Law Review, 88*(1).

Mach, L. T. (2019). The Rise of Professional Facebook Content Generators in Vietnam: A Fake News Campaign against the Betibuti Founder. In I. E. Chiluwa & S. A. Samoilenko (Eds.), *Handbook of Research on Deception, Fake News, and Misinformation Online* (pp. 209-225). Hershey, PA: IGI Global.

Marsh, E. J., Cantor, A. D., & Brashier, N. M. (2016). Believing that Humans Swallow Spiders in Their Sleep: False Beliefs as Side Effects of the Processes that Support Accurate Knowledge. *Psychology of Learning and Motivation, 64,* 93-132.

Pal, A., & Banerjee, S. (2019). Understanding Online Falsehood from the Perspective of Social Problem. In I. E. Chiluwa & S. A. Samoilenko (Eds.), *Handbook of Research on Deception, Fake News, and Misinformation Online* (pp. 1-17). Hershey, PA: IGI Global.

Reynard, L. J. (2019). Troll Farm: Anonymity as a Weapon for Online Character Assassination. In I. E. Chiluwa (Ed.), *Handbook of Research on Deception, Fake News, and Misinformation Online* (pp. 392-419). Hershey, PA: IGI Global.

Reznik, M. (2013). Identity Theft on Social Networking Sites: Developing Issues of Internet Impersonation. *Touro Law Review, 29*(2), article 12.

Solo, A. M. G. (2011). The New Fields of Public Policy Engineering, Political Engineering, Computational Public Policy, and Computational Politics. In *Proceedings of the 2011 International Conference on e-Learning, e-Business, Enterprise Information Systems, and e-Government (EEE'11)*. Watkinsville, GA: CSREA.

Solo, A. M. G., & Bishop, J. (2011). The New Field of Network Politics. In Proceedings of the 2011 International Conference on e-Learning, e-Business, Enterprise Information Systems, and e-Government (*EEE'11*). Wakinsville, GA: CSREA.

Solo, A. M. G. (2014). The New Interdisciplinary Fields of Political Engineering and Computational Politics. In A. M. G. Solo (Ed.), *Political Campaigning in the Information Age* (pp. 226-232). Hershey, PA: IGI Global.

Solo, A. M. G., & Bishop, J. (2014). Conceptualizing Network Politics following the Arab Spring. In A. M. G. Solo (Ed.), *Handbook of Research on Political Activism in the Information Age* (pp. 231-239). Hershey, PA: IGI Global.

Solo, A. M. G., & Bishop, J. (2016). Network Politics and the Arab Spring. *International Journal of Civic Engagement and Social Change (IJCESC), 3*(1), 23-27.

Solo, A. M. G. (2017). An Overview of the New Interdisciplinary Fields of Political Engineering and Computational Politics for the Next Frontier in Politics. In *Proceedings of the 2017 International Conference on Computational Science and Computational Intelligence (CSCI'17)*. Piscataway, NJ: IEEE CPS.

Solo, A. M. G., & Bishop, J. (2017). Conceptualizing Network Politics following the Arab Spring: An African Perspective. In J. Bishop (Ed.), *The Digital Media Reader* (pp. 205-212). Swansea, GB: The Crocels Press Limited.

Solo, A. M. G. (2019a). Brief on Effectively Combatting Cyberbullying and Cyberlibel by Online Hate Groups for the Study on Online Hate of the Standing Committee on Justice and Human Rights for the House of Commons of Canada. Standing Committee on Justice and Human Rights, House of Commons of Canada. URL : https://www.ourcommons.ca/Content/Committee/421/JUST/Brief/BR1 0520155/br-external/SoloAMG-e.pdf

Solo, A. M. G. (2019b). Mémoire sur la lutte efficace contre les actes de cyberintimidation et de diffamation en ligne commis par des groupes haineux présenté au Comité permanent de la justice et des droits de la personne de la Chambre des communes du Canada dans le cadre de son étude sur la haine en ligne. Standing Committee on Justice and Human Rights, House of Commons of Canada. URL: https://www.noscommunes.ca/Content/Committee/421/JUST/Brief/BR 10520155/br-external/SoloAMG-10061182-f.pdf

Solo, A. M. G. (2019c). Combating Online Defamation and Doxing in the United States. In *Proceedings of the 2019 International Conference on Internet Computing and Internet of Things (ICOMP'19)*. Watkinsville, GA: CSREA.

Solo, A. M. G. (2019d). The Interdisciplinary Fields of Political Engineering, Public Policy Engineering, Computational Politics, and Computational Public Policy. In A. M. G. Solo (Ed.), *Handbook of Research on Politics in the Computer Age*. Hershey, PA: IGI Global.

Stengel, R. (2019). *Information Wars: How We Lost the Global Battle Against Disinformation and What We Can Do About It*. New York, NY: Grove Press.

Vosoughi, S., Roy, D., & Aral, S. (2018). The spread of true and false news online. *Science, 359* (6380), 1146-1151.

Watts, C. (2018). Messing with the Enemy: Surviving in a Social Media World of Hackers, Terrorists, Russians, and Fake News. New York, NY: Harper.

The Impact of the Internet on Transnational Civil Society Networks: The Anonymous Movement Unmasked

Shefali Virkar

Abstract

The last quarter of the twentieth century was a time of significant upheaval. Unprecedented advances in computer technology began to collapse vast geographical distances and differences in time and made it possible for people from different parts of the world to form connections in manner not thought possible before. Centred around information, this technological revolution has today transformed the way in which people around the world think, work, share, and communicate. The rise in the number of non-state actors, particularly the emergence of civil society bodies such as NGOs, and the increase of their political influence has thrown up significant questions about how best the Internet and its associated technologies may be harnessed to aid the activities of such organisations and facilitate the formation of international networks.

Introduction

Can the Internet truly augment the effects of those activists, hacktivists, and cyberprotestors seeking to alter the landscape of international relations and political advocacy? This book chapter attempts to answer this question through an examination of the possibly the most iconic, cutting-edge transnational civil society network of the 21st Century: The Anonymous Movement, and the manner in which the collective's participants and constituent elements have successfully harnessed and have in turn been impacted by the Internet and its associated digital platforms and technologies. The research dealt with herein aims to showcase the various intersecting circumstances that help advance Anonymous' contemporary geopolitical power, and in doing so, to contribute to that body of empirical political science which recognises the impact and significance of Information and Communication Technologies and their associated digital platforms on transnational protest and advocacy ever since their development and rapid global proliferation in the mid-1990s. These include Encyclopedia Dramatica, 4chan and 8chan.

New technology is changing the world. Although the idea of a communications network spanning the globe is not new, the past three decades have seen the emergence of a vast global network of computers whose effect on the global political arena has been more significant than any previous technological revolution. Following closely on the heels of the advent of the Internet and the rapid global proliferation of the new digital Information and Communication Technologies (ICTs), are important questions concerning the manner in which transnational civil society networks and movements have been able to harness the potential benefits of complex computer systems and of online networking to mount international campaigns for social change. Is the power of the Internet merely a chimera, unable to deliver on its promises?

In attempting to evaluate the significance of the new digital communications technologies, and their role in transforming global social, political, and economic history, this journal research article will take a brief look at possibly the most iconic transnational civil society network of the 21st Century: *The Anonymous Movement*, and the way in which the collective's participants and constituent elements have successfully harnessed and have been impacted by the Internet and its associated digital platforms, "the biggest technological juggernaut that ever rolled" (Gilder, 1999).

This research showcases the various intersecting elements that contribute to Anonymous' contemporary geopolitical power: the ability of the movement to land mainstream media attention, its bold and recognizable aesthetics, its participatory openness, its use of the Internet and the new digital information and communication technologies to self-organise, and the propaganda and misinformation that surrounds the collective's key participants and constituent structural elements. One feature of this cutting-edge political movement stands out: Anonymous' amorphous unpredictability.

Plugging In: A Brief Background to the Internet

In 1962, an academic at the Massachusetts Institute of Technology (MIT), J.C.R. Licklider, circulated a series of memos elaborating an idea that he called the "Galactic Network", a concept that envisioned "a globally interconnected set of computers through which everyone could quickly access data and programs from any site." He later became the first person to head the computer research programme at the Advanced Research Project Agency (ARPA), a division of the U.S. Department of Defence, where he quickly convinced his successors about of the importance of his idea. His ideas soon converged with those of Paul Baran, an engineer at the American think-tank RAND Corp., whose work stemmed from the concern that a leader of an unfriendly state would be tempted to take advantage of the ease with which military communications could be disrupted and launch a pre-emptive nuclear strike on the USA circumventing its current digital arrangement. As an alternative to conventional circuit switching technology, therefore, which focused on a single line of communication, Baran suggested the creation of a nationwide network of computers to head off such a catastrophe (Abbate, 2001).

Licklider and Baran's ideas were soon put to the test with the creation of the ARPANET, which commenced operations in the early 1970s. The aim of ARPANET was to make research on military defence related issues efficient by enabling researchers and their government sponsors to share resources without having to physically deliver them. The informal collegial, non-hierarchical working relationships that evolved were the chief cause of ARPANET's early success, ultimately resulting in that of the Internet and its associated technologies as we know it today (Warkentin, 2001). ARPANET's users were also involved in its development: the most significant addition being the introduction of *electronic mail* or *e-mail*, an application that very soon became the most popular feature of the project. From a means of sharing data, the ARPANET thus became a medium of instantaneous and rapid communication.

The late 1980s saw a boom in the sale of personal computers (PCs) and a gradual opening of the Internet to public access. The creation of the World Wide Web in the mid-1990s, following the almost complete privatisation of the ARPANET a few years earlier, completed the transformation of the Internet from a purely defence-related research tool into a popular communication medium that allowed for "information gathering, social interaction, entertainment, and self-expression" as well as the overall interaction of many with many on a global scale. Today, the Internet is shaping and is constantly being shaped by the activities of its users like never before. It is inexpensive and increasingly popular - current estimates suggest that over 2.5 billion people were online as of September 2012, up from a little over 600 million in September 2002 (Internet World Stats, 2012). From its inception, the people and groups who use the Internet have had their own 'agendas, resources, and visions' for its future, making its history 'a tale of collaboration and conflict amongst a remarkable variety of players' (Abbate, 2001).

The explosion in the number of civil society networks dependent on the Internet and its associated technologies over the last few years has been touted as one of the most dramatic and intriguing changes in current world politics (Warkentin, 2001). These groups and their ideas proliferate across borders, and infiltrate nearly all major political arenas, thereby altering the landscape of international political economy with their promise of forging a global civil society that is altogether more just and equitable. Delivering this promise, however, depends on the ability of these groups and networks to communicate with each other quickly over vast expanses of space and time; and it is in this endeavour that new communication technologies, particularly the Internet, have played and will continue to play, a crucial role (Frangonikolopoulos, 2012).

One of the more innovative means used by global civil society for mobilisation and communication has been the Internet, which, since its initial inception and subsequent commercialisation, has provided unprecedented opportunities for the exchange of information outside the control of the dominant mainstream media (Fenton, 2007). The prevalence of such information and resources no other available in the mainstream media, which stemming from alternative sources that may otherwise not be heard or easily accessed, has thus the potential to greatly enhance the quality of action in global civil society and the tools available to actors involved in social and political grassroots struggles.

Political observers and social critics are divided, however, as to the nature and ultimate significance of such citizen networks; with the more optimistic (encompassing a broad spectrum ranging from Gramscians to liberals) seeing these networks as being by-and-large positive expressions of democracy in arenas dominated by nation-states and cross-border companies and as having an ever increasing significance on world affairs (Diebert, 2000). A second line of argument takes a more cautious approach, and vocalises an oft-muted concern that, instead of citizen-focused mass democracy, the global arena will be dotted with millions and millions of niche interests.

More particularly, there are those who associate the advent of the Internet with the idea of the information 'haves' and 'have-nots', who are wary of the consequences ensuing from the so-called 'digital divide' (Zinnbauer, 2001). Finally, there those who believe that, far from being constructive, the Internet is harmful to true global civil society, and in that an increasingly digital society results in a gradual decline in an individual's social circle and in the ultimate destruction of social capital which can only be built up and maintained through continuous face-to-face interaction (Huysman & Wulf, 2004).

This research article examines the significance, structure, and impact that the use of the Internet, Internet-based platforms and technologies, and their opportunities for global networking have had on a radically different type of modern day social activist network: the Anonymous Movement collective, borne out of a sustained and successful series of attempts by informally-organised actors and online group to patrol the World Wide Web in a configuration of behaviours that has since the mid-1990s come to be known as 'trolling' (Virkar, 2014).

Networks and Networking: Connecting for Success

The Internet is altering the landscape of political discourse and advocacy in a way no other technology has done before (Virkar, 2014). It has proved of great use to those who wish to influence foreign policy and the international decision-making process, particularly non-state actors - both individuals and organisations. Cyber activism (otherwise known as Internet activism or *hackitivism*) involves *a normal, non-disruptive use of the Internet in support of an agenda or cause* (Hampson, 2012); such as the use of the Web as an information resource, the construction of user-friendly websites and the posting of material for public viewing, the use of e-mail to disseminate information and electronic publications and letters, and the use of the World Wide Web as a place to discuss issues, form alliances, and to plan and co-ordinate activities (Jordan & Taylor, 2004).

Coupled with a steadily growing online community, the Internet has become a powerful, inexpensive medium through which ideas and agendas may be communicated (Virkar, 2011). The beauty of the Internet lies in its ability to cross national boundaries, enabling people and organisations from diverse geographical regions to come together to influence foreign policy anywhere in the world (Denning, 2001). Today, many virtual communities are focused on shared political beliefs, and there are a number of websites encouraging online activism (Wall, 2007). The owners of some websites, such as Netaction.com, have even published online 'how-to' guides and training programmes, which *inter-alia* aim to adapt and popularise the use of e-mail, cyberspace networking, internet relay chats, instant messaging and intranets as a means of expanding and sustaining the cyber activist community. As 'The Virtual Activist training manual' proclaims:

"... Although you'll need some special skills to build and maintain a Web site, e-mail is easily mastered even if you have little or no technical expertise. If you can read and write and your computer has a modem, you can be a Virtual Activist!" (Krause et. al., 2007)

The successful use of the Internet by civil society organisations lies chiefly in the key organisational process of *networking* (Hampson, 2012). A critical concept, particularly in the context of collective action in the Information Age, the idea of a network is fundamental to an understanding of the dynamics of both online communication and collaboration and to the work that civil society organisations carry on offline (Wall, 2007). In theory, a network consists chiefly of a number of nodes connected to each other in a loose, horizontal, flexible structure that may expand and integrate new nodes and satellites, as long as communication and information flows between the key nodes is maintained (Castells, 1996).

It is easy to infer, therefore, that the emergence of the Internet would greatly benefit the setting up and maintenance of civil society networks in the today's world. Effective use of the Internet and its associated technologies does indeed seem to mitigate traditional difficulties of conventional civil society networks, particularly those issues pertaining to the co-ordination of functions, focusing its resources on specific goals and restraints placed on it due to its size and complexity (Van Laer & Van Aelst, 2010). Scholars of digital society such as Castells often credit the Internet as being the technological basis of form that civil society networks take in the Information Age. Accordingly, the use of technology results in networks having a potent combination of "flexibility and task performance, co-ordinated decision-making and decentralised execution, of individual expression and global horizontal communication which provide a superior form for human action" (Castells, 2001:2).

Networking Dissent: Cyber Activists use of the Internet

The Internet may be put to a variety of uses by civil society organisations (Arquilla & Ronfeldt, 2001). The five main modes of Internet usage listed and elucidated upon below. These modes are by no means unrelated and are frequently used in combination by civil society networks to enhance their efficacy (Harwood & Lay, 2001).

Collection

The Internet is a vast storehouse of information, most of it available for free. Today, fact-sheets, policy statements, legislative documents, academic papers, critiques and analyses, and other items relating to a wide variety issues are available for download online. Activists can get hold of whatever material they need at the click of a button, using one of the many search engines, e-mail lists, or chat services available online. News channels providing almost minute-to-minute updates are also available and prove especially invaluable to groups wishing to monitor ongoing events. In addition, websites provide activists with information on how to use the Internet, its associated applications and digital technologies more effectively.

Publication

Organisations use the Internet to post and distribute information for public consumption. They can create interactive websites that provide global audiences may include fact-sheets, reports, lectures, and interviews. They may publish online journals, create mailing lists, online discussion groups, and bulletin boards. By using the Internet to publish and disseminate information, civil society groups can take advantage of its relatively low costs whilst at the same time reaching out a global audience. The interwoven nature of the World Wide Web, with its links, attachments, and hypertext, enhances its effectiveness as a medium of effective and far-reaching information dissemination.

Dialogue and Debate

E-mail, newsgroups, web forums, chat rooms, and the like provide to civil society multiple forums for the discussion and debate of various issues. For instance, the use of chat rooms has been a subject of robust debate amongst social scientists; with some scholars touting on the one hand virtual discussions as being as good for the building of social capital amongst network members as face-to-face conversations, and with others believing that the only outcome of such impersonal communications is a gradual decline in the quality of interpersonal relationships.

Organising and Mobilising

Advocacy groups use the Internet to increase awareness and mobilise people to rally around an issue. The Net also enables groups to co-ordinate action among members and with other organisations and individuals, across borders and across time-zones. Plans of action may be circulated via e-mail or posted on websites, which exist solely to facilitate better co-ordination between different members of a network.

Lobbying Decision-Makers

The Internet facilitates the lobbying of those in power and has contributed to the success of many online campaigns. In particular, the use of e-mail has become very popular with, for example, e-mails containing sample protest letters being sent to people on electronic mailing lists, or through the setting up of e-mail boxes by activist groups to gather signatures for petitions. These days, almost everyone who's anyone in the echelons of power and civil society has an e-mail address, and some websites meticulously compile a list of such government officials and urge people to write in to them. It is not clear how successful such lobbying campaigns are. It is possible that, with e-mail software to block certain types of incoming electronic mail, and the use of standard, automatically generated replies used to respond to electronic petitions, campaign success depends on how well augmented the use of the Internet and associated platforms is with more traditional offline methods; backing the argument made by some that the Internet alone is not an adequate tool for public political movement.

There are, however, several disadvantages or potential drawbacks to the use of the Internet that can limit its usefulness to grassroots groups engaged in political action. More specifically, many of these "downsides" depend on what facets of the Internet are used and the context within which they are applied. Much like the advantages of the Internet discussed above, some have to do with the medium's unique characteristics.

The Internet is a Single Source of Communication

Although the Internet was designed for robustness during the time of emergency, disruptions in the global network of networks can and have occurred. In July 1997, for example, Internet traffic "ground to a halt" across much of the United States because of a freak combination of technical and human errors, forewarning what some Internet experts believed could someday be a more catastrophic meltdown (Chandrasekaran & Corcoran, 1997). Similarly, at a micro-level, Internet crashes and outages are a regular feature of everyday life the world over. Other, older, technologies such as the facsimile and the telephone continue to have an advantage over the Internet in given situations, particularly if a sender needs immediate acknowledgement or if information is required urgently or covertly or both (Larmer, 1995).

Communications Over the Internet Can Be Easily Monitored

Public platforms and Internet websites are easy to monitor and control, particularly by state organisations or individuals with the appropriate technical know-how. Further, private one-to-one electronic messages may be slightly more secure, however, these again can be hacked by anyone with sufficient technical knowledge. Whilst data encryption packages may provide a solution to individuals and organisations exchanging private or classified information, these programmes and their related technologies might for a while remain out of reach of the majority of Internet users (Danitz & Stobel, 2001).

Opponents May Try to Use the Internet for Sabotage

This disadvantage is related to many of the concerns discussed above, but also represents a more active use of the Internet by activists, hacktivists and cyber criminals alike to trick, disrupt, or otherwise sow dissension (de Armond, 2001). This is because the Internet allows for anonymity and makes it possible for provocateurs posing as someone or something else to try to cause dissension or sidetrack the campaign by posting messages for that purpose (Kalathil & Boas, 2010).

Information on the Internet is Unmediated

One of the advantages of the Internet for activists and many other users, of course, is the fact that it allows them to dispense with the traditional filters for news and information (Virkar, 2014). It allows users to self-select information they are interested in and retrieve data in far more detail than available in a newspaper or, certainly, a television programme. This same lack of structure, however, can present dangers, allowing for wide and rapid dissemination of information that is of questionable accuracy, being factually incorrect or propagandistic, including material that is racist, sexist, or otherwise hateful and incendiary (Arquilla & Ronfeldt, 2001).

Access to the Internet and Technical Know-How is Not Equal

Not all who wish to play a role in a campaign for change, have access to the most modern tools of communication, including computers, modems, and the necessary telephone lines or other means to connect to the Internet. As already noted, access to encryption methods that allow for more secure communication may be limited, and technical knowledge concentrated in a small pool of hacktivists bent on causing destruction (Norris, 2001).

The Internet Cannot Replace Face-to-Face Contact

Put simply, the Internet and other communications media cannot replace human interaction. Rather, the Internet has its own set of advantages and disadvantages, with Internet campaigns, because of their decentralized electronic nature, being decidedly unstable (Juris, 2005). Whilst the use of the Internet may supplement face-to-face interactions, it cannot wholly substitute for them as personal interactions constitute nearly-all initial campaigning groundwork (Kalathil & Boas, 2010).

Have transnational civil society networks been able to harness the potential benefits of the Internet and online networking to mount international campaigns for social change? Or is the power of the complex computer systems networking illusory, unable to deliver on its promises? This research article examines the significance, structure, and impact that the use of the Internet, Internet-based platforms and technologies, and its opportunities for global networking have had on a radically different type of modern day social activist network: the Anonymous Movement collective, borne out of a sustained and successful series of attempts by informally-organised actors and online group to patrol the World Wide Web in a configuration of behaviours that has since the mid-1990s come to be known as 'trolling' (Virkar, 2014).

The research paper is divided into three sections. The work commences with a brief overview of the concept of digital networking, moving on to discuss the advantages of the Internet, Internet-based platforms, and digital communications technologies accruing to transnational social networks; in their formation, maintenance, and evolution. The second section, within the framework elucidated, examines in detail The Anonymous Movement and the collective's antecedents. The research first proposes a fairly straightforward, narrative account of Anonymous from 2005 to the present, with key emphasis given to the major events and turning points that define both its constitution and the group's subsequent evolution as a global social movement.

This chronology might be considered particularly necessary given the intrinsic nature of Anonymous as a chimera within the given panoply of identifiable protest movements online and the high degree of misinformation surrounding it, in direct contrast to the nature of the technological network the collective claims to harness near-exclusively and the civil liberties it professes to defend. The core features of the Anonymous movement, which in turn shed light on its political significance, together with the strengths and weaknesses of Anonymous as a protest movement of recognisable success are also briefly considered. Finally, the research article concludes with an assessment of the broader implications that the Internet revolution holds for civil society networks in the 21st century.

The Anonymous Movement Case Study: Net Resistance = Net Benefits?

The following in-depth case study examines the use of the Internet and its associated platforms and technologies by the global civil society network collective, Anonymous, worldwide. Though seemingly different to the traditional socio-anthropological ideal of transnational civil society groups, the Anonymous Movement nonetheless possesses uncanny similarities to other grassroots protest movements of the digitally networked modern era. Firstly, the Anonymous collective's actions and activist interventions centre around and focus on the impact that the advent of the Internet and the rapid proliferation of Information and Communication Technologies (ICTs) have had on global market forces and globalisation, issues at the heart of recent events in international political economy, and concerns that are bound to increase in importance during the years to come.

Political commentators might also see the rise of the Anonymous movement as proof that transnational citizen networks offer a counter-hegemonic, activist alternative in the grassroots rebellion that has sparked against capitalism, authority, and the State. Secondly, the nature and scale of Anonymous operations has pre-empted, in many instances, resounding if temporary success; Multinational Corporations and national governments have been pushed onto the back foot as a consequence of hacker strike attacks and through the organisation of mass protest, whilst the importance of transnational multilateral agreements and their ensuing discussions lessened as a direct result of operational fallout.

The final common denominator, and the real reason behind the choice of the Anonymous Movement as a case study, is the base fact that the documented, major successes borne out of the committed participation of the collective's constituent elements have been attributed wholly to the Internet and to the rapid transnational proliferation of digital technologies. The high correlation between these successes and the manner of use of the World Wide Web by members of Anonymous, together with the potential lessons that future campaigns might learn from the further elucidation of these experiences are hence the two chief reasons that make the chosen research case study key to a holistic understanding of the role that Internet and its associated technologies play in the shaping of global political architecture.

Anonymous in Context: The Power and the Politics Behind the Mask

The Anonymous Movement is difficult to pin down and to describe. When considered either as an umbrella term or a rallying cry, the word Anonymous signifies a banner used by individuals and groups to organize diverse forms of Internet-based collective action; ranging from street protests to distributed denial of service (DDoS) campaigns to covert hacking attacks.

Unlike self-professed or registered members of Anonymous, many individual hackers and Internet-based hacktivists work part-time, informally, and surreptitiously. Similarly, organizations whose websites, online databases, and digital repositories have been either hacked or partially compromised usually get to decide whether or not to disclose the precise details of their circumstances and situations to the general public. The Anonymous Movement, in direct contrast, is an informal collective of undisclosed individuals and groups that seeks publicity and attention from the mainstream media before and after every successful action. The fundamental paradox at work here is that state-supported or state-sponsored activism and hacking is altogether much better organized and sufficiently funded and, in most respects, far more powerful than the symbolic action undertaken by the Anonymous collective.

More precisely, a significant proportion of Anonymous participants, known colloquially as "Anons", work independently, whilst yet others work in small teams full-time, or join in as part of a swarm of demonstrators during a flashmob or other large-scale campaign. Further, the Anonymous Movement lacks the human and financial resources required for the general collective to engage in either the long-term strategic thinking or the planning required to code, to operate, and to sustain military grade hardware and software. More particularly, Anonymous possesses neither the steady income nor the fiscal sponsorship necessary to support a dedicated team tasked with recruiting individuals, coordinating activities, and developing sophisticated computer networks.

Considered within broad framework of its *modus operandi*, Anonymous tends to ride and to amplify the wave of any existing events or activist causes currently trending. However, even if its involvement magnifies and extends the scope of an event or of an occurrence, sometimes so remarkably as to alter the very nature or base significance of the happenstance, tradition dictates that the constituent elements of the Anonymous Movement do not sustain their participation until the bitter end, and that the campaign is eventually discontinued before popular interest wanes.

Oftentimes Anonymous members opt to miss out on the wave completely or choose to act against the grain of the *vox populi*, particularly when the mainstream media fails to rise entirely to the proffered bait and report especially on the specifics of the movement's operations. Wherein, therefore, lies the real power of Anonymous? Without the wholehearted support of the mainstream media and of the general public, how has the movement in successfully accomplishing its objectives managed to strike such fear into corporations, governments, and other groups and activist collectives?

V for Vendetta and The Rise Of Anonymous: 2005 - 2014

Anonymous' ancestry lies in the often obnoxious, occasionally humorous, generally murky, and at times terrifying world of Internet trolling, wherein malicious pranking and cyber-bullying abounds. More precisely, when located within the contextual framework of the movement, the term Internet Trolling is particularly indicative of pathological patterns of digital interaction that consist primarily of acts which deliberately try to chronically distress a person online through the periodic indulgence of frequently inflammatory and abusive behaviour, although usually just to cause disruption without direction and too often do so anonymously (Virkar, 2014).

Internet-based groups and movements like Anonymous have called themselves 'trolls' in order to legitimise their regular abusive behaviour and organised protest action (Bishop, 2014) although in contrast, when more generally surveyed, trolling may be considered as a favourite Internet-based pastime of the bored, the insecure, and the antisocial; usually attempting to bait and to subsequently harm members of the virtual community, collective, or given digital environment into descending to the level of the aggressor or to a similar state of mind.

The Anonymous Movement first made headlines in 2005 when, following the release worldwide of the movie V for Vendetta, the collective adopted the central character's signature mask as the future emblem of the network and as the symbol of a faceless rebel horde (Olson, 2013). First published in 1982, the comic series V for Vendetta charted a masked vigilante's attempt to bring down a fascist British government together with its complicit media (Moore, 2012). Today, it would appear that the central character's charismatic grin has furnished, for members of the Anonymous Movement, a ready-made identity for likeminded, highly motivated protesters (Colter, 2011); one that at once embodies resonances of anarchy, romance, and of theatre – sentiments that are clearly well-suited to the contemporary *cyberactivism* and hacktivist action of the network, from Madrid's Indignados to the Occupy Wall Street movement (Kushner, 2014).

By 2007, Anonymous had become so well known for organised irreverent or casual trolling that Fox News dubbed the collective "the Internet hate machine" (Coleman, 2013). Anonymous mockingly embraced this hyperbolic title (Anonymous, 2007). Six months later, following the adoption of the media epithet by the collective, individuals – primarily participants from 4chan.org – began to operate under the Anonymous banner and to use the imagery, symbolism, and the iconography associated with the movement whilst trolling online and during their appearances at public mass demonstrations and protests (Olson, 2013).

The online trolling campaign against the Church of Scientology was first launched under the banner of Anonymous in 2008, sparked off by a now infamous recruitment video featuring Tom Cruise praising the organisation's efforts to "create new and better realities" (Coleman, 2013). The video, leaked by critics of the church, promptly went viral (Olson, 2013). When the Church of Scientology threatened legal action, members of Anonymous commenced a sustained trolling and DDoS campaign that eventually gave way to Project Chanology (Stone, 2014); a prolonged and earnest political campaign against the church and its supporters hosted on 4chan.org (Fuchs, 2013).

Following a successful start to its hacktivist action, Anonymous in 2009 and 2010 focussed on building on its involvement with Operation Chanology (otherwise known to 4chan.org participants as OpChanology) (Stone, 2014). Trolling activity began to wane by mid-2010, when Anonymous' political portfolio began to diversify following Operation Titstorm, a DDoS attack on the Australian government protesting against legislation aimed at curbing online pornography via the institution of mandatory filters for Internet Service Providers (ISPs) (Coleman, 2013).

In September 2010, self-organising in the name of Internet freedom, a small group of Anons set their eyes on protesting against the Anti-Counterfeiting Trade Agreement (ACTA); the pro-copyright, multilateral agreement on the enforcement of intellectual property rights (Ackerman, 2012). The faction eventually managed to establish a sizable street team of participants and supporters, and a dedicated IRC server in November 2010 called AnonOps (Coleman, 2013).

AnonOps came to the notice of the wider public in December 2010, following the collective's opposition to the recent censorship of the whistle-blowing organisation WikiLeaks (Fuchs, 2013). In response to their refusal to accept payments and donations in the name of the WikiLeaks founder Julian Assange, Anonymous via the AnonOps platform, launched a series DDoS attacks aimed at PayPal, MasterCard, and Visa (Stone, 2014).

By 2011, both Anonymous and WikiLeaks became names emblematic of free speech in the face of censorship (Coleman, 2013). Individual participants began to organise in dedicated AnonOps chat rooms and over channels, teaming up with local activists and hackers in countries like Tunisia, Libya, Egypt, Algeria, and Syria, for a series of campaigns in what came to be known as "Freedom Ops". AnonOps that year also diversified its political portfolio; transitioning to include subtler Web-based hacking activity against corporate security firm HBGary (Olson, 2013) and database DDoS attacks in opposition to changes made by the San Francisco Bay Area Rapid Transit (BART) (Coleman, 2013).

The winter of 2011-2012 stood witness to yet another increase in online activity amongst members of Anonymous, wherein Anons were in action against a slew of errant corporations and legislative measures (Sembrat, 2011); including the global intelligence firm Stratfor, protests against the looming copyright bill –

Stop Online Piracy Act (SOPA), the establishment of a new leaks platform

Par:AnoIA (Potentially Alarming Research), a flurry of international operations

including OpQuebec and OpIndia, and the Occupy Wall Street movement

(Stone, 2014). Most recently, participant hackers of the Anonymous movement

have become embroiled in Operation Last Resort which, in 2013, comprised of

a series of web defacements and hacks commemorating the memory of activist

and hacker Aaron Swartz (Coleman, 2013).

Theorising Anonymous: From Trolling for the Lulz to the Theory of Organised Chaos Online

Consider, for example, the birth of the movement as an activist endeavour.

Prior to 2008, the name Anonymous was deployed almost exclusively as a

generic umbrella term alternative to the locution "trolling", which in Internet

parlance refers to the pulling of oft-harmful pranks targeting people and

organizations, the desecration and slander of reputations, and the revelation of

harmful, humiliating, or personal information online (Virkar, 2014).

During the early years of the Internet, configurations of trolling behaviour were

coordinated over online platforms, often on the image board 4chan.org, for the

sake of "the lulz"; that is, in order to elicit "malicious laughter" (Virkar, 2014).

Anonymous accidentally, if altogether dramatically, however, first cut its teeth

and enlarged its repertoire of tactics during the summer of 2008 (Olson, 2013).

That year, several of the collective's participants came together over, and the movement sprouted a concerted activist sensibility during, a full-fledged pranking campaign against the Church of Scientology (Bishop, 2014). Two years later, by 2010, distinct and stable activist nodes of the Anonymous Movement had emerged (Coleman, 2013). The name Anonymous was also increasingly being used to herald online activist and hacktivist action and activity, particularly those exploits that often in several ways defied the expectations of both the general public and the mainstream media (Parker, 2014).

At the heart of Anonymous' success as an amorphous, online hacktivist movement or collective, and as staple component of both its contemporary activist programmation and historical development, are continued to be found the key complex network traits of mutability and of dynamism (Coleman, 2013). In consequence, it is altogether difficult to predict, trend, or to forecast *where*, *when*, or *why* the Anonymous movement will strike, *if* a new node will appear in the network, *whether* a campaign will be successful, and *how* the constituent elements of the collective might change direction or alter tactics during the course of an operation (Olson, 2013). A by-product of the Internet, and of the rapid global proliferation of the medium, Anonymous is reputed to rise up and act most forcefully and to garner the most popular support and media coverage whilst defending the fundamental democratic values and human rights associated with this global communications platform, such as free speech and privacy (Fuchs, 2013).

However, the Anonymous movement has repeatedly demonstrated that it is not bound by tradition to either this modus operandi or to any other political imperative (Parker, 2014). Over the last five years, Anonymous has contributed decisively to an astonishing array of *causes celebres*; from the publicisation of rape cases in small-town Ohio and Halifax to the aiding and abetting of rebellion in the Arab and the African Spring of 2011 (Kushner, 2014). It is this continuous and constant cycle of growth, circulation, and ongoing metamorphosis that makes the next steps of the Anonymous collective difficult to ascertain and to effectively combat.

Further, despite media reports to the contrary, the Anonymous movement, although nimble, flexible, and emergent, is neither random, shadowy, nor chaotic (Coleman, 2013). Whilst Anonymous, both as a rallying banner under which hacktivists and cyberprotestors gather and as the sum total of the composite individual participants of the collective, may be devilishly unpredictable and difficult to study, the key campaigns of the movement still comprise a number of recognisable core features (Fuchs, 2013).

In contextualizing the Anonymous movement collective within the framework of both recent and historic global socio-political and economic currents and trends, it is altogether unsurprising that a fiery protest movement, closely wedded to the Internet and involving the hyper-networked medium's central features and significant benefits, has arisen at this time in history and in this particular form. As indicated by its very name, Anonymous underlines, highlights, and dramatizes the importance of anonymity and privacy in an era when these civil liberties and other similar fundamental democratic rights are perceived as being rapidly eroded as a consequence of the emergence and development of new, highly sophisticated digital information and communications technology, coupled with a parallel rise in increased government secrecy and in systematic security surveillance.

The Anonymous Movement has also been extremely vocal and forthright on issues of international import during a period of especial, tumultuous global unrest and discontent, evident in the increasing high-frequency of large scale popular uprisings that have occurred across the world; most recently, the 15-M Movement in Spain (2011), the Arab and African Spring (2011), and the Occupy Movement in the U.S.A. (2011) (Kushner, 2014). Over the last two years, in keeping with global economic and historical cyclical convention, sharp inequalities in economic performance the world over have been met by a tide of grassroots protest activity online (Virkar, 2014).

Whilst remaining independent and distinct from this historical tradition, Anonymous considers itself still part and parcel of the general global trend; symbolically showcasing its conception of the ideal for privacy and other civil liberties, together with acting as both the popular face of global digital unrest and the rallying cry across these various protest movements. In this manner, Anonymous demonstrates and exercises the power of symbolic Internet-based digital engagement within the broader political contextual framework of direct social action.

The Logic of Anonymous: Global Civil Society And 'The Weapons Of The Geek'

Relying on a fairly predictable stereotype, most commentators, from scholars to field practitioners and working professionals, usually think of the Anonymous movement as consisting of an evasive and shadowy group of hackers (Parker, 2014). This truncated description often runs contrary to discussions of sociological reality, to the very real social composition of the collective (Fuchs, 2013). Although Anonymous is certainly home to hackers of various hues, a great many Anons are neither proficient at programming nor are difficult to find (Parker, 2014). True to fact, if one wants to talk with Anonymous participants, simply log onto one of their IRC networks (Kushner, 2014).

della Porta and Diani (1999) define social movements as possessing four major characteristics: social movements are (1) informal networks, based upon (2) shared beliefs and a sense of solidarity, wherein (3) constituent actors mobilize around (4) controversial, contentious, and emotive issues, through (5) the frequent employ of various forms of protest (della Porta & Diani 1999). In other words, social movements might be defined as "networks of informal interactions between a plurality of individuals, groups and/ or organizations, engaged in political or cultural conflicts, on the basis of shared collective identities" (Diani 1992: 13).

In studying hypermodern global social movements like Anonymous, Fuchs (2006) further identifies a number of defining aspects necessary to the advancement of this typography of actor-network relationship. These include the presence of: societal problems; the negation of dominant values, institutions and structures; dissatisfaction; adversaries; shared collective identities; orientation towards social change; triggers of protest, their repercussions, and the effects of contagion; network mobilization through protest practices and collective action; protest methods and their deployment; and extra-parliamentary politics and politicking.

A specific characteristic of Anonymous is that the collective considers itself to be at once a *global social movement* and an *anti-movement* (Fuchs, 2013); its activist interventions and political action are based upon and constituted out of a shared common identity and group identification with a common set of basic values which include fundamental civil liberties and freedom of the Internet that results in protest practices online and offline against common adversaries, whilst simultaneously involving many of the regular participants on

Anonymous platforms there to engage primarily in individual play and in entertainment (Kushner, 2014). In this respect, Anons participate in collective action predominantly 'for the lulz'; traditionally to elicit malicious fun for the participant-users concerned (Virkar, 2014), but from time-to-time to convert individual action into collective political intervention (Bishop, 2014).

In keeping with the collective's reputation as a global social or protest movement, Anonymous' political actions are grounded in a number of shared, pivotal, base political values that are elucidated upon in *5 Principles: An Anonymous Manifesto*, the movement's core political polemic (Fuchs, 2013). The group's stated values might be further summarised as being a struggle for an "open, fair, transparent, accountable and just society", in which information is "unrestricted and uncensored", and wherein Anonymous in central to the upholding of citizens' "rights and liberties" and to underwriting of a guarantee to strengthen the "privacy of citizens" so that "citizens shall not be the target of any undue surveillance" (Coleman, 2013). Anonymous further operates on the basis of three concurrent principles: that (1) the media should not be attacked; that (2) critical infrastructure should not be attacked; and that (3) individual action should work for justice and freedom (Fuchs, 2013).

Scholars of global civil activism and their practitioner-activist counterparts each possess their own separate interpretations and judgements concerning these basic, fundamental values of freedom and justice set down in the

Anonymous Manifesto. The overall impression of Anonymous when examined from the perspective of the scholarly community is that of a collective functioning according to exceedingly loose principles and moral standards, very much unlike a highly formalised party-political programme (Fuchs, 2013). While this degree of flexibility might also be characteristic of other contemporary social movements, Anonymous diverges from them in maintaining a high level of anonymity amongst, for, and within its various activists and differing protest practices (Parker, 2014).

Conventional social movements, in the manner of political party networks, tend to encourage and be sustained through the establishment and maintenance of personal relations, face-to-face meetings, discussions, and actions (Fuchs, 2006). Similarly, their campaigns are often focused on the targeting of strategic adversaries (Fuchs, 2013.). In contrast, the highly decentralized and informal character of the Anonymous network often results in multiple independent and parallel campaigns that can become networked and coordinated but can also exist independently (Coleman, 2013), wherein people who share in a basic value are allowed to declare an action in the movement's name (Kushner, 2014).

Anonymous, similar to its other global civil society counterparts, conforms to permutations in "logics of action" that might be combined in different ways (della Porta & Diani 2006; Fuchs, 2013). Within this framework, Anonymous' chosen methods of protest are unconventional, if not hypermodern. Protests can take place either online, primarily as conversation in Internet Relay Chat (IRC) rooms or through the hacking of websites, the publishing personal of data, DDoS attacks, and/ or offline, as street protests or mass demonstrations (Fuchs, 2013). The logic of the Anonymous movement is that of collective action organised and executed at a distance (Sembrat, 2011). The first logic of action requires, therefore, that the collective achieve temporal synchronicity, difficult to co-ordinate when there are distributed actions conducted over the Internet remotely (Fuchs, 2013). The second logic of protest action associated with the movement is that which coordinated and planned online, but which makes use of temporal and spatial co-presence both on- and offline (Kushner, 2014).

Irreverent Activism and the Notion of Digital Direct Action

Invented in 1989, Internet Relay Chat (or *IRC*) is still used by geeks and hackers to develop collaborative software and, as its name suggests, to chat or to converse (Coleman, 2013). IRC, unlike other rich-text media, consists of only bare-bones functionality: the medium is entirely text-based, generally free of brightly colour, icons, cute noises, and interaction is conducted in-window with its own mix of text commands and norms of communication (Glenny, 2011). In being ideal for real-time communication and for coordinating protest action and operations, many Anons become regulars within various stable IRC networks, where they converse and find fellowship on public or private channels (Olson, 2013). In many regards, these channels function similar to online social clubs, open round the clock. Anons aren't required to collaborate over IRC (Stone, 2014); some prefer to act alone, whilst others turn to Web forums, open platforms like Twitter or .delicious, or to other chat protocols (Olson, 2013). Truly illegal activities are orchestrated over by-invite-only, encrypted communication channels (Glenny, 2011).

Hackers, from programmers to security researchers to system administrators, are essential to maintaining the lifeblood of Anonymous' networks: they erect and maintain communications infrastructure, infiltrate servers to expose weak security, or in their hunt for information, leak data (Parker, 2014). Nevertheless, compared to other spheres of hacker activity wherein contributions, and often respect, require and are determined by the prevalent degree of technical skill, Anonymous is more participatory, in that what sustains the movement is its dynamism and flexibility (Kushner, 2014). No particular abilities are advertised as being required. Whilst hackers obviously wield more technical power, and their opinions carry weight online, this subset of participants do not either erect barriers to entry or control the evolution of Anonymous (Coleman, 2013).

Individuals without technical skills may participate collectively through actively recruiting new volunteers, writing press communiqués, giving media interviews on IRC, designing propaganda posters, editing videos, and by mining information that is publicly available but difficult to access (Kushner, 2014). Organizers also emerge from within the ranks to advise, inspire, and to corral troops; and sometimes to broker between different groups and networks in the formation of inter-network *ad hoc* teams (Parker, 2014). Although the structure of the Anonymous network may at times appear to be chaotic, participants rarely choose targets at random (Olson, 2013). Operations tend to be reactive, whereby existing local, regional, and international events and causes can trigger action from Anonymous groups worldwide (Kushner, 2014). Given this, all types of collective operations can usually be linked to a particular IRC network, including *AnonOps*, *AnonNetor*, *Voxanon* or related Twitter accounts, such as *@OpLastResort*, dedicated to the particular operation at hand (Olson, 2013).

Being part of Anonymous

In order to be part of Anonymous, therefore, one needs to simply self-identify as being Anonymous. No single group or individual can dictate the manner and direction in which the name or the iconography of the Anonymous movement is used, much less claim legal ownership over its pseudonyms, aliases, icons, and actions. The Weapons of the Geek remain out of public reach.

We Are Legion: Anonymous, From Flash Crowd to Slashdot

The Anonymous Movement considers itself as being nothing short of "21st century enlightenment" personified (Fuchs, 2013). True. The collective cannot be simply described as being a mere 'part-and-parcel' of the enlightenment dialectic of modern-day, turn-of-the-century informational capitalism (Taylor, 2013). In both demanding and opposing the very rights and values that capitalism, its constitutions, and its adherents profess, the movement and its constituent participatory elements have demonstrated and have publicly disclosed – through positions taken and held with relation to the methods of direct action employed, means of indirect intervention resorted to, and stance taken in terms of moral reasoning – the contradictions inherent within Anonymous' equation with the general *vox populi* and with hypermodern-day society at large; manifest and expressed in terms of degrees of freedom observable and the differences intrinsic to the spectrum of conventional liberal ideology.

Only a handful of actions performed under the banner of the Anonymous movement have been atypical and radically non-conformist (Parker, 2014). Hence, whilst predictions of chaos unleashed by malicious or maladjusted hackers loom large within the ambit of the state's anxieties regarding Anonymous, they remain largely unrealized. That's not to say that all of Anonymous' operations are laudable, effective, or, indeed, publicly acknowledged. On the contrary, as the base character and tactics of each Anonymous operation are usually distinct, blanket moral judgments are hard to make, and related pronouncements tend to be overly simplistic as against either nuanced or sophisticated (Fuchs, 2013).

The majority of individual Anons never break the law; however, since Anonymous cannot and will not generally police participants as a collective, it's possible that some may do so (Stone, 2014). Further, despite the given unpredictability of the movement, its past actions provide no sound basis for predicting the future. Nonetheless, reckless operations meant to endanger lives have, thus far, never been part of Anonymous' overt moral calculus or tactical repertoire (Coleman, 2013). Certain factions have certainly done so covertly; wherein any vulnerability has been exploited, and any advantage generally leveraged (Ackerman, 2012).

Unlike other criminal groups who want to remain hidden, Anonymous seeks the limelight regularly to publicize its campaigns and the direct action employed therein (Olson, 2013). Both the mainstream and grassroots media also contribute towards the achievement of this public relations agenda, frequently featuring and sometimes highlighting the more controversial acts of the collective within their reportage and, in doing so, invariably boosting the Anonymous movement's global profile and public image (Kushner, 2014).

Partly as a consequence of its maverick image, and in part the nature and scale of its transgressive antics, Anonymous has attracted significant international attention, sometimes admiration, sometimes caution, and oftentimes fear (Parker, 2014). As an entity, the Anonymous collective intends itself to be amorphous, indestructible, slippery, evasive, and even invisible; if at the same time both international and, within its sphere of influence, omnipotent (Fuchs, 2013). Anonymous' overarching principle of organisational structure — *anonymity*, or more technically put, *pseudonymity* — makes it difficult to tell just how many people are involved overall (Coleman, 2013).

As a result, misinformation regarding Anonymous abounds. Some of it is self-created, some has been foisted upon the movement. Although core participants exist, and chat channels are overtly dedicated to reporters and to movement reportage, Anonymous reputed to comprise a shifting cast of characters (Ackerman, 2012). Some individuals routinely change their online nicknames (Olson, 2013). Catching up can prove frustrating, and certainly time consuming once a participant leaves for a spell, even more so for an outside observer (Kushner, 2014). Journalists, even those reporting for reputable news outlets, have at times incorrectly identified and typecast Anonymous direct action (Parker, 2014).

To disguise itself further, deflect media attention, and to even confound anonymous participants internal to and embedded within the collective,

Anonymous also seeds false propaganda (Taylor, 2014). It can be hard, at times, to distinguish fib from fact, truth from lies. However, this obfuscation only adds to the collective's mystique and, thence, to the innate power of The Anonymous Movement.

Conclusions: Anonymous and the Future of the Internet

"The world at large is exactly what is at stake. Geographical borders seem to be of no importance whatsoever to the new media - they simply haven't been invited to the global ICT party."

Source: Sarai Report to The Waag

Never before in the history of mankind has any invention shot from obscurity to global fame in quite the way the Internet has. Never before has any new technology given us a peek into the future in quite the same manner: a glimpse into a highly interconnected world where the cost of transmitting and accessing an infinite amount of information is reduced to virtually nothing, where material boundaries are no longer limits to human action, and constrained physical space is replaced by a virtual '*cyberspace*' which is not subject to traditional hierarchies and to conventional power relations. And where there is place for all regardless of gender, sexual orientation, nationality, ethnicity, or religion. In short, the Internet promises us a rapid movement towards a just and prosperous world, and the development of a truly global, comprehensively networked civil society.

At the same time, there are roadblocks to be overcome if the Internet, together with the medium's associated applications and platforms, is to deliver on its promises. Contrary to the claims of cyber romantics, equality and empowerment are not inevitable consequences of the use of technology and its application to day-to-day living. The present bias of the Internet towards the West, with the predominance of English as the major *lingua franca* online, reinforces the existing global digital divide and reflects the lopsided power relationships currently prevalent in contemporary world politics. This imbalance is a formidable barrier to a truly international and hyper-networked civil society, and there is no guarantee that alteration to modern society will see it rectified in the near future. Furthermore, issues of Internet regulation and security have, particularly after its effective use by criminal and terrorist networks such as Al-Qaeda, become hotly debated issues in both scholarly and practitioner circles.

In the Information Age, societies and civilisations find themselves highly interconnected. The days of closed-door negotiations and secret repression are drawing to an end. As many national governments and supranational agencies have found out the hard way, the digital technology has empowered those Non-Governmental Organisations, protest movements, and advocacy groups that have embraced the Internet and which are now electronically networked across borders. Information technology has become, and looks set to remain, a critical ingredient of networking activity and mass protest in today's world. Civil society networks, buttressed by the power of the Internet, information and communications technologies, and digital platforms, have found themselves able to defy existing boundaries. We can no longer remain isolated from the networks of power and resistance that criss-cross and envelop our increasingly interconnected world.

Transnational movements of the 21st century enlightenment have recognised this and are increasingly expanding their presence on the Internet. From the more traditional movements of the era such as the Labour Movement, to more recent ones such as the Campaign Against Climate Change, and then to hypermodernity of the Anonymous Movement collective, there is a growing acknowledgement of the Internet's dynamism and versatility, and an increased recognition of its advantages and contribution to the shaping of modern society in its role as a medium of international communication. The ease with which information can be exchanged, together with the fluency of the logistics planned between partners thousands of miles apart, promises activists new opportunities for vigorous coalition-building and other similarly related civil rights protest and advocacy activities. By the same logic, the Internet has also become an increasingly important tool for facilitating and for cementing the social relations that serve as the basis for global civil society.

The contemporary world is in the midst of a historical change. The Information Revolution has given way today to new powers and to new responsibilities and to a whole new host of unrecognisable actors who, through embracing the Internet and digital technologies, are fast becoming central to the new, electronically hypernetworked modern-day civil society. Whilst Internet access in the developed world still far outstrips that of the developing world, predictions made of the expected growth in the number of Internet users online worldwide annually remain phenomenal, and the potential and promise of the Internet as a tool to combat underdevelopment and inequality in the future is yet considered immense. The Internet today, in its avatar as the chief weapon within the Armoury of the Geek, constitutes a significant part of global socio-political and economic interactions, and will continue to play an increasingly important role in the shaping of world politics and current affairs in the years to come.

References

Arquilla, J. & D. Ronfeldt (2001), *Networks and Netwars: The Future of Terror, Crime, and Militancy*. Santa Monica, C.A.: RAND Publications.

Bishop, J. (2014). My Click is My Bond: The Role of Contracts, Social Proof, and Gamification for Sysops to Reduce Pseudo-Activism and Internet Trolling. In J. Bishop (Ed.), *Gamification for Human Factors*

Integration: Social, Education and Psychological Issues (pp. 1–16). Hershey, PA: IGI Global.

Blatherwick, D.E.S. (1987). *The International Politics of Telecommunications*, Research Series #68, Institute of International Studies. Berkley, C.A.: University of California.

Cairncross, F. (1997). The Death of Distance: How the Communications Revolution is Changing Our Lives. Boston, M.A.: Harvard Business School Press.

Castells, M. (1996). The Information Age: Economy. Society and Culture Volume 1- The Rise of the Network Society. Oxford: Blackwell Publishing.

Castells, M. (2001). The Internet Galaxy: Reflections on the Internet, Business and Society, Oxford: Oxford University Press.

Chandrasekaran, R. & E. Corcoran (1997). Human Errors Block E-Mail, Web Sites in Internet Failure: Garbled Address Files From Va. Firm Blamed. *The Washington Post,* July 18, 1997. p. A1.

Cleaver Jr., H. M. (1998). The Zapatista Effect: The Internet and the Rise of an Alternative Political Fabric. *Journal of International Affairs, 51*(2), 621-640.

Coleman, G. (2013). Anonymous in Context: The Politics and Power Behind the Mask. *Internet Governance Papers – Paper No. 3, September 2013.* The Centre for International Governance Innovation (CIGI).

Conway, S., Combe, I., & D. Crowther (2003). Strategizing Networks of Power and Influence: The Internet and the Struggle over Contested Space. *Managerial Auditing Journal, 18*(3), 254-262.

Danitz, T. & W.P. Stobel (2001). Networking Dissent: Cyber Activists Use the Internet to Promote Democracy in Burma. In J. Arquilla & D. Ronfeldt (eds.) *Networks and Netwars: The Future of Terror, Crime, and Militancy* (pp. 129-170), Santa Monica, C.A.: RAND Publications.

de Armond, P. (2001). Netwar in the Emerald City: WTO Protest Strategy and Tactics. In J. Arquilla & D. Ronfeldt (eds.) *Networks and Netwars: The Future of Terror, Crime, and Militancy* (pp. 201-238), Santa Monica, C.A.: RAND Publications.

Deibert, R. J. (2000). International Plug 'n Play?: Citizen Activism, the Internet and Global Public Policy. *International Studies Perspectives, 1*(3), 255-272.

della Porta, D. & M. Diani (1999). *Social Movements: An Introduction, First Edition.* Malden, M.A.: Blackwell Publishing.

Denning, D. E. (2001). Activism, Hactivism and Cyberterrorism: The Internet as a Tool for Influencing Foreign Policy. In J. Arquilla & D. Ronfeldt (eds.) *Networks and Netwars: The Future of Crime, Terrorism and Militancy* (pp. 171-199), Santa Monica, C.A.: RAND Publications.

Diani, M. (1992). The Concept of Social Movement. *The Sociological Review, 40*(1), 1-25.

Fenton, N. (2007). Contesting Global Capital, New Media, Solidarity and the Role of a Social Imaginary. In B. Cammaerts & N. Carpentier (eds) *Reclaiming the Media* (pp. 225-242)*,* Brussels: ECREA Series - Intellect.

Frangonikolopoulos, C.A. (2012). Global Civil Society and Deliberation in the Digital Age. *International Journal Electronic Governance, 5*(1), 11–23.

Fuchs, C. (2006). The Self-Organization of Social Movements. *Systemic Practice and Action Research, 19*(1), 101-137.

Fuchs, C. (2013). The Anonymous Movement in the Context of Liberalism and Socialism. *Interface: A Journal For and About Social Movements, 5*(2), 345-376.

Glenny, M. (2011) *DarkMarket: CyberThieves, CyberCops, and You.* London: The Bodley Head.

Hampson, N.C.N. (2012). Hacktivism: A New Breed of Protest in a Networked World. *Boston College International & Comparative Law Review, 35*(2), 511-542.

Harris, E (1999). Web Becomes a Cybertool for Political Activists. *Wall Street Journal,* 5th August 1999, p. B11.

Harwood, P. G., & L. J. Celeste (2001). Surfing Alone: The Internet as a Facilitator of Social and Political Capital?. *Paper prepared for delivery*

at the 2001 Annual Meeting of American Political Science Association,
Aug-Sept. 2001.

Huysman, M. & V. Wulf (2004). *Social Capital and Information Technology*,
Cambridge M.A.: M.I.T. Press.

Johnston, J. & G. Laxer (2003). Solidarity in the Age of Globalization:
Lessons from the Anti-MAI and Zapatista Struggles. *Theory and
Society, 32*(1), 39-91.

Jordan, T. & P.A. Taylor (2004). *Hacktivism and Cyberwars: Rebels with a
Cause?*, London: Routledge Press.

Juris, J.S. (2005). The New Digital Media and Activist Networking within
Anti—Corporate Globalization Movements. *The ANNALS of the
American Academy of Political and Social Science, 597*(1), 189-208.

Kalathil, S. & T. C. Boas (2010). *Open Networks, Closed Regimes: The
Impact of the Internet on Authoritarian Rule*. Washington, D.C.:
Carnegie Endowment for International Peace.

Kraut, R., Patterson, M. Lundmark, V., Kiesler, S., Mukhopadyay, T., & W.
Scherlis (1998). Internet Paradox: A Social Technology That Reduces
Social Involvement and Psychological Well-Being?. *American
Psychologist, 53*(9), 1017-1031.

Kumar, C. (2000). Transnational Networks and Campaigns for Democracy. In
A. M. Florini (ed.) *The Third Force: The Rise of Transnational Civil*

Society (pp. 115-142). Tokyo: Japan Centre for International Exchange

and Washington D.C.: Carnegie Endowment for International Peace.

McChesney, R. W., Wood, E. M., & J. B. Foster (1998). Capitalism and the

Information Age: The Political Economy of the Global

Communications Revolution. New York, N.Y.: Monthly Review Press.

Norris, P. (2001). Digital Divide: Civic Engagement, Information Poverty,

and the Internet, Cambridge: Cambridge University Press.

Olson, P. (2013). WE ARE ANONYMOUS: Inside the Hacker World of

LulzSec, Anonymous, and the Global Cyber Insurgency. London:

Random House.

Sembrat, E. (2011) How to Respond and Build Around Hacker Communities.

IS 8300 – Disaster Recovery and Contingency Planning, Fall 2011,

October 21, 2011.

Taylor, B.C. (2013). *No More Suffering Fools*. Rahleigh, N.C.:

PostPaper/Lulu Enterprises Inc.

Tehranian, M. & R. Falk (1999). Global Communication & World Politics:

Domination, Development and Discourse. London: Lynne Rienner

Publications.

Uimonen, P. (2003). Networks of Global Interaction. *Cambridge Review of*

International Affairs, 16(2), 273-286

Van Laer, J. & P. Van Aelst (2010). Internet and Social Movement Action

Repertoires. *Information, Communication, & Society. 13*(8), 1146-1171.

Virkar, S. (2011). The Politics of Implementing e- Government for Development: The Ecology of Games Shaping Property Tax Administration in Bangalore City. Unpublished Doctoral Thesis. Oxford: University of Oxford.

Virkar, S. (2014). Trolls Just Want To Have Fun: Electronic Aggression within the Context of e-Participation and Other Online Political Behaviour in the United Kingdom. *International Journal of E-Politics*, *5*(4), 21-51.

Walter, A. (2000). Unravelling the Faustian Bargain: Non-State Actors and the Multilateral Agreement on Investment. *Working Paper 4ᵗʰ Draft*, London School of Economics and Political Science, August 2000.

Wall, M. A. (2007). Social Movements and Email: Expressions of Online Identity in the Globalization Protests. *New Media Society, 9*(2), 258-277.

Wartenkin, C. (2001). Reshaping World Politics: NGOs, the Internet and Global Civil Society. Oxford: Rowman and Littlefield.

Zinnbauer, D. (2001). Internet, Civil Society and Global Governance: The Neglected Political Dimension of the Digital Divide. *Information and Security: An International Journal*, *7*, 45-64.

Documentation

Ackerman, E. (2012). Why Anonymous is Winning Its War on Internet Infrastructure. *www.forbes.com*. Available at: http://www.forbes.com/sites/eliseackerman/2012/02/21/why-anonymous-is-winning-its-war-on-internet-infrastructure/ (Accessed on: 20/01/2015).

Colter, A. (2011). V for Vendetta Inspires Anonymous, Creator David Lloyd Responds. Comics Alliance Online, 04 August 2011. Available at: http://comicsalliance.com/v-for-vendetta-anonymous-david-lloyd/ (Accessed on: 10th February 2015).

Deibert, R. J. (2002). The Politics of Internet Design: Securing the Foundations for Global Civil Society Networks, *Paper presented at the Institute of Intergovernmental Relations*. Available at: http://www.iigr.ca/conferences/archive/pdfs1/deibert.pdf (Accessed: 3rd October 2013).

Internet Society (2013). All About the Internet: A Brief History of the Internet. Available at: http://www.isoc.org/internet/history/brief.shtml#Origins (Accessed: 2nd October 2013).

Koliba, C. (2000). Collaboration, Technical Assistance and Interactive Media: Trends in U.S. Civil Society. *Institute of Development Studies Civil Society and Governance Case Study Papers (USA) #20.* Available at: http://www.ids.ac.uk/ids/civsoc/final/usa/Chris%20Koliba2.doc,

(Accessed: 3rd October 2013).

Krause, A., Stein, M., Clark, J., Chen, T., Li, J., Dimon, J., Kanouse, J. &
J.Herschman (2006). The Virtual Activist 2.0: A Training Guide.
NetAction.Org. Available at: http://www.netaction.org/training/v-
training.html (Accessed: 1st October 2013).Kushner, D. (2014). The
Masked Avengers: How Anonymous Incited Online Vigilantism from
Tunisia to Ferguson. *The New Yorker*, 08 September 2014. Available at:
http://www.newyorker.com/magazine/2014/09/08/masked-avengers
(Accessed on: 20/01/2015).

Longworth, R.C. (1999). Activists on Internet Reshaping Rules for Global
Economy. *Chicago Tribune*, 5 July, 1999. Available at:
http://www.economicjustice.org/resources/media/trib070599.html (Accessed:
5th October 2013).

Moore, A. (2012). Viewpoint: V for Vendetta and the Rise of Anonymous.
BBC News Online – Technology, 10 February 2012. Available at:
http://www.bbc.co.uk/news/technology-16968689 (Accessed on:
20/01/2015).

Organisation for Economic Co-operation and Development (1997). *Towards
A Global Information Society – Global Information Infrastructure,
Global Information Society: Policy Requirements*. Paris: Organisation
for Economic Cooperation and Development.

Parker, C. (2014). Anonymous Unmasked. *The Huffington Post*, 01 April 2014. Available at: http://www.huffingtonpost.com/high-times/anonymous-unmasked_b_5065038.html (Accessed on: 20/01/2015).

Stone, J. (2014). What Is Anonymous? 'Hacktivist' Involvement In Mike Brown Shooting Proves Vigilante Justice Is Now Routine. *International Business Times* (Online), 15 August 2014. Available at: http://www.ibtimes.com/what-anonymous-hacktivist-involvement-mike-brown-shooting-proves-vigilante-justice-now-1660052 (Accessed on: 20/01/2015).

Surman, M. & K. Reilly (2003). Appropriating the Internet for Social Change: Towards the Strategic Use of Networked Technologies by Transnational Civil Society Organisations. *Social Science Research Council Report, November 2003*. Available at: http://www.ssrc.org/programs/itic/publications/knowledge_report/final_entire_surman_reilly.pdf (Accessed: 2nd October 2013).

The Economist (2001). Globalisation: Making Sense of An Integrating World. London: Profile Books Ltd.

Evaluating two successful and two failed multi-organisation e-learning software development projects using service-orientated approaches

Jonathan Bishop

Abstract

This chapter discusses how developing information society services, including information systems that take the form of e-learning software, is not an exercise where success is guaranteed. It evaluates two successful and two failed projects. What is common among the project was that a standardised methodology, namely PRINCE2 and ITIL, were adapted to account for the organisational context of the organisation responsible for the project management. The chapter carries out interviews with the stakeholders in the projects to establish their experiences in taking part in them. These experiences are verified through reference to the literature. The chapter concludes that it is necessary to take into account the organisational culture, including organisational architecture, of all organisations participating in a project, even where a common project management methodology is used.

Introduction

If there is one thing that is certain about software projects, it is that many of them fail to realise their original objectives and expectations (Zaman, Jabbar, Nawaz, & Abbas, 2019). The reasons for project failure and numerous and include business case deterioration, different opinions on the project's purpose and objectives, unhappy/disinterested stakeholders and steering committee members, continuous criticism by stakeholders, changes in stakeholders without warning, no longer a demand for the deliverables or the product, invisible sponsorship, delayed decisions resulting in missed deadlines, high tension meetings with team and stakeholders, finger pointing and poor acceptance of responsibility, lack of organisational process assets, failing to close lifecycle phases properly, high turnover of personnel, especially critical workers, unrealistic expectations, failure in progress reporting, technical failure, having to work excessive hours and with heavy workloads, unclear milestones and other requirements, poor morale, everything is a crisis, poor attendance at team meetings, surprises as well as slow identification of problems and constant rework, poor change control process (Kerzner, 2014).Literature Review

Standardised project management methodologies

There are a number of standardised project management methodologies on the market, some of which have been tailored to the development of information systems, such as structured systems analysis and design methodology (SSADM) and Information technology infrastructure library (ITIL). Other methodologies, such as Projects in Controlled Environments version 2 (PRINCE 2) are suited to any project management environment.

Structured systems analysis and design (SSADM)

Structured Systems Analysis and Design Methodology (SSADM) is a software project management methodology that offers information system practitioners a structured way to develop new systems, whether electronic or otherwise (Weaver, Lambrou, & Walkley, 2002, p.vii). Despite the existence of PRINCE2 as a project management methodology for projects beyond software, SSADM is still used in some government departments and non-governmental contractors to achieve a *"disciplined engineering approach and improve the quality of the entire system that is developed"* (Iorliam, 2019). It's use today is primarily in results orientated analysis as it is still accepted as a project management methodology for software engineering (Abereola, 2019).

Projects in controlled environments version 2 (PRINCE2)

Whilst Projects in Controlled Environments version 2 (PRINCE2) is seen as the successor to SSADM, it has a number of flaws in that it is not automatically tailored for the design of information systems in the way SSADM is, as it is a general project management methodology for use in any type of project, especially complex ones (Marshall & Hughes, 2008).

Information technology infrastructure library (ITIL)

The Information technology infrastructure library (ITIL) is regarded as the information technology framework that is most widely used by organisations across the world for implementing information society services (Sharifi, Ayat, Rahman, & Sahibudin, 2008). In the context of this study, ITIL is treated no differently to any other project management methodology, even though it is regarded as a service delivery methodology because it is generally accepted as a complementary approach to organisational management (Cater-Steel, Toleman, & Tan, 2006).

Organisation-specific methodologies

Even though there are standardised project management methodologies, many organisations will have developed their own approaches to delivering projects. Each organization has a culture to how it does things and many have codified these in models and frameworks that they have attempted to communicate to their stakeholders as best practice.

Crocels Community Media Group

The organisation that led the projects discussed in this chapter was the Crocels Community Media Group (known simply as 'Crocels'). Crocels has adopted a number of approaches to delivering blended learning and e-learning projects. These include a strategic design approach called PASS (Bishop, 2004), a systematic methodological approach called MAPEL (Bishop, 2005), an iterative methodological approach called the Star Lifecycle (Bishop, 2007) and an approach to designing online communities called OCD5 (Bishop, September 08 2009).

Crocels's Persuasive, Adaptive, Sociable and Sustainable Model

The Persuasive, Adaptive, Sociable and Sustainable model (Bishop, 2004) was devised as part of the Digital Classroom of Tomorrow Project, which was an initiative in Wales that led to the Classroom 2.0 initiative across Europe in the early- to mid-2000s (Bishop, 2012a; Falcinelli & Laici, 2012; Taddeo & Tirocchi, 2012). The aim of the PASS approach is making learning more engaging for the learners and more manageable for the educators (Bishop, 2004).

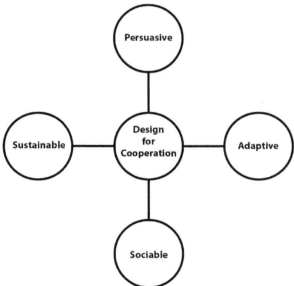

Figure 1 Crocels's Persuasive, Adaptive, Sociable and Sustainable (PASS) Model

Crocels's Mediating Artefacts for Persuasive E-Learning Model

The Mediating Artefacts for Persuasive E-Learning model (Bishop, 2005) was Crocels Community Media Group's first attempt at creating a project management methodology specifically for e-learning, namely persuasive e-learning systems. It was based on a goal-orientated approach that accounts for situation awareness (Endsley, M. R., 1988; Endsley, Mica R. & Jones, 2012).

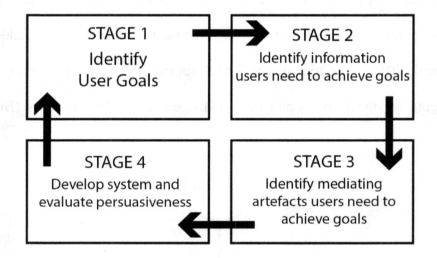

Figure 2 Crocels's Mediating Aretfacts for Persuasive E-Learning (MAPEL) Model

Crocels's Star Lifecycle

The Star Lifecycle for E-Learning Development (Bishop, 2007) was the Crocels Community Media Group's second attempt at developing a project management methodology specifically for developing e-learning products, though in this case not necessarily persuasive.

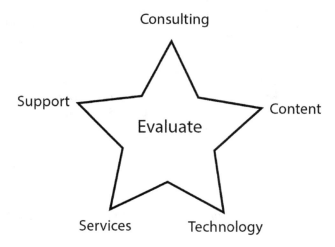

Figure 3 Crocels's Star Lifecycle

Crocels's Five-Factor Online Community Development Model

The Five-Factor Online Community Development Model (OCD5) was developed for the effective operation of information society services that take the form of web-based communities (Bishop, 2009a; Bishop, 2009b). Once a virtual environment has been built with for instance message boards or chat groups, this model shows how the information system can be operated so as to promote community. It need not necessarily be for e-learning systems, but those based around them often benefit from e-tivities (Salmon, 2003b) and e-moderating (Salmon, 2003a) and the OCD5 model can help manage such forms of online learning.

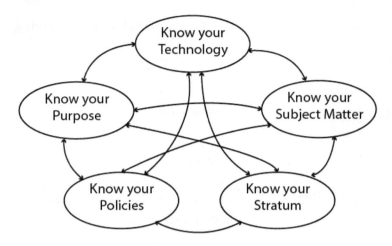

Figure 4 The 5-Factor Online Community Development model (OCD5)

Crocels's Learn, Create, Communicate Model

Crocels's Learn, Create, Communicate (LCC) model (Bishop, 2009b) does for e-learning communities what OCD5 does for online communities. It provides an approach for the effective operation of e-learning communities as information society services. Because it has an educational context it can be seen as a pedagogical approach (Coomey & Stephenson, 2002) .

Figure 5 Crocels's pedagogical model: Learn, create, communicate (LCC)

Towards synthesised models

This section shows how two of the standardised methodologies, namely PRINCE2 (Bentley, 2005; Hedeman, van Heemst, & Fredriksz, 2006) and ITIL (Cater-Steel et al., 2006, have been adapted to account for the way that Crocels does things using its models (Bishop, 2004; Bishop, 2005; Bishop, 2007;

Bishop, 2009). Even though these standardised methodologies were adapted by Crocels, they were not adapted for the organisations that partnered with Crocels and this is one of the limitations discussed later in the chapter.

An approach based on PRINCE2

PRINCE2 is increasingly becoming known as a project management methodology that is structured and provides a clear and flexible approach to running projects using accepted approaches (Graham, 2008). This section sets out a five-part amalgamation of PRINCE2 with Crocels's MAPEL, Star Lifecycle and OCD5 methods to produce a software development methodology called C2-Tech-S2 for delivering web-based learning (Weller, 2002). Table 1 presents an amalgamation of PRINCE 2 and Crocels's MAPEL, Star Lifecycle and OCD5 methods as part of the C2-Tech-S2 methodology.

Table 1 Making PRINCE2's starting up a project stage fit with Crocels's methods and tasks to create a new methodology

Star Lifecycle Iteration (OCD5 Stage)	Stage Aim (MAPEL Stage)	Stage tasks (Task Methods)

A. Consulting (OCD5.3 Know your Stratum)	I. Identify User Goals (MAPEL Stage 1)	1. Starting up a project 1.1. Discuss the suitability of given systems in terms of style, ease of use and the end user (User Experience Analysis) 1.2 Produce a design concept in terms of customer, purpose and target audience (Scenario Based Design) 1.3. Prepare flow diagrams showing navigation through system (Requirements Analysis)

Table 2 presents an amalgamation of PRINCE 2 and Crocels's MAPEL, Star Lifecycle and OCD5 methods along with the relevance processes of Crocels to form part of the C2-Tech-S2 methodology.

Table 2 Making PRINCE2's initiating a project stage fit with Crocels's methods and tasks to create a new methodology

Star Lifecycle Iteration (OCD5 Stage)	Stage Aim (MAPEL Stage)	Stage tasks (Task Methods)

B. Content (OCD5.2. Know your subject matter)	II. Identify Information Users need to Achieve Goals (MAPEL Stage 2)	2. Initiating a project 2.1 Collect a range of source materials (e.g. text, graphics, forms, processes) that can be used and modified in various contexts (Business Activity Modelling) 2.2 Create index of source material identifying copyright status and other meta data of each, indicating relevance to requirements, and ensuring recognition of user participation (Current Environment Analysis). 2.3 Select the most appropriate, consider file size, customs and practice, and save files in appropriate format to maintain user interest (Entity Behaviour Modelling) 2.4 Store files in a preparation folder for easy access in a range of contexts (Requirements Cataloguing).

Table 3 presents an amalgamation of PRINCE 2 and Crocels's MAPEL, Star Lifecycle and OCD5 methods as well as Crocels processes to form part of the C2-Tech-S2 methodology.

Table 3 Making PRINCE2's managing product development stage fit with

Crocels's methods and tasks to create a new methodology

Star Lifecycle Iteration (OCD5 Stage)	Stage Aim (MAPEL Stage)	Stage tasks (Task Methods)
C. Technology (OCD5.1. Know your technology)	III. Identify Mediating Artifacts Users need to Achieve Goals (MAPEL Stage 3)	3. Managing product development 3.1 Create a simple system that can accommodate different users (User Task Analysis and Prototyping)

		3.2 Create hyperlinks as mediating artefacts to avoid dead links (Third-Party Resource Refinement and Tuning) 3.3 Create text and image based mediating artefacts to enhance participation (User Scenario Testing).

		3.4 Create persuasive links for e-mail and other applications (Social Planning and Modelling).

Table 4 presents an amalgamation of PRINCE 2 and Crocels's MAPEL, Star Lifecycle and OCD5 methods as part of the C2-Tech-S2 methodology.

Table 4 Making PRINCE2's managing product delivery stage fit with Crocels's methods and tasks to create a new methodology

Star Lifecycle Iteration (OCD5 Stage)	Stage Aim (MAPEL Stage)	Stage tasks (Task Methods)

D. Services (OCD5.4. Know your policies)	IV. Develop System (MAPEL Stage 4)	4. Managing product delivery
		4.1 Create a homepage or menu screen and other nodes compliant with standards (Two-Tree Modelling).
		4.2 Create and format system nodes to ensure compliance with policies and law (Connected-Dots Modelling).
		4.3 Create tables and format cells, columns and rows that take account of accessibility and multi-platform

		standards (Nuts and Bolts Audit). 4.4 Set text colour, font styles and heading size and size, location, borders of images, to accommodate those with disabilities and other needs (Design Matters Audit).

Table 5 presents an amalgamation of PRINCE 2 and Crocels's MAPEL, Star Lifecycle and OCD5 methods as well as Crocels processes to form part of the C2-Tech-S2 methodology.

Table 5 Making PRINCE2's closing a project stage fit with Crocels's methods and tasks to create a new methodology

Star Lifecycle Iteration	Stage Aim (MAPEL Stage)	Stage tasks (Task Methods)

(OCD5 Stage)		
E. Support (OCD5. Know your purpose)	V. Evaluate Persuasiveness (MAPEL Stage 4)	5. Closing a project 5.1 View results in preview environment and run testing sequences (Inspection/Walkthrough). 5.2 Collect feedback, from at least three users, in terms of suitability for purpose, ease of use and style (User Focus Groups and Interviews). 5.3 Test out system in real world, showing regard for effect on body posture, potential eyestrain and positioning of user hardware (Direct Observation).

Figure 6 is an illustration of the amalgamation of PRINCE 2 and Crocels methods as part of the C2-Tech-S2 methodology.

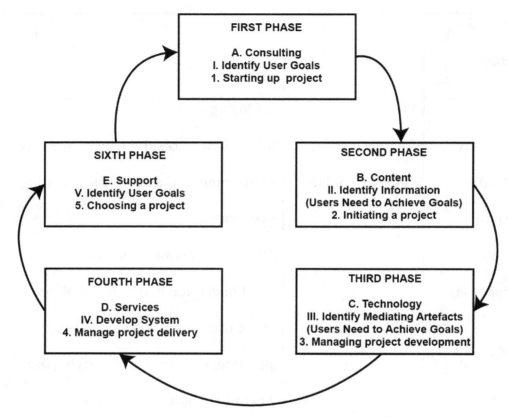

Figure 6 Illustration of an amalgamation of PRINCE 2 and Crocels methods

as part of the C2-Tech-S2 methodology

An approach based on ITIL

This section sets out a five-part amalgamation of ITIL with Crocels's MAPEL, Star Lifecycle and OCD5 methods to produce a software development methodology called MOLPSL-S5 for delivering web-based learning (Weller, 2002) Figure 7 presents an illustration of this model and Table 6 presents the links between ITIL and Crocels's methods.

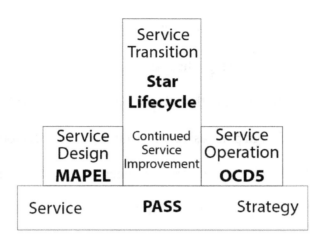

Figure 7 Illustration of service-orientated e-learning software project

management based on ITIL (MOLPSL-S5)

Table 8 Service-orientated e-learning software project management based

on ITIL (MOLPSL-S5)

ITIL Factor	Crocels Methodology
Service Design	MAPEL
Service Operation	OCD5 (Online communities) / LCC (E-Learning)
Service Strategy	PASS
Service Transition / Continued Service Improvement	Star Lifecycle

Service Design / MAPEL

The ITIL Service Design stage has as its purpose to design IT services (Bannerman et al., 2013b). It is therefore a perfect match for MAPEL, which has as its purpose to design persuasive e-learning systems (Bishop, 2005). Table 9 shows how ITIL's service design stage has been fused with Crocels's MAPEL model and its relevant processes to form an element of the MOLPSL-S5 methodology.

Table 9 Making ITIL Service Design take account of MAPEL as part of the MOLPSL-S5 methodology

ITIL Service Design Element	MAPEL Element	Tasks
A. Capacity management	I. Identify user goals (MAPEL Stage 1)	1.1 Discuss the suitability of given systems in terms of style, ease of use and the end user (User Experience Analysis).
B. Service catalogue management	II. Identify mediating artefacts users need to achieve goals (MAPEL	1.2 Produce a design concept in terms of customer, purpose and target audience (Scenario Based Design).
C. Information security		

management	Stage 2)	
D. Design coordination	IV. Develop system (MAPEL Stage 3)	1.3 Prepare flow diagrams showing navigation through system (Requirements Analysis)
E. Supplier management		1.4 Create a simple system that can accommodate different users (User Task Analysis and Prototyping).
F. Service level management		1.5 Create and format system nodes to ensure compliance with policies and law (Connected-Dots Modelling).
G. Availability management	V. Evaluate persuasiveness (MAPEL Stage 4)	1.6 Collect feedback, from at least three users, in terms of suitability for purpose, ease of use and style (User Focus Groups and Interviews).
H. IT service continuity management	I. Identify user goals (MAPEL Stage 1)	1.1 Discuss the suitability of given systems in terms of style, ease of use and the end user (User Experience Analysis).

Service Operation / OCD5/LCC

ITIL service operation has as its purpose to "co-ordinate and carry out the activities and processes required to deliver and manage services" to users and for the "ongoing management of the technology that is used to deliver and support services" (Bannerman et al., 2013c). Table 10 presents and amalgamation of ITIL's service operation elements with Crocels's OCD5 approach. Table 11 presents and amalgamation of ITIL's service operation elements with Crocels's LCC approach for use with e-learning systems.

Table 10 Making ITIL Service Operation take account of OCD5 (Online communities) as part of the MOLPSL-S5 methodology

ITIL Service Operation Element	OCD5 Element	Tasks
I. Event Managemen t	XII. Know Your Technolog y (OCD5 Stage 1)	2.1 Create index of source material identifying copyright status and other meta

		data of each, indicating relevance to requirements, and ensuring recognition of user participation (Current Environment Analysis).
J. Incident Managemen t	XIII. Know Your Policies (OCD5 Stage 4)	2.2 Create hyperlinks as mediating artefacts to avoid dead links (Third-Party Resource Refinement

		and Tuning)
K. Request Fulfilment	XIX. Know Your Strata (OCD5 Stage 3)	2.3 Select the most appropriate, consider file size, customs and practice, and save files in appropriate format to maintain user interest (Entity Behaviour Modelling)
L. Problem Management	XIII. Know Your Policies (OCD5 Stage 4)	2.4 Store files in a preparation folder for easy access in a

		range of contexts (Requirements Cataloguing).
M. Access Management	XX. Know Your Subject Matter (OCD5 Stage 2)	2.5 Create text and image based mediating artefacts to enhance participation (User Scenario Testing).

Table 11 Making ITIL Service Design take account of LCC (E-Learning Systems) as part of the MOLPSL-S5 methodology

ITIL Service Operation Element	LCC Element	Tasks
N. Event	XI. Create /	2.1 Create index of source material

Management	Communicate (LCC Stages 2 & 3)	identifying copyright status and other meta data of each, indicating relevance to requirements, and ensuring recognition of user participation (Current Environment Analysis).
O. Incident Management	XII. Learn / Communicate (LCC Stages 1 & 3)	2.2 Create hyperlinks as mediating artefacts to avoid dead links (Third-Party Resource Refinement and Tuning)
P. Request Fulfilment	XII. Learn / Communicate (LCC Stages 1 & 3)	2.3 Select the most appropriate, consider file size, customs and practice, and save files in appropriate format to maintain user interest (Entity Behaviour Modelling)
Q. Problem Management	XIII. Learn / Create (LCC Stages 1 & 2)	2.4 Store files in a preparation folder for easy access in a range of contexts (Requirements Cataloguing).
R. Access	XI. Create /	2.5 Create text and image based

Management	Communicate (LCC Stages 2 & 3)	mediating artefacts to enhance participation (User Scenario Testing).

Service Strategy / PASS

Service strategy in the case of ITIL has as its purpose to "define the perspective, positions, plans and patterns that a service provider needs" to meet an organisation's outcomes (Bannerman et al., 2013d). Table presents and amalgamation of ITIL's service strategy elements with Crocels's PASS approach.

Table 12 Making ITIL Service Strategy take account of PASS as part of the MOLPSL-S5 methodology

ITIL Service Strategy Element	PASS Element	Tasks
S. Define Services	XXI. Adaptable (PASS Stage 2)	3.1 Create a homepage or menu screen and other nodes compliant with standards (Two-Tree Modelling).
T. Service	XXII.	

Providers	Sustainable (PASS Stage 4)	
U. Customers and Services	XXIII. Sociable (PASS Stage 3)	3.2 Create persuasive links for e-mail and other applications (Social Planning and Modelling).
V. Customer Satisfaction	XXIV. Persuasive (PASS Stage 1)	

Service Transition / Star Lifecycle

Service transition in the case of ITIL has as its purpose the "improvement of capabilities for introducing new and changes services into supported environments (Bannerman et al., 2013e). Table 13 presents an amalgamation of ITIL's service transition elements with Crocels's Star Lifecycle elements.

Table 13 Making ITIL Service Transition take account of Star Lifecycle (1) as part of the MOLPSL-S5 methodology

ITIL Service Transition	Star	Tasks

Element	Lifecycle Element	
W. Change Management	XXV. Consulting (SL Stage 1)	4.1 Set text colour, font styles and heading size and size, location, borders of images, to accommodate those with disabilities and other needs (Design Matters Audit).
X. Service Asset and Configuration Management	XXVI. Content (SL Stage 2)	4.2 Collect a range of source materials (e.g. text, graphics, forms, processes) that can be used and modified in various contexts (Business Activity Modelling)
Y. Release and Deployment Management	XXVII. Technology (SL Stage 3)	4.3 Create tables and format cells, columns and rows that take account of accessibility and multi-platform standards (Nuts and Bolts Audit).
Z. Transition Planning and Support	XXVII. Services	4.4 View results in preview environment and run testing

AA. Service Validation and Testing	(SL Stage 4)	sequences (Inspection/Walkthrough).
AB. Change Evaluation	XXVIII.	4.5 Test out system in real world, showing regard for effect on body posture, potential eyestrain and positioning of user hardware (Direct Observation).
AC. Knowledge Management	Support (SL Stage 5)	

Continued Service Improvement / Star Lifecycle

Continued service improvement in ITIL has as its purpose to "align IT services with changing business needs by identifying improvements are required to IT services" that support the processes of the organisation (Bannerman et al., 2013a).

Table 14 presents an amalgamation of ITIL's continued service improvement elements with those of Crocels's Start Lifecycle.

Table 14 Making ITIL Continued Service Improvement take account of Star Lifecycle (2) as part of the MOLPSL-S5 methodology

ITIL Continued Service	Star Lifecycle Element	Tasks

Improvement Element		
AD. Identify the strategy for improvement	XXV. Consulting (SL Stage 1)	1.1 Discuss the suitability of given systems in terms of style, ease of use and the end user (User Experience Analysis).
AE. Define what will be measured	XXVI. Content (SL Stage 2)	1.2 Produce a design concept in terms of customer, purpose and target audience (Scenario Based Design).
AF. Gather the data	XXVII. Technology (SL Stage 3)	4.2 Collect a range of source materials (e.g. text, graphics, forms, processes) that can be used and modified in various contexts (Business Activity Modelling)
AG. Process the data		2.3 Select the most appropriate, consider file size, customs and practice, and save files in appropriate format to maintain user interest (Entity Behaviour Modelling)
AH. Analyse the	XXVII. Services	2.1 Create index of source material identifying copyright status and other

information and data	(SL Stage 4)	meta data of each, indicating relevance to requirements, and ensuring recognition of user participation (Current Environment Analysis).
AI. Present and use the information		3.1 Create a homepage or menu screen and other nodes compliant with standards (Two-Tree Modelling).
AJ. Implement improvement	XXVIII. Support (SL Stage 5)	4.5 Test out system in real world, showing regard for effect on body posture, potential eyestrain and positioning of user hardware (Direct Observation).

Evaluation of two successful and two failed projects

This section evaluates two successful and two failed projects using the software development methodologies devised above from combining standardised project and service management methodologies with the organisational architecture and working practices of the Crocels Community Media Group.

Participants

The participants in the projects varied. They included on the one hand content and technology creators and on the other services and support staff. Both groups were supported by a project manager who led the consulting side of the project. Table 15 sets out the participant details. All participants have been anonymized.

Table 15 Anonymised participants in the projects

Pseudonym of Participant	Descriptives
"Angie"	Angie is a middle-aged woman who took the role of parent-educator.
"Argie"	Argie is a man in his 20s who took the role of content production.
"Damal"	Damal is man in his 30s who took the role of video production and supervision.
"Garda"	Garda is a middle-aged woman who took the role of parent-educator.
"Gloc"	Gloc is a middle-aged man who took the role of content production.
"Morgsie"	Morgsie was a supervisor and educator who was a

	retired civil servant.
Person T	Person T was a university manager in charge of managing project funds.
Person D	Person D was a man in his 30s who took the role of project manager.

Methodology

The methodological approach was an online questionnaire where after participating in the projects those involved were invited to take part in a social audit of how they responded to the organisational architecture of Crocels and how they responded to its working practices. The outcomes of these questionnaires were synthesised to understand how the specific individual experienced the different methodologies in the different projects.

Results

The results of the project found different outcomes for each project with the responses to the online questionnaires reflecting whether or not the specific project was deemed successful in terms of outcomes.

Successful C2TechS2: The Emotivate Project @ Treforest Underpass

The Emotivate Project @ Trefforest Underpass was the first major project that Crocels undertook when it incorporated for the first time in 2007. It formed part of its Clicks and Mortar Environments for Learning and Leisure Experiences (CAMELLE) Project, which was based on Classroom 2.0.

Organisational architecture

Organisational architecture is not just about organisational structure, but includes people, processes and technology (Cox, 2019) In this project there were a number of different organisations involved, across the public, private and people sector. Each organisation had its own structures, but it was possible through using the C2-Tech-S2 software project management methodology to bring them all together to deliver the didactic goal – of young people using computers to create collages that result in two murals reflecting the community – one mural reflecting the past and one reflecting the ideal future.

Rhondda Cynon Taf County Borough Council

The local authority for the community of Pontypridd, where the project was conducted, was highly cooperative. They provided a grant to the project and were active in the opening of the underpass when complete by providing a photographer and arranging for their mayor, Councillor Rob Smith, of the Rhondda ward in the community of Pontypridd, to cut the ribbon to officially open it.

Figure 8 Rhondda Cynon Taf's mayor Councillor Rob Smith opening the St Dyfrig's Underpass (Courtesy: BBC News)

Crocels Community Media Group

The organisational architecture of Crocels at the time was a single company, called Glamorgan Blended Learning Ltd and the brand from which Crocels is abbreviated, namely 'Centre for Research into Online Communities, E-Learning and Socialnomics.' It had what is now called a 'MDAC' or 'Managed Direct Action Committee', which was a task-and-finish group that came together on a voluntary basis with a dedicated Project Manager leading the project. The project manager had direct authority to make decisions as they were on the board of directors of the incorporated Crocels company.

Pedagogical and Management Issues

Effective working practices exist in organisations that are learning-centred and thus promote greater motivation among the staff that form part of them (Moody, 2012). It has been argued that management and pedagogy should be separated

(Lumby & Tomlinson, 2000), but in the case of this project pedagogy was at the heart of the delivery and so effective project management was needed to keep the project on track so that stakeholders did not go in directions other than the didactic one chosen (Bishop, 2012b).

Rhondda Cynon Taf County Borough Council

Rhondda Cynon Taf County Borough Council is a local authority in Wales structured as a unitary authority, unlike many areas in England, which have both county and district councils in addition to parish, town or neighbourhood councils (i.e. local councils as opposed to local authorities).

Crocels Community Media Group

The Digital Classroom of Tomorrow (DCOT) Project was the Classroom 2.0 project in Wales (Bishop, 2004; Bishop, 2012; Bishop, 2014; Bishop, 2015; Bishop, 2017a).

Failed C2-Tech-S2 Project: QPress – A Q-methodology plugin for WordPress

QPress was intended to be a Q-methodology plugin for WordPress. It's aim was on the one hand to collect research data in the form of q-sorts and on the other to be a more effective means of replicating the Duke University preferential card study into extra sensory perception (Rao, 1962) , where participants would have to replicate the position of the cards on a grid and not just try to guess or judge which symbol is behind a card. It could also have been used as a means to conduct the James Randi Educational Foundation's 'One Million Dollar Paranormal Challenge' (Farha, 2003).

Organisational architecture

For organisational architecture to be successful it needs to be systems and process-based (Savage, Franz, & Wasek, 2019). The organisational architecture of all those parties involved in the research and development of QPress were fundamental in the project's failure to be realised.

Cardiff Metropolitan University

The contribution of Cardiff Metropolitan University to the failure of the QPress project was significant. Despite the project having been approved by the Research Director, there were interventions from other departments to try and change the scope of the project and limit the resources available to it. One manager shall be called Person T. *"Unfortunately some of his [project specifications were] instigated prior to him arriving at UWIC and it was continued [...] here,"* was one comment made by Person T. To one of the principal members of the project team, Person T contacted them to say, *"I understand you are involved in [Person D's research project, would] it be possible to meet up briefly to discuss his research [...]? He's raised some requests for software [...] and I need to check out the justification for those items."* This intervention led to the project being delayed by three months initially as Person T sought to block the expenditure on the software needed to program and test QPress as well as that required to derive a parametric user model from it (Bishop, 2017b) .

Crocels Community Media Group

The Crocels Community Media Group was in a difficult position in that it had signed a contract with Cardiff Metropolitan University and provided funding directly to them for the research project. Funding had also been obtained from two Welsh Government funded schemes. However, even though the funding was in place, Person T took it upon themselves to try to veto the funding that they believed was used in a way contrary to their own public policies on how public funding should be used (Robson, 2003), which was different from the policies of the Welsh Government. Problems with funding had an evidential impact on Crocels staff. *"With the exception of the delayed payments Crocels has a negligible influence on my career ambitions,"* Person W said.

iFlair Web Technologies

The WordPress plug-in software developer, iFlair Web Technologies were called upon to develop QPress when the lead project manager between Cardiff Metropolitan University and Crocels Community Media Group (i.e. Person D) suffered a deterioration in mental health as a result of the actions of Person T. Despite there being funding available so that Crocels Community Media Group could be reimbursed for the costs of engaging iFlair, the non-cooperation of

Person T meant that funding was not accessed even though all the evidence required to claim it was in place. Despite meetings being held between Person T, Person D and a senior researcher involved in the project, an extension of time request was submitted to delay the project by a year because of Person T's non-cooperation and the effect Person T was having on Person D's wellbeing. At the Alpha Testing stage of QPress a representative said, "It's good experience to work with Crocels!"

Working practices and management style

In software development projects, effective working practices are highly dependent on the exchange of information, especially where outsourcing is involved (Lonsdale, Barrar, & Gervais, 2006).

iFlair Web Technologies

At the Alpha Testing stage of QPress, iFlair seemed quite upbeat about completing the project. "*According to me, it (QPress) should be very much user friendly in terms of user interface and with rich style which can easily attract users to visit the website again and again,*" they said. "*I can say that when [the] client sees the outcome, he should feel that it is the same what s/he has visualized which fulfills all the above aspects of purpose and target audience,*" they continued. "*Site map should not be very much detailed but it should give the better idea of the complete website features/ functionality navigation,*" they added, "*I would say nice content and attractive graphics should be used,*" concluding, "*It should be pretty much organized and structured*" and "*website should be attractive in terms of design and look and fill (sic).*"

The confidence of iFlair at the Alpha stage was without doubt. "*It should be auto recognizable which should describe what it will display before we click on it. It should be attractive and not boring,*" a representative said. "*It should be correctly linked! It should be very well designed and informational which should make the user eager to visit other pages,*" they continued, "*All the styles, look and fill (sic) and cosmetics of [the] website should match and appeal the website purpose and motive,*" adding, "*Browser compatibility is must. It should be created with following default patterns and well defined structure,*" saying finally, "*According to me, it should be very much user friendly in terms of user interface and with rich style which can easily attract users to visit the website again and again.*"

Crocels Community Media Group

Not all members of the Crocels Community Media Group appreciated its working practices. One worker, whom we shall call Gloc, was critical of how Crocels had evolved from a small single-company entity into a nanoconglomerate of multiple firms with a group structure. "*I was not aware 'world peace' featured in Crocels mission,*" they said about the global outlook of Crocels. "*The constraint placed [on working practices] is one of threat - i.e.*"

'comply or take the consequences': those of displeasure at least," is how Gloc felt about the way Crocels had standardised around flexible working. *"Since my reduction in my hours worked for Crocels impinges very little on my life beyond my research interests into EI & ERD,"* was Gloc's attitude about being a contingent worker who had less work assigned to them following completion of their side of the project.

Successful MOLPSL-S5 Project: Comprend 2.0 during the Emotivate Project for Efail Isaf Underpass (Emotivate'16)

Comprend 3.0 is the successor to the ASP.Net-based Comprend (Bishop, 2004) and Moodle-based Comprend, namely virtual learning environments developed around Crocels's persuasive, adaptable, sociable and sustainable (PASS) approaches. What makes version 3 of Comprend, which is derived from the French word for 'understand', different from the earlier version is that it is based on a service orientated architecture that supports the principal that whilst all learners might not be thrice exceptional (3E) all learners have the same three needs (3N), namely to have their level of intelligence accommodated, their learning abilities accommodated and any neurological or mental health differences.

Organisational architecture

A key part of organisational architecture is putting in the processes that motivate people to work together (Helper, Martins, & Seamans, 2019). Often organisational architecture is driven at the executive level in order to strategically manage resources and direct their use within the firm or other structure (Brickley, Smith Jr, & Zimmerman, 2002). Organisational architecture is the most holistic way to understand an organisation and through it, it is possible to understand and accommodate different protected characteristics (Guy, 1994).

Crocels Community Media Group

By the time Comprend 2.0 was being designed the organisational changes at Crocels had all but been complete. The Crocels Community Media Group now existed as an organisation with most of its workers being on flexible working contracts, as either casual, contingent or composite workers. The first means they are on a zero-hours contact, the second that they are self-employed and the third that they could be either self-employed or incorporated, but work according to their own contractual terms. Their relationship with Crocels is more arm's length than contingent or casual workers in other words. They form part of the pedagogical side of School 3.0 that was Classroom 2.0, as opposed to the facilities side, discussed in the next section in relation to the 2016 Emotivate Project, which is the site that provides social context through enhancing situational awareness.

"Damal"

The worker called "Damal" (not their real name) provided a 3E/3N mentor to support the delivery of the sessions to ensure that any communication issues were overcome. He also ensured proper records of how the participants were feeling were kept for reflective review at a later date by the project manager who was also the lead tutor. *"The project was a one-off, rather than a regular thing,"* they said, adding, *"sometimes have to mix in things that I may not be interested or like into those things I'm particularly good at."* It is known that where there are skills shortages in an organisation that flexible working can be a key factor in attracting the right workers (Anderson & Kelliher, 2009), but as Damal said in this case, it is not always possible to have all the skills necessary.

Some things that stood out for Damal included, *"Unique strategies that I (they) can analyse to implement or learn from - a good balance of them,"* *"Being given the opportunity helped to see what other things I could deal with"* and *"(The project) Made me (them) more bold in my (their) approaches to goals in my (their) life."* Flexible working allows workers to enhance their learning on a continuous basis, which can add to the organsiation in terms of the knowledge available to it (Idris, 2014), and this seemed to be what Damal experienced.

"Argie"

The worker called "Argie" (not their real name) was the library support worker for the project, assisting with compiling materials for the instructional design. Argie said, *"working with Crocels allows me to work any time, even when ill if I can manage it,"* continuing, *"Working with Crocels has helped me understand the world of work where no other potential employer was giving me the chance to do so,"* indicating that he felt Crocels *"allows me (him) to work at my own pace and when I am able,"* and that *"Working for Crocels has brought discipline into my life, allowing me to help plan my work day or even future plans."*

"Garda"

The worker called "Garda" (not their real name) were responsible for the provision of classroom tuition to support the project manager who was also leading as an educator. *"I like work relationships and prefer more contact although I am given a lot of freedom,"* they said, which are known strengths and weaknesses of lone working, especially with teleworking (Mann, Varey, & Button, 2000) . *"As a whole it is a very positive experience and all experiences are learning opportunities,"* Garda concluded. It is known that teleworking and other forms of remote working offer the opportunity for personal development not afforded for in other forms of working (Fleetwood, 2007).

External Partner Organisations

It is becoming more common for organisations external to one another to partner in order to provide combined knowledge and other resource advantages (Whicker & Andrews, 2004). Public-private partnerships were an innovation of the New Labour Government to provide mutual benefit to collaborations between the private sector and the public sector (Pongsiri, 2002). In terms of this 2016 specific project, there was not as great a partnership with the public and private sector as in the 2009 project, as the facilities were used rather than there being any financial or human resources being utilised outside of Crocels's own budget.

Colleges and Libraries

Colleges and libraries were used in parts of Taf Ely where other facilities were not being used. In the case of the college it was in Nantgarw – where the project manager is a councillor – and in the case of the library it was Beddau and Tynant community library, located where the project manager previously stood for election and campaigned to keep the library open.

Community Centres and Churches

Like with the original Emotivate Project (Bishop, 2012) there was partnership with a religious organisation. In this case, Castle Square United Reformed Church. A community centre was also used, in the form of Tonyrefail Community Resource Centre. The former had no computer equipment, whereas the latter did, along with worktops next to them to allow for greater blended learning.

Home-based Learning

An important part of the DCOT concept was that through the Classroom 2.0 approach that learners at home could take part in classroom-based at the same time as other learners using PCs or other devices in the classroom itself. In the case of this project two learners were supported by their grandmother at home, whose professional background in childcare made her suitable to assist in an educational context.

Pedagogical and management issues

Effective working practices are created when project managers who can recognise and tap into the diversity of the human resources that they have access to (De Vries, Manfred F R Kets, Rook, & Engellau, 2016).

Crocels Community Media Group

This Emotivate project was based around School 3.0, where pedagogy and buildings infrastructure co-exist. Forming part of the Clicks and Mortar Environments for Learning and Leisure Experiences Project (CAMELLE), which is School 3.0 in Wales (Bishop, 2012; Bishop, 2007), the project accounted for three-needs (3N) learning by providing learning that accounts for ability, learning style and personality type.

By using the multi-site version of WordPress so that different types of resource were stored under different domain names, it would then be possible to use specialist domain names, such as emotivate.org.uk and crocels.ac.uk, to provide tailored experiences to different user groups. The benefit is that the multi-site domains are stand-alone websites that operate in their own right, with the most popular ones being news.crocels.com and base.crocels.com, which are mapped to www.crocels.news and www.crocels.info respectively. This makes it possible for learners to explore authorised content accordance to their 3N learning plan.

"Morgsie"

The worker called "Morgsie" (Not their real name) played a role as a home-based educator. "*I helped participants to choose websites,*" they said about their role. "*I helped the participants understand the questions and activities,*" they continued. "*I supported participants by taking breaks from the screen,*" they pointed out. The concept of parents as teachers is usually confined to early stage development (Pfannenstiel & Seltzer, 1989). However, in this project a grandmother assisted her grandchildren by following the curriculum of the project. Morgsie said, "*I helped participants to choose images and other media relevant to them,*" and that they "*helped participants when things went wrong, such as content not being available,*" as well as saying they "*pointed out to the (lead) instructor when participants needed help that I couldn't provide.*" It is known that with schemes involving parents or grandparents as teachers still needs the support of outside agencies or formally trained educators (Wagner & Clayton, 1999).

"Garda"

"*I like work relationships and prefer more contact although I am given a lot of freedom,*" they said. "*I work to earn money but also to have a life away from my domestic duties largely concerning disability.*" Teleworking is regarding as an option for people with disabilities to gain access to employment (Murray & Kenny, 1990). As technology advances so do the opportunities for workers with disabilities taking part in teleworking (Moon, Linden, Bricout, & Baker, 2014).

Failed MOLPSL-S5 Project: Prototyping Comprend 3.0 during the Cotswolds Easter Academy

This section discusses a failed implementation of POLPSL-S5 with a pilot of Comprend 3.0, which is relies on an enhanced approach to blended learning. Unlike the first Comprend, which applied PASS automatically (Bishop, 2004), this first trial of School 3.0 as part of the CAMELLE Project (where buildings are as important as computers) relied on two educators in two different localities learning the learning of learners who were eTwinned from each device via Google Hangouts, rather than each class being eTwinning via magic whiteboards or other forms of screen projection.

Organisational architecture

The right organisational architecture is no guarantee of success as for a project to success those involved need to be motivated to do so at a high level (Ngwa, Adeleke, Agbaeze, Ghasi, & Imhanrenialena, 2019). An entrepreneurial attitude often forms part of successful organisational architectures (Urban & Verachia, 2019).

Crocels Community Media Group

The Crocels organisational architecture – based around using the Cloud to support communication and collaboration across multiple locations – allows for working, teaching and studying to occur around a range of locations, from home-based, school based to being based in an office or community building. Some offices are leased on a long-term basis, whereas community venues may only be used for a specific workshop. In the case of this project there was a bit of both with supervision taking place in learners' homes and a public library and eTwinning in a central location for the project manager and lead educator.

"Angie"

Angie (not their real name) was responsible for data management and delivering learning. Their role was as a 'community member' meaning they were not paid for the work they did. They liked the way the organisation was based around flexible working. "I *am able to adjust the times and days that I participate at short notice, maintaining a balance very easily between live events and work,*" they said. "*I am able to take part as a volunteer in all areas of Crocels and I have a greater understanding of e-learning.*" Flexible working is not common in most organisations (Anderson & Kelliher, 2009; Kelliher & de Menezes, 2019), but has been used to good effect in projects managed by Crocels. Angie also liked the work-life balance they could achieve through Crocels and continuing professional development opportunities. "*Having a very busy personal life working with Crocels has allowed me to volunteer and take part in a business without having any disruption to my life,*" adding, "*I am able to maintain and update my e learning abilities and knowledge for future use.*" Work-life balance is known to be important in worker satisfaction (Håkansson,

Milevi, Eek, Oudin, & Wagman, 2019) and was certainly the case with workers at Crocels.

"Garda"

Garda, who was involved in content creation and grant funding, did not like the additional bureaucracy that came with their role. "*The accounting is sometimes chaotic and repetitive and I've frequently had to fill in worksheets several times*," they said about the fact there are internal records kept in addition to ones given to external funding bodies. Garda did not like the fact their content creation role did not involve working with others. "*I would therefore appreciate more face-time and contact through work*," they said. Teleworking, as is available to workers (and eTwinning to learners) at Crocels is not always an effective means to improve quality of life (Macía Arce & Quintá, 2012). However, as can be seen in Garda's case there is the benefits of being able to work in spite of having a disability, but that remote setting that can make compliance and sociability issues more obviously problematic.

Dursley Library

Durley Library's organisational architecture is that it is part of Gloucestershire County Council, in stark contrast to Beddau & Tynant Community Library, which was a wholly community-owned library. Community-owned libraries were once uncommon (Burlingame, 1995), with publicly financed libraries being the dominant model (Moyers & Patchett, 2014). This changed when public finances became tighter, but the move from public funding meant that those who took part in Beddau and Tynant probably had a better experience (Bishop, 2016).

Pedagogical and management issues

When working with open educational and other online resources it is essential to have effective working practices to accommodate the challenges arising from them (White, Leon Urrutia, & White, 2015). This particular project had a policy of bring-your-own-device and making use of public Wi-Fi and open communication platforms like Google Hangouts, which was particularly distinct from when Comprend 2.0 was used in community settings as a stand-alone platform.

Crocels Community Media Group

"Garda"

Garda was not totally satisfied with the fact that Crocels operated as a nano-conglomerate, with multiple locations, but not necessarily the staff numbers of larger conglomerates. "*I like work relationships and prefer more contact although I am given a lot of freedom,*" they said. The quality of relationships at work is a know factor when it comes to satisfaction and managing work related stress (Einarsen, Raknes, & Matthiesen, 1994). "*I work to earn money but also to have a life away from my domestic duties largely concerning disability,*" Garda continued. "*I would therefore appreciate more face-time and contact through work.*" It is the case many organisation that working relationships are based on exchange (Buunk, Doosje, Jans, & Hopstaken, 1993), or in other words transactional in nature, meaning although there is reciprocity, it is not necessary that Garda would get what they wanted from more time with other workers.

Garda concluded that on the whole the fact that Crocels is an e-learning organisation makes up for the fact staff are distributed over many locations. *"As a whole it is a very positive experience and all experiences are learning opportunities,"* they said. In a teaching environment where there is strong morale, educators, like Garda, can feel very positive about their activities (Mackenzie, 2007). Because Crocels's management style and pedagogical approach is very much based around encouraging people to take an individual approach rather than conform to a specific model then workers like Garda can enhance their individual development while developing electronic resources and supporting the delivery of educational activities.

"Argie"

Argie (not their real name) was involved in content production, but was not entirely satisfied with their experience. *"I was approached quite late at times to scan and prepare photos for the project, but did so willingly,"* they said. *"I was required to upload them to a cloud folder, where at least once an upload error caused problems,"* noting they *"had remained awake to the point exhaustion prevented me seeing the failed uploads)."* Despite the problems faced by Argie, it is known that creating learning objects, especially on a sustainable basis, is a viable instructional design activity as it promotes retention of concepts (Crow, 2006)

Argie said making use of historical documents posed extra challenges. *"Often there just wasn't much that could be used as the photos used were old and so not many exist of the objects/places,"* they said. *"Dropbox can sometimes be horrible in its refusal to upload,"* they concluded. Often for destroyed buildings, historical photographs are the only option available (Brauer-Burchardt & Voss, 2002). By placing historical photographs online, it serves as an objective record of the past that newer photographs are unable to do (Schindler & Dellaert, 2012).

Dursley Library

Dursley Library, unlike Beddau and Tynant Community Library, is a public library that is owned and run by the county council for the area, namely Gloucestershire County Council. Unlike at Beddau and Tynant there was no option to book the computers, meaning a meeting room had to be used and Bring Your Own Device was as much of a necessity as a testing condition. The fact that a community library existed in one of the locations meant it was able to function as a resource and social centre (Gould & Gomez, 2010).

A proposed conceptual framework for organisation-centered project management

This chapter has investigated three projects using tow tailed software development methodologies. What is clear from the results is that adapting standardised project management methodology to take proper account of organisational architecture and an organisation's working practices and management style is essential to a project being successful. As is presented in Figure 9, this is only possible when this organisation culture of all the collaborating organisations is considered.

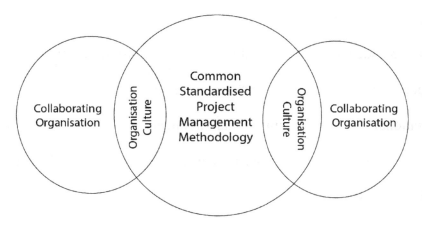

Figure 9 A conceptual framework for organisation-centered project management

What was common across all the projects in this chapter is that it was Crocels Community Media Group acting as the project manager and specifying the project management methodology to be used, which was tailored to the way it did things. What is proposed by the conceptual framework in Figure 9 is that the standardised project management methodology needs to be tailored for all collaborating organisations. In other words, the organisational practices of each participating organisation needs to be used to modify the standardised approach that all parties would otherwise share. On that basis they have both a standardised methodology and one that takes account of the organisational context.

Discussion

This chapter has investigated two successful and two failed projects that were based around customising standardised project management methodologies to the organisational context. The projects were all software projects, with some involving blended learning where the successfully produced software products were put into practice. Three aspects were explored in detail in terms of organisational culture; organisational architecture, pedagogical issues and management issues. Several issues were drawn out from the investigations, including attitude of participants to teleworking, the effectiveness of involving parents and grandparents in the education process, and the importance of having software teams motivated and who buy in to the software product being produced, even if it is as simple as adding content to a website or producing a PowerPoint presentation. The chapter concludes that even where a common software project management is used that the organisational culture and architecture of all participating organisations needs to be considered and not just the one leading the project management of a project.

Limitations and directions for future research

This chapter has shown that project-based organisations with flexible approaches to working have the benefit of allowing workers to work from home when they are not needed to work at a different physical location, but how at the same time they feel they need more contact with other people outside of contact time with workshops and tutorials. Future research should investigate how organisational architecture can be better integrated into project management approaches so that all organisations involved in a project have their different cultural practices accounted for as the human-side of software development seems essential to project success.

References

Abereola, O. (2019). Design and construction of a GSM based home automation system. (PhD, Federal University Oye-Ekiti).

Anderson, D., & Kelliher, C. (2009). Flexible working and engagement: The importance of choice. *Strategic HR Review, 8*(2), 13-18.

Bannerman, E., Basham, M. R., Gray, R. P., Hunt, M. R., McCarthy, R. J., Steel, J. T. J., et al. (2013a). *ITIL continual service improvement*. Norwich, GB: The Stationery Office.

Bannerman, E., Basham, M. R., Gray, R. P., Hunt, M. R., McCarthy, R. J., Steel, J. T. J., et al. (2013b). *ITIL service design*. Norwich, GB: The Stationery Office.

Bannerman, E., Basham, M. R., Gray, R. P., Hunt, M. R., McCarthy, R. J., Steel, J. T. J., et al. (2013c). *ITIL service operation*. Norwich, GB: The Stationery Office.

Bannerman, E., Basham, M. R., Gray, R. P., Hunt, M. R., McCarthy, R. J., Steel, J. T. J., et al. (2013d). *ITIL service strategy*. Norwich, GB: The Stationery Office.

Bannerman, E., Basham, M. R., Gray, R. P., Hunt, M. R., McCarthy, R. J., Steel, J. T. J., et al. (2013e). *ITIL service transition*. Norwich, GB: The Stationery Office.

Bentley, C. (2005). *Practical PRINCE2*. London, GB: The Stationery Office.

Bishop, J. (2004). The potential of persuasive technology for educating heterogeneous user groups. (MSc, University of Glamorgan). (Available online)

Bishop, J. (2005). The role of mediating artifacts in the design of persuasive e-learning systems. *The 1st International Conference on Internet Technologies and Applications (ITA'05),* Wrexham, GB. pp. 54-62.

Bishop, J. (2009a). Enhancing the understanding of genres of web-based communities: The role of the ecological cognition framework. *International Journal of Web Based Communities, 5*(1), 4-17.

Bishop, J. (2009b). The role of multi-agent social networking systems in ubiquitous education: Enhancing peer-supported reflective learning. In T. T. Goh (Ed.), *Multiplatform E-learning systems and technologies: Mobile devices for ubiquitous ICT-based education* (pp. 72-88). Hershey, PA: IGI Global.

Bishop, J. (2009c). Increasing membership in online communities: The five principles of managing virtual club economies. *Proceedings of the 3rd International Conference on Internet Technologies and Applications - ITA09,* Wrexham, GB. pp. 12-20.

Bishop, J. (2012a). Cooperative e-learning in the multilingual and multicultural school: The role of 'Classroom 2.0' for increasing participation in education. In P. M. Pumilia-Gnarini, E. Favaron, E. Pacetti, J. Bishop & L. Guerra (Eds.), *Didactic strategies and technologies for education: Incorporating advancements* (pp. 137-150). Hershey, PA: IGI Global.

Bishop, J. (2012b). Lessons from the emotivate project for increasing take-up of big society and responsible capitalism initiatives. In P. M. Pumilia-Gnarini, E. Favaron, E. Pacetti, J. Bishop & L. Guerra (Eds.), *Didactic strategies and technologies for education: Incorporating advancements* (pp. 208-217). Hershey, PA: IGI Global.

Bishop, J. (2014). Microeconomics of education and the effect of government intervention: The role of classroom 2.0 in facilitating the UK government's schools policies. In J. Bishop (Ed.), *Transforming politics and policy in the digital age* (pp. 39-51). Hershey, PA: IGI Global.

Bishop, J. (2015). Managing behaviour in networked learning environments: Lessons from the classroom 2.0 project. *Enhancing Student Engagement through Online Learning Communities,* Cardiff, GB. pp. 3.

Bishop, J. (2016). The impact of physical and virtual environments on human emotions: A pilot study in an adult and community education setting. *The 2016 International Conference on Computational Science and Computational Intelligence (CSCI'16),* Las Vegas, NV. pp. 306-314.

Bishop, J. (2017a). Devising parametric user models for processing and analysing social media data to influence user behaviour: Using quantitative and qualitative analysis of social media data. In S. Hai-Jew (Ed.), *Social media data extraction and content analysis* (pp. 1-41). Hershey, PA: IGI Global.

Bishop, J. (2017b). Classroom 2.0 and beyond: Education, health, economic and justice policies for exeter. *The Third International Congress on the Internet, Trolling and Addiction (ITA'17),* Exeter, GB.

Bishop, J. (2007). Evaluation-centred design of E-learning communities: A case study and review. *The 2nd International Conference on Internet Technologies and Applications (ITA'07),* Wrexham, GB. pp. 1-9.

Brauer-Burchardt, C., & Voss, K. (2002). Facade reconstruction of destroyed buildings using historical photographs. *International Archives of*

Photogrammetry Remote Sensing and Spatial Information Sciences, *34*(5), 543-550.

Brickley, J. A., Smith Jr, C. W., & Zimmerman, J. L. (2002). Business ethics and organizational architecture. *Journal of Banking & Finance, 26*(9), 1821-1835.

Burlingame, D. (1995). Raising money for public libraries: Insights from experience. *New Directions for Philanthropic Fundraising, 1995*(9), 95-107.

Buunk, B. P., Doosje, B. J., Jans, L. G., & Hopstaken, L. E. (1993). Perceived reciprocity, social support, and stress at work: The role of exchange and communal orientation. *Journal of Personality and Social Psychology,* *65*(4), 801.

Cater-Steel, A., Toleman, M., & Tan, W. (2006). Transforming IT service management-the ITIL impact. Paper presented at the *Proceedings of the 17th Australasian Conference on Information Systems (ACIS 2006),* Adelaide, AU.

Coomey, M., & Stephenson, J. (2002). Online learning: It is all about dialogue, involvement, support and control - according to the research. In J. Stephenson (Ed.), *Teaching & learning online: Pedagogies for new technologies* (pp. 37-52). London, GB: Kogan Page Limited.

Cox, S. A. (2019). A framework for exploring IT-led change in morphing organizations. In M. Khosrow-Pour (Ed.), *Advanced methodologies and* technologies in business operations and management* (pp. 296-310).

Hershey, PA: IGI Global.

Crow, R. K. (2006). Student-created digital learning objects as an elaborative

strategy for promoting conceptual understanding. (Doctor of

Philosophy, University of South Carolina).

De Vries, Manfred F R Kets, Rook, C., & Engellau, E. (2016). Coaching

across the gender divide—creating people-friendly organizations. In De

Vries, Manfred F R Kets, K. Korotov, E. Florent-Treacy & C. Rook

(Eds.), *Coach and couch* (pp. 241-252). New York, NY: Springer

Publishing.

Einarsen, S., Raknes, B. r. I., & Matthiesen, S. B. (1994). Bullying and

harassment at work and their relationships to work environment quality:

An exploratory study. *European Journal of Work and Organizational

Psychology, 4*(4), 381-401.

Endsley, M. R. (1988). Design and evaluation for situation awareness

enhancement. *Human Factors and Ergonomics Society Annual Meeting

Proceedings, , 32.* (2) pp. 97-101.

Endsley, M. R., & Jones, D. G. (2012). *Designing for situation awareness:

An approach to user-centered design* (2nd ed.). London, GB: CRC

Press.

Falcinelli, F., & Laici, C. (2012). ICT in the classroom: New learning

environment. In P. M. Pumilia-Gnarini, E. Favaron, E. Pacetti, J.

Bishop & L. Guerra (Eds.), *Didactic strategies and technologies for education: Incorporating advancements* (pp. 48-56). Hershey, PA: IGI Global.

Farha, B. (2003). Psychic dodge ball: The sylvia browne chronology. *Skeptic (Altadena, CA), 10*(2), 19-22.

Fleetwood, S. (2007). Re-thinking work–life balance: Editor's introduction. *The International Journal of Human Resource Management, 18*(3), 351-359.

Gould, E. A., & Gomez, R. (2010). Community engagement & infomediaries: Challenges facing libraries, telecentres and cybercafés in developing countries.

Graham, N. (2008). *PRINCE2 for dummies*. Chichester, GB: John Wiley & Sons Ltd.

Guy, M. E. (1994). Organizational architecture, gender and women's careers. *Review of Public Personnel Administration, 14*(2), 77-90.

Håkansson, C., Milevi, S., Eek, F., Oudin, A., & Wagman, P. (2019). Occupational balance, work and life satisfaction in working cohabiting parents in sweden. *Scandinavian Journal of Public Health, 47*(3), 366-374.

Hedeman, B., van Heemst, G. V., & Fredriksz, H. (2006). *Project management based on Prince2* Van Haren Publishing.

Helper, S., Martins, R., & Seamans, R. (2019). Who profits from industry 4.0? theory and evidence from the automotive industry. *Theory and Evidence from the Automotive Industry (January 31, 2019),*

Idris, A. (2014). Flexible working as an employee retention strategy in developing countries: Malaysian bank managers speak. *Journal of Management Research, 14*(2), 71.

Iorliam, A. (2019). Proposed digital surveillance software. *Functional and constraint logic programming* (pp. 45-55). New York, NY: Springer.

Kelliher, C., & de Menezes, L. M. (2019). Flexible working in organisations: A research overview Routledge.

Kerzner, H. (2014). Project recovery: Case studies and techiques for overcoming project failure. Chichester, GB: John Wiley and Sons Ltd.

Lonsdale, C., Barrar, P., & Gervais, R. (2006). Risk mitigation and outsourcing: Alternative models for managing supply risk. Paper presented at the *Global Outsourcing Strategies: An International Reference on Effective Outsourcing Relationships,* pp. 221-230.

Lumby, J., & Tomlinson, H. (2000). Principals speaking: Managerialism and leadership in further education. *Research in Post-Compulsory Education, 5*(2), 139-151.

Macía Arce, J. C., & Quintá, A. (2012). Consumption of advanced internet services in the enterprises sector: The spread of telework in the metropolitan area of madrid. *Journal of Urban & Regional Analysis, 4*(1)

Mackenzie, N. (2007). Teacher morale: More complex than we think? *The Australian Educational Researcher, 34*(1), 89-104.

Mann, S., Varey, R., & Button, W. (2000). An exploration of the emotional impact of tele-working via computer-mediated communication. *Journal of Managerial Psychology, 15*(7), 668-690.

Marshall, R., & Hughes, R. (2008). Project management in nursing and residential care: An introduction. *Nursing and Residential Care, 10*(11), 556-560.

Moody, R. (2012). Experiential learning–creating learning experiences with business impact. *Development and Learning in Organizations: An International Journal, 26*(3), 16-18.

Moon, N. W., Linden, M. A., Bricout, J. C., & Baker, P. (2014). Telework rationale and implementation for people with disabilities: Considerations for employer policymaking. *Work, 48*(1), 105-115.

Moyers, B., & Patchett, A. (2014). *The public library: A photographic essay.* San Francisco, CA: Chronicle Books.

Murray, B., & Kenny, S. (1990). Telework as an employment option for people with disabilities. International Journal of Rehabilitation Research, 13(3), 205-214. doi:10.1097/00004356-199009000-00003 [doi]

Ngwa, W. T., Adeleke, B. S., Agbaeze, E. K., Ghasi, N. C., & Imhanrenialena, B. O. (2019). Effect of reward system on employee performance among selected manufacturing firms in the litoral region of cameroon. *Academy of Strategic Management Journal, 18*(3)

Pfannenstiel, J. C., & Seltzer, D. A. (1989). New parents as teachers: Evaluation of an early parent education program. *Early Childhood Research Quarterly, 4*(1), 1-18.

Pongsiri, N. (2002). Regulation and public-private partnerships. *International Journal of Public Sector Management, 15*(6), 487-495.

Rao, K. R. (1962). The preferential effect in ESP. *The Journal of Parapsychology, 26*(4), 252.

Robson, K. (2003). Putting institutional frameworks in place: Good practice in assessing students with disabilities. *Exchange, 2003*(4), 16-18.

Salmon, G. (2003a). *E-moderating: The key to teaching & learning online.* London, GB: Taylor & Frances Books Ltd.

Salmon, G. (2003b). *E-tivities: The key to active online learning.* London, GB: RoutledgeFalmer.

Savage, G., Franz, A., & Wasek, J. S. (2019). Holacratic engineering management and innovation. *Engineering Management Journal, 31*(1), 8-21.

Schindler, G., & Dellaert, F. (2012). 4D cities: Analyzing, visualizing, and interacting with historical urban photo collections. *Journal of Multimedia, 7*(2), 124-131.

Sharifi, M., Ayat, M., Rahman, A. A., & Sahibudin, S. (2008). Lessons learned in ITIL implementation failure. Paper presented at the *2008 International Symposium on Information Technology, , 1.* pp. 1-4.

Taddeo, G., & Tirocchi, S. (2012). Learning in a "Classi 2.0" classroom: First results from an empirical research in the italian context. In P. M. Pumilia-Gnarini, E. Favaron, E. Pacetti, J. Bishop & L. Guerra (Eds.), *Didactic strategies and technologies for education: Incorporating advancements* (pp. 57-67). Hershey, PA: IGI Global.

Urban, B., & Verachia, A. (2019). Organisational antecedents of innovative firms: A focus on entrepreneurial orientation in south africa. *International Journal of Business Innovation and Research, 18*(1), 128-144.

Wagner, M. M., & Clayton, S. L. (1999). The parents as teachers program: Results from two demonstrations. *Future of Children, 9,* 91-115.

Weaver, P. L., Lambrou, N., & Walkley, M. (2002). *Practical business systems development using SSADM: A complete tutorial guide.* Harlow, GB: Pearson Education Limited.

Weller, M. (2002). Delivering learning on the net: The why, what & how of online education. London, GB: RoutledgeFalmer.

Whicker, L. M., & Andrews, K. M. (2004). HRM in the knowledge economy: Realising the potential. *Asia Pacific Journal of Human Resources, 42*(2), 156-165.

White, S., Leon Urrutia, M., & White, S. (2015). MOOCs inside universities: An analysis of MOOC discourse as represented in HE magazines.

Zaman, U., Jabbar, Z., Nawaz, S., & Abbas, M. (2019). Understanding the soft side of software projects: An empirical study on the interactive effects of social skills and political skills on complexity–performance relationship. *International Journal of Project Management, 37*(3), 444-460.

A United Kingdom Perspective

Microchips Law in the UK and Animal Liability Post-2016

Ivan Mugabi

Abstract

This work examines pros and cons underlying the legal Obligation to microchip dogs from in Wales, England, Scotland and Northern Ireland. These include The Microchipping of Dogs (Wales) Regulations 2015, Regulation 3, Dangerous Dogs Act 1991 c. 65 sec. 3 see also Dogs (Amendment) Act (Northern Ireland) 2011 c. 9 sec.2, Microchipping of Dogs (England) Regulations 2015/108, cf. Western Australia Sec. 14 Cats to be microchipped As at 01 Nov 2013 and Western Australian The Dog Act 1976 For example by 6 April 2016, on importing a dog keeper who must ensure that the dog is microchipped within 30 days of importing the dog unless a veterinary surgeon certifies that microchipping would significantly compromise the dog's health. The powers under the Animal Welfare Act also mentioned in this paper because of being the parent statute rationalising the legality of varied legislative enactments in Wales and England through authorising the formulation of different national authorities, as well as suggesting the local or regional procedures that are desirable when dealing with animal matters at decentralised levels. The likely articles also comprises of practical challenges differences in enforcing compulsory microchipping of dogs. An account of how similar developments have happened other parts of the World such as microchipping of cats in some jurisdictions. Scientific counter arguments for the development of this law. However, these final observations are neither conclusive nor the most authoritative but a clear reflection of observations based on the available law and evidence at the time of writing.

Introduction

The 2013 Department of Environment Food and Rural Affairs (hereafter Defra) Government report indicated that more than 100,000 dogs are dumped or lost each year costing taxpayers and welfare charities about £57millions (Caroline, 2014). Consequently, the Defra made recommendations (Caroline, 2014). Among others, those recommendations included a proposal that every dog owner in England ought to have their dog microchipped from 2016. That would be under the plans intended to counter the increasing number of dogs that were being dumped (Caroline, 2014). In the preliminary stages, it was also proposed that the legislation on microchips must require coding the data base with the owners' details (Caroline, 2014). Owners that would fail not comply could face fines of up to £500 (Caroline, 2014). The other rationale underlying this development was overcoming the legal loophole of ensuring that owners are prosecuted for an attack caused by their dogs on private lands (Caroline, 2014). The RSPCA (which is one of the main charities) (Caroline, 2014) was in support if these proposals though it expressed considerable misgivings that the proposed legislation alone would make owners more responsible or ensure fewer dogs bite people (Caroline, 2014). In fact, the microchipping procedure was estimated to be at a cost of about £20-£30 at a private veterinary clinic, this estimation was in repose to the concerns raised by of the pet charities in the primary stages of proposing this legislation. Unlike the UK, in some of the State within Europe, for example, Slovenia, legalisation of compulsive microchipping predates 2005. The legislation helped in controlling illicit trading of animals to Romania and Poland but using Slovenia as the passage route.

For purposes of connecting this development with the UK's common law legal history, it is imperative to understand that the law of animal nuisance has been in place in quite a while. In this regard, it is worthwhile highlighting that since the Ryland v. Fletcher[14] rule of nuisance and trespass to private property.

Wales and law on compulsory microchipping

Everywhich is older than 8 weeks shall be implanted with a microchip from the 6 April 2016 unless a health certificate has been provided by a veterinary officer. This law came into force in Wales on the 25 December 2015.

(i) Obligation to microchip dogs in Wales.

Subject to a certificate issued under paragraph (2) or (3), from 6 April 2016 every keeper of a dog which has not been implanted with a microchip by that date which is older than 8 weeks according to Regulation 3 (1)(a) of the Microchipping of Dogs (Wales) Regulations 2015. Secondly, which is not a certified working dog for the purposes of *Section 6 (3)* of the Animal Welfare Act of 2006 must ensure that it is microchipped (Harding, 2014). According to the aforementioned section 6(3), it must be pointed out that working dog must be less than 5 days old at the time when the veterinary surgeon makes that certification (Harding, 2014). Examples of the working animals include dogs that have been proved to be useful in the context of working in the following; law enforcement (Harding, 2014), activities of Her Majesty's armed forces (Harding, 2014), emergency rescue (Harding, 2014), lawful pest control (Harding, 2014), or lawful shooting of animals (Harding, 2014). It is important to stress that a veterinary surgeon is expected to comply with the Regulations enacted by the responsible national authorities (Harding, 2014). In that context, it must be mentioned that those authorities tend to vary depending on whether that surgeon is in Wales England and Scotland. Take for instance according to the law in Wales the dog can be exempted from the Microchipping requirement long as a veterinary surgeon has certified on a form approved by *the Welsh Ministers* as opposed to the secretary of the State that microchipping activity would significantly compromise the dog's health (Harding, 2014).

Subject to paragraph (4), from 6 April 2016 a keeper who imports a dog must ensure that the dog is microchipped within 30 days of importing the dog unless a veterinary surgeon certifies, on a form approved by the Welsh Ministers that microchipping would significantly compromise the dog's health (Harding, 2014).

A certificate issued under paragraph (2) or (3) must state the period for which the dog will be unfit to be microchipped (Harding, 2014).

A dog is microchipped where a microchip which complies with Regulation 4 has been implanted in the dog (Harding, 2014). The details set out in *Regulation 5* are recorded on to a database by a database operator meeting the conditions set out in *Regulation 6* (Harding, 2014).

The law identifies the authorities for implanter of microchips in Wales.

(1) No person may implant a microchip in a dog unless they are a veterinary surgeon or a veterinary nurse acting under the direction of a veterinary surgeon (Harding, 2014). Alternatively, such a person could be a student of veterinary surgery or a student veterinary nurse acting under the direction of a veterinary surgeon. Additionally, microchip implanters must be been assessed on a training course approved by the Welsh Ministers for that purpose. The fourth but less important requirement at this date, required that the microchip implanter ought to have received training on implantation which included practical experience of implanting a microchip before the day on which these Regulations come into force.

As a matter of administrative law, the Welsh Ministers may (this power is discretionary) serve a notice on that person prohibiting them from implanting microchips in dogs in case it appears to the Welsh Ministers, is unable to do so to a satisfactory standard on the basis of information provided pursuant to *Regulation 10* and any other information, that a person who may implant microchips pursuant to paragraph (1) (c) or (1) (d) (Harding, 2014). That prohibition to implant microchips can be withdrawn after the person has received further training on a course approved by the Welsh Ministers.

Lastly, for purses of clarity *"student, veterinary nurse"* (*"myfyriwrnyrsiomilfeddygol"*) and *"veterinary nurse"* (*"nyrsfilfeddygol"*) have the same meanings as given by Schedule 3 to the Veterinary Surgeons Act 1966. A *"student of veterinary surgery"* (*"myfyriwrmilfeddygol"*) has the same meaning as in Regulation 3 of the Schedule to the Veterinary Surgeon (practice by student relations order of council of 1981. Finally, a *"veterinary surgeon"* (*"milfeddyg"*) means a person registered in the register of veterinary surgeons, or the supplementary veterinary register, kept under the Veterinary Surgeons Act 1966.

England and dog microchip legislation

According to the law of England the term "microchipped" has been defined to mean ensuring an implanted with a microchip the details are set out as per Regulation 5 are recorded on a database by a database operator meeting the conditions set out in Regulation 6 (Harding, 2014). In that context, Regulation 5imposes several obligations on the operator of the microchip. Among those include; Ensuring that the details to be recorded on databases with the details to be recorded on a database are, the full name and address of the keeper where applicable, the fact that the keeper is also the breeder; if the keeper is the breeder and is licensed by the local authority under the Breeding of Dogs Act 1973 (Harding, 2014). The relevant details include the breeder's licence number and the name of the local authority by which they are certified (Harding, 2014). More over the name or identification number given to the dog (Harding, 2014). Additionally, the contact telephone number if available the name given to the dog by the keeper (Harding, 2014). That is different to the details recorded pursuant to the sex of the dog (Harding, 2014). The breed of the dog or a description if it is a crossbreed (Harding, 2014). The colour of the dog and the most accurate estimate of its date of birth that the keeper is capable of giving thus implanting the unique number of the microchip implanted in the dog (Harding, 2014).

In addition to the above, it is imperative to point that according to Regulation 6 there are ten obligations that must be met database operator from 6th April 2015 (Harding, 2014). These duties include the ability have storage and retrieve the details of the keepers where required

The benefit to evidential issues

Microchipping of dogs might increase the possibility of collecting credible evidence by law enforcement officers. In fact, such evidence might useful to the owners of the dog in cases of disputes on missing pets. This argument might be perceived with considerable reservations since in some cases the assurance of such evidence might make some dog keepers even less vigilant with their dogs. Simply because this microchipping law will increase the possibility of bio-trucking in the event of lost and found pets. On the other hand, in such evidence gains more public to be used in tracing the dog keepers or owners for animal negligence, then, that might increase vigilance to be seen as an obligation than discretionary moral responsibility. It might be too early to predict how the conduct of the publicmight be reshaped by this development.

The increase in the role of empirical evidence in regulating dog-ownership relationship.

The reliance of compulsory microchipping of dogs might not only reduce the cost of charities but shall enable better policies and practices of empirically accessible data bases in monitory the relationship between the dog owners and their animals. This polices seems to apply to notion of private ownership and bearing of risk. In essence, the risk associated with the misconduct of the dog are legally and undisputedly transferable to the rightful individuals. The view of capitalism and ownership are somehow strengthened. Bearing in mind that capitalisms emphases private ownership although with limited state interference.

The future of microchipping law in Scotland

After Wales and England legislating on the issue of compulsory microchipping, there is a possibility for the Scottish law to emulate that approach in this area. This year shows possible momentum for such reforms following the anticipated benefits that policy makers in Scotland have attributed to microchips.

Rural Affairs secretary Richard Lochhead said:

"Scotland is a nation of animal lovers and so we must do all we can to safeguard dog welfare and promote responsible ownership. [...] two-thirds of dogs in Scotland had already been microchipped voluntarily and claimed that in 2014, over 10,000 dogs in the UK were reunited with their owners as a result of a microchip. This is an impressive figure, but it could be improved on dramatically by ensuring that all dogs are microchipped and, equally important, that their details are kept up-to-date" (Harding, 2014).

In the above regard is apparent that voluntary microchipping of dogs is the norm in Scotland laws rather than the compulsory requirement. After April, it is microchipping is anticipated that obligatory microchipping shall take greater strides in Scotland. It is possible that with the regime of voluntary microchipping only a person with an inherently dangerous or previously harmful dog might be reluctant to take positive action. In fact, it might be interesting to establish whether dog owners whose dogs have been served with dog control notices had or might willingly or voluntarily under take dog microchip out of their own volition. Moreover, there is evidence that the law of Scotland has made an effort to address the usual problems that such dangerous dogs have previously caused.

Consequently, section 9 relates to the dangerous or unresponsive dogs and it applies where an authorised officer is responding in relation to a dangerous dog that is out of control by serving a dog control notice (or a further dog control notice) (Harding, 2014). Accordingly, the local authority by summary application apply to the sheriff for an order that would have two implications. Firstly, appointing a person to undertake the dog's destruction is one possible the outcome (Harding, 2014). Another supplementary act is requiring the dog to be delivered up for that purpose. *Dickson v. Brown* (Harding, 2014) and *Scottish Borders Council v. Johnstone* (Harding, 2014) are classic examples of cases where such orders have been imposed. It unclear but supposedly unlikely that dog owners who have been red flagged with such notices would voluntarily embrace microchips in their dogs or even future off springs of such dogs for fear of liability or legal battles.

Furthermore, if the sheriff declines to make an order under subsection (2), the case may, if the sheriff thinks fit, be remitted to the local authority for a dog control notice (or a further dog control notice) to be served (Harding, 2014).

In this context, it is imperative to note that the above trends have seen the presence of more concerted efforts to support legislation in this area. Those efforts account for the enactment of the Microchipping of Dogs (Scotland) Regulations 2016 (Harding, 2014). The entire context and contents of this legislation have a number of similarities with the legislation on dog microchip in other part of the UK, those are explained in further details in another section of this study.

Additionally, considering the situation in Scotland, there is apparent that pet charities have expressed their commitment to financially support the microchipping arrangements. It is vital to highlight that the contemporary changes of the law on this issue might increase the need for microchips services and charities might at some stage become overwhelmed and subsequently desirous of being exonerated from the cost. There is a high likelihood that such support might be hardly sustainable in the long run and making dog owners take responsibility for covering the expenses involved.

Law on Microchipping of dogs in Northern Ireland

In Article 6 of the Dogs Order (issue of dog licences) at the end paragraph, 7 is added that obligates the district council never to issue either a dog licence or issue a transfer certificate in respect of a dog which has not been microchipped (Harding, 2014). Secondly, a licence or a transfer is void in respect of a new dog unless that dog has been microchipped (Harding, 2014). The process of licensing and transfer has been used by authorities in enforcing the registration of animals in Northern Ireland. It is apparent the Wales and England has adopted the same approach

Bio-tracking and its role to guide dogs before and after situations of emergencies

Persons with disabilities are among the group of people that can benefit from microchipping dogs. Catastrophic situations of disasters have often caused displacement in both developed and developing and developed countries. However, such situations are known for making blind and deaf lose truck of their guides. Note that under normal circumstances the assistance animal will hardly depart from the service users (Harding, 2014), the occurrence of displacement makes such separation inherently inevitable. However, after experiencing such situations, it might be possible to identify the rightful owners of the guide animals in such cases. Therefore, in such cases microchipping assistance animals can enhance the reunion with service beneficiaries.

Counter voices to the 2016 law on compulsory microchipping

There are some arguments that have been made by some of the animal activist groups in in contesting the microchipping (Harding, 2014). The vires can revolve around the legality, credulity, morality and ethical aspects underlying legislation on compulsory microchipping.

> *"Whilst fully respecting those that have [had, emphasis mine] their dogs microchipped and regard the database a good thing, I do not think the majority of people would have been advised of the risks involved by their veterinary practitioner (Harding, 2014)."*

In light of the first criticism, it seems apparent that the above observation by Hawkins about has a point to make however, that observation might simply imply emphasizing the duty of microchip implanters to inform the dog owners with the possible risks. Perhaps such a legal obligation remains a central principle of most medical professions. It is arguable that, the absence of the legal provision in the law that specifies the duty of discussing possible side effects must not be used in portraying the measure of as liability than being an asset of social engineering. Secondly, it would be a question of reforming and revisiting the training of professional implanters in the UK. Perhaps this might be another emerging discipline where the law on animal nuisance and veterinary professionals might be portrayed as developing complementary relationships.

Furthermore, this analyst of the 2016 UK law on compulsory dog microchipping has made more useful assertions worthwhile highlighting. Primarily this law might seem to serve the interests of local authorities whereas exposing the health and lives of these loyal companions to one or more of the following medical conditions.

"Adverse tissue reaction, migration of implanted transponder, electrical hazards, and compromised information security are a few of the FDAidentified Potential health risks associated with such devices. Should your dog experience any of the above, then an operation would be required. At least three studies conducted since the 1990s have reported tumours at the site of implantation in laboratory dogs, rats and mice (Harding, 2014)."

The concept of tissue migration is a concern although it seems apparent that more scientific research and improvements might happen in this area will deal with these concerns (Harding, 2014). For example, some of the guidelines and more instruction given to veterans in terms of the expectation and possible liability in case of professional negligence of their part as medical experts in this sector.

It appears there would have been a professional discontent from countries where laws on animal microchipping are implemented. For instance, the use of microchips has remained undoubtedly accredited by several experts from the international Organisation for standardisation of Radio Frequency Identification Devices (RFID) to be one of the most effective devises for suck ownership tracking and tracing related-work (Harding, 2014).

"[...] research reviewed in this report indicates a clear causal link

between microchip implants and cancer in mice and rats. It also appears

that microchips can cause cancer in dogs, as they have done so in at least

one case, and quite likely in two (Harding, 2014)."

Nonetheless, the findings of most of these results are showing a remote possibility. The extent of this health threat remains hardly ascertainable to justify disregarding the meritorious anticipations that the laws on compulsory microchipping might bring to enforcing the tort of animal negligence and public nuisance (Harding, 2014). Moreover, several products used by mankind rely on microchip technology. Thus, the applications in other aspects of life and law should not be constrained

The lack of prescriptive uncertainty of the standards of devices another criticism Hawkins has associated the new legislation in addition to the above.

"There are also many other microchips with different build and

qualities that are aligned to different scanners and databases, so it is very important that you understand the risks and implications these devices may

pose to you and your dog. It should also be mandatory and the duty of all

veterinary practitioners and/or animal welfare societies to advise dog

owners of any health risk that may arise from microchipping. This does not

seem to be the case (Harding, 2014)."

In as much there is some truth that several brands and specifications of microchip products on the market it must be pointed out that these discrepancies are less of a problem. That is simply because considerable efforts have been devoted to identifying products that can promote good practice standards in the event of compulsory microchipping. In fact, the 2016 law against which Hawkins lodged his online petition requires veterinary professionals to ensure that the type of microchip used is consistent with a frequency of 132.4 KHz (Harding, 2014). It might be argued that as long as the guidelines are complied with by those concerned (see Petlog website) the anticipated health risks might be minimised. Of course, it is vital to stress that the concerned stakeholders range from veterinary nurses to everyone qualifying as veterinary surgeons (As per the Petlog website). This might raise questions as to whether these developments have long-term impacts and implications on the monitoring and supervisory powers of veterinary council (see Petlog website).

Comparing and contrasting the microchip legislations

Reference to the Equality Act's 173 interpretation (1). In that interpretation section the Equality Act section it should be highlighted that accessibility requirements have same the meaning as that given under section 167(5) of the Act. In the context of Equality, section 167(5) of the Act defined accessibility requirements as those requirements for securing that as much as possible the disabled persons in wheelchair are to get into and out of vehicles in safety, and to travel in vehicles in safety and reasonable comfort by staying in their wheelchairs or not (depending on which they prefer).

In that same vain and probably more important in this context Section 173 (1) of the Equality Act defines an "assistance dog" to mean firstly a dog which has been trained to guide a blind person. In other cases, an assistance dog can be a dog which has been trained to assist a deaf person. Additionally, an assistance dog could be dog that is trained by a prescribed charity to assist a disabled person who has a disability that consists of epilepsy or otherwise affects the person's mobility, manual dexterity, physical co-ordination or ability to lift, carry or otherwise move everyday objects. The above definition encompasses a dog of a prescribed category that has trained to assist a disabled person who has a disability (other than one falling within paragraph of a prescribed kind. It is striking to note that the interpretations of assistance dogs in the Act in both Wales and England.

Differences in the microchip laws of Wales and England.

In as much as both in both jurisdiction there is a definition authorised persons under Regulation 2 as well as a requiring those persons are permitted to enforce of the Regulations as provided Regulation 11. There is a jurisdiction difference as to who can authorise under Regulation 11. For example, in Wales the Welsh ministers instead of the Sectary of the State exercise discretionally powers in making written authorisation for an authorised person whom the Regulations are also bilingually translating as ("person awdurdodedig") as per Regulation 11(1) of The Microchipping of Dogs (Wales) Regulations 2015. Whereas in England that Regulation mandates those authorisation powers to the secretary of the State as per Regulation 11(1) of the Microchipping of Dogs (England) Regulations 2015. Other persons authorised are the same in their status legal standing in both of the legislations. Those include; the local authority in terms of Regulation 11(2), police constable in terms of Regulation 11(3) and community support officer in terms of Regulation 11(4). Save that in the Welsh law, those authorised categorises are translated to bilingual texts such as the reference to the community support offer as ("swyddogcymorthcymunedol").

In terms of the implications of that jurisdiction discrepancy it creates a situation in which the power of authorisation granted to a person under Welsh law by devolved or delegated powers to the Welsh Ministers can only be exercised within Wales and supposedly such a power ceases to be an authorised persons as soon as they relocate or travel to England and vice versa. Relocation between the two regions is a usual likely due to education, marriage or job transfers. It appears if a person under paragraph 1 of Regulation 11, from either of the jurisdictions is to continue functioning as a legally authorised persons (person awdurdodedig), they would be possibility have to secure another authorisation from the approved authority in the jurisdiction Regulation 11 of the Microchipping of Dogs (Scotland) Regulations 2016 Regulations that apply.

Differences in dealing with adverse reactions and failures in microchips

The term 'adverse reactions' refers to situations in which the implanting of a microchip in the dog leads to any unnecessary pain or suffering, or any pathology on the part of a dog under Regulation 10(2) (a) of the Microchipping of Dogs (England) Regulations 2015 and Regulation 10 (2) of the Microchipping of Dogs (Wales) Regulations 2015. That same term is also used when referring to the migration of a microchip from the intended body site in which it was originally implanted in accordance with Regulation 10(2)(b) of the Microchipping of Dogs (Wales) Regulations 2015, Regulation 10. In accordance with Regulation 10(3) of the Microchipping of Dogs (Wales)

Regulations 2015, 'Failures in microchips' refers to those situations in which the microchip when scanned by an appropriate transceiver. In as much as both the Walsh and the English legislation envisaged the importance of reporting adverse reactions from microchips and failures in microchips, nonetheless there is evidence of a differences in terms of the administrative institutions to which those adverse reactions or microchip failures are reported. Welsh Ministers are mandated to receive reports in the event of adverse reactions ("adwaithanffafriol") relation to dog microchipping from within Wales, or failures in microchips ("methiantmicrosglodyn") implanted from within Wales. Where as in England reports on similar issues are directed and received by the Secretary of the State in accordance with Regulation 10 (1) of the Microchipping of Dogs (England) Regulations 2015.

The implications of the above differences are continued in latter discussion recommendations.

Wales and Northern Ireland and microchip legislation

Similarities in the use of dog microchipping in Wales and Northern Ireland. In the context of Northern Ireland, the Dogs (Amendment) Act (Northern Ireland) 2011 define the use of microchipping as a means of identification of a dog and its keeper. In this case, the law related the issues microchipping act as means of enabling the possibility of knowing or identity of the owner. Furthermore, the role of use microchips for identifying in Northern Ireland is instrumentally important ensuing that the persons that have been licensed to be in charge of that dog are accurately identifiable (Dickson & Graeme, 2013).

Additionally, the law on using dog microchipping in Northern stipulates the rationale as well as guiding grounds upon which acts pf microchipped must be justified Dickson & Graeme, 2013. Those considerations include that a dog is microchipped for the purposes of Article 6(7) (Dickson & Graeme, 2013). If in the first instance the microchip is of a prescribed class or description or of a class or description approved by a prescribed body or person (Dickson & Graeme, 2013). Related to that condition is the obligatory duty to ensure that the microchip being implanted in the dog is of a prescribed class or description (Dickson & Graeme, 2013). In contrast, the law related to the use of dog microchipping in Wales contains a provision describing expected contents of the accepted microchips (Dickson & Graeme, 2013). Furthermore, microchip must comply with the conditions as prescribed for keeping and those on making of the information contained in the microchipped data available for use by councils for purposes of identifying of keeper or licensed and authorised person a dog (Dickson & Graeme, 2013). It must be pointed out that law in Wales also outlines law relate to the stage of data related to the dog. It is imperative to high that those details more included the section the duties of the data base operator (Dickson & Graeme, 2013). The law in Wales and England seems clearer in terms of explaining the expected and the accepted duties in relation to keeping and the storage of data (Dickson & Graeme, 2013). For example, Regulation 6 in Wales refers to a duty of having sufficient database with capacity of electronically storing and retrieving the details as provided to it by keepers (Dickson & Graeme, 2013). Additionally, storage involves some duties to do with ensuring that such information is backed on the daily basis (Dickson & Graeme, 2013). The law in Northern Ireland remains silent on those issues of backing up and having sufficient storage and such silence might lead to lack of clarity of when, where and how liability might arise in these cases.

Adverse effects on health of dog in both jurisdictions. In the laws of both jurisdictions, the possibility of adverse effects on the health of the dog can be e ground for the exemption of the dog from subject to the microchipping legal requirement. However, it will be striking to understand how there are different on how to report, what to report, who can report and to whom such reports must became in the respective jurisdictions.

Differences in the use of microchip in Wales and Northern Ireland.

In Northern Ireland subject to fulfilling the microchipping, the power the issue the certificate or authorisation license of the dog given to the eleven local councilsthat comprise Northern Ireland (Dickson & Graeme, 2013). The district councils include; Antrim and Newtownabbey Borough Council, Ards and North Down Borough Council, Armagh City, Banbridge and Craigavon Borough Council, Belfast City Council, Causeway Coast and Glens Borough

Council, Derry City and Strabane District Council and finally Fermanagh and Omagh District Council, Lisburn and Castlereagh City Council, Mid and East Antrim Borough Council, Mid Ulster District Council, Newry, Mourne and Down District Council. Note the certificate and a license in Northern Ireland are issued as evidence that a particular dog has been microchipped. On the other hand, it must be noted that in Wales the certificate is only issues as evidence that a dog should or shall be exempted from microchipping. Here is there a clear difference in terms of when and why a certificate can or should be issued. In Northern Ireland, certificates or licenses can be issued by local councils as approval of compliance but could also be issued by the veterinary surgeons as signs of exemption from this duty. In Northern Ireland, there is hardly a reference to the exemption of working dogs based on the same grounds those mentioned the section 6(3) of the Regulations in Wales and England with reference to the animal welfare Act of 2006.

Differences in terms of reporting adverse effects

It is imperative to note that there are clear variances in the manner in which reporting is made, who can make them and to who they must be made. For example, in Wales, there is some element of Communal or collective based reporting.

"Anyone who identifies an adverse reaction to a microchip or the failure of a microchip must report that reaction or failure [...]" (Dickson & Graeme, 2013)

It is apparently evident in the above context that the reporting duty is neither limited to one person that is termed as an authorised person nor to the licensed breeder of the dog. It is apparent in the present context the anyone that seems to connate more of a collective reporting obligation as opposed to leaving to this duty to only one specific person on law. On the contrary, the law in Northern Ireland seems to suggest an individual-centered reporting approach in relation to the presence of such adverse effects.

"Microchip" does not apply if the keeper of the dog produces to the council a certificate signed by a veterinary surgeon to the effect that implantation (or continued implantation) of a microchip in the dog would have an adverse effect on the health of the dog" (Dickson & Graeme, 2013)

Similarity of the law in Wales and that of Scotland

Both of the laws have a provision related to statutory offences with respect to the following persons. In this, section the law of Wales and that of England are under the same category for purposes of making the comparative analysis easier. That is ideal given the several similarities in most contents of the microchipping Regulations for both of those jurisdictions. A difference can be seen with respect to an authorised person in Regulation 11. According to Regulation 11, it is stated that:

"[...] the following persons are "authorised persons" for the purposes

of the Regulations any person authorised in writing by the Scottish

Ministers."

The authorised persons will also imply any person authorised in writing by a local authority in respect of its area. Finally, in the Scottish context an authorised person can be constable. It is imperative to note in the above context community support officers are never the list of authorised persons according to Regulation 5 of Microchipping of Dogs (Scotland) Regulations 2016:

"An individual who identifies any of the following in respect of a

compliant microchip implanted in a dog must report it to the Scottish

Ministers"

However, in the Welsh and the English law they have powers to undertake microchips. See for instance Microchipping of Dogs (Wales) Regulations 2015, Regulation 11 (4) c.f. Regulation 11. (4)

Unlike in Wales in Scotland where the law appears unclear as to whether the extent and purpose of authorisation can be limited is explicitly clear under the Scottish law that the purpose and extent of making someone an authorized person in process of authorisation. The lawfulness of actions performed or undertaken by an authorised person can only be legitimate if in compliance with the extent and purposes mentioned in their written authorisation by the concerned Scottish ministers or local authority as per Regulation 11(2). The importance of those differences is appropriate in terms of suggesting good practice. The continued analysis of the same issue is contained in the subsequent sections.

According to Regulation 5, an individual who identifies any of the following in respect of a compliant microchip implanted in a dog must report it to the Scottish Ministers within 21 days beginning with the day of identifying an adverse reaction, migration, or a failure of a microchip. It seems after the lapse of the period stated in the Regulation 5 then it becomes evident that the person is liable for the statutory offence identifiable in Regulation 13, and which on summary becomes punishable by a fine note exceeding level 2 on the standard scale according to Regulation of the Scottish Regulation. On contrary, in this respect it imperative acknowledge that is much as a similar statutory offence and punishment is created under the Microchipping of Dogs (Wales) Regulations 2015 and Microchipping of Dogs (England) Regulations 2015. Although there is hardly a conditional for ensuring that reporting of those adverse effects in done in 21 days from the time of identifying those effects especially in the context of Wales and England Regulations respectively.

Offences and microchipping dogs in the United Kingdom

A database operator and offences in relation to microchipped data

According to Regulations 13 of the Microchipping of Dogs (Scotland) Regulations 2016, it is a punishable offence for a database operator in the event of defaulting or failing to recording on database, the details notified to them by keepers of dogs, by virtue of a dog that is older than 8 weeks that must be microchipped. It is an offence for a database operator to default or fail recording on its database details notified to them by a keeper who brings a dog into Scotland must ensure that the dog that ought to be microchipped within 30 days of the date on which it is brought into Scotland. Scottish Regulation also contain statutory offences against the database operator is cases of failure to comply of the database as provided under the Regulation 8. In other wards the data operator committee the offence in Regulation 13 in case of pretending or from the time of stopping to meet the conditions under Regulation 8.

There are some discrepancies in some of these conditions. For example, it is an offence under the Scottish Regulations for a database operator to destroy or delete the data concerning a dog before a minimum of 30 years from its time of birth. This 30-year period is not applicable in the context of Wales and England. The database operators would also committee an offence in case of the omission to publicly publish its data retention policy or fail in the obligation of securing the database in relation to the storage of this data. Those are simply a few examples of the 11 conditions listed in Regulations 8. Most important for now it suffices to mention there are many other conditions that are mentioned under Regulation 8. On summary conviction that offence is punishable by a fine not and exceeding level 4 on the standard scale.

A data base operate is also held to have committed a statutory offence under Regulation 13 if he/she has been served with a notice by the Scottish Ministers under Regulation 9(1) but refuses to surrender the details held of their data base for inspection to the authorised persons. Similarly, it would be an offence in case a *person* unlawfully continues pretending and misleading the general public that that they are data operators in spite of serving on them as notice requesting them to stop carrying out the work of data operators but he or she continues doing that work thence undermining that notice by utter contempt. In the context of Scotland it must understood that there is a likelihood of strict liability for the statutory the moment the data base operator falls pay of the conditions that are outlined in Regulation 8, note that for this offence to be committed it is not a prerequisite that the ministers will be expected to first service this is a remarkable difference with the situation in Wales as we shall see latter.

In contrasting the above Scottish Regulations with those of Wales, namely the Microchipping of Dogs (Wales) Regulations 2015, similar offences seem to apply in relation to database operators are evident Regulations 13 of the microchipping. The major different being that it is rather unclear if the data operate will be held data base operator ("gweithredwrcronfaddataperthnasol") would be held liable for the violating the expected standards in the data base in Regulation 6 unless the this matter has been satisfactorily confirmed and dealt with by the Welsh minsters as provided in Regulation 7(2) of the Microchipping of Dogs (Scotland) Regulations 2016.

It is an offence, punishable on summary conviction by a fine not exceeding level 4 on the standard scale, to fail to comply with a notice served under regulation 7. From 6 April 2016, as a result of the Microchipping of Dogs (Wales) Regulations 2015, the Welsh Ministers may serve a notice on a database operator requiring it to provide to them with any information recorded on the database, or any information relating to the functioning of the regulatory regime established by the Regulations. Additionally the Welsh ministers can request the data operator in Wales to tender any information necessary to demonstrate that it is meeting the conditions in Regulation 6. It must be reiterated that the conditions in Regulation 6 relate to standards that database operator ("gweithredwrcronfaddataperthnasol") is expected to uphold with regards data relating to the dogs microchipped in Wales.

Paragraph 2 of Regulation 7 prescribes the action that must be undertaken by the ministers is Wales in the event of a failure the data operator ("gweithredwrcronfaddataperthnasol") to meet or comply with the excepted standards. Such as supplying the electronic data to the mister or another data base operator. It apparent that Minsters are expected to take action and it is upon the refusal to comply with ministerial directive that a data base operator will committee the offence in Regulation 13.

It appears as if this in the context of Wales there is hardly clarity as to whether there will be offence prima facie as matter of strict liability unless there has been a failure to comply with a service given to a data base operator ("gweithredwrcronfaddataperthnasol") that is offending the conditions through the assistance of the Walsh ministers. This seems to subject the committing of the offence as a consequence of the failure by the data base operator ("gweithredwrcronfaddataperthnasol") with the service made against them. Otherwise in the absence of that obligations.

Keeper and offences in relation to offences of microchipped data

According to Regulation 13 (5)(a) of the Microchipping of Dogs (Scotland) Regulations 2016, it is a punishable offence for the Keeper of the dog, notify to a database operator any of the details set out in Regulation 7 knowing those personal details to be false in material particulars, or acting recklessly notify to the database operator any of the details set out in Regulation 7 which are false in a material particular, fail to comply with Regulation 10(2). It Imperative to recall that Regulation 10(2) is to the effect that from the 6th April 2016, no keeper may transfer a dog to a new keeper until that dog has been has been microchipped and ensure the details that are to be recorded on the database. It is an offence for a keeper of a dog to intentionally obstruct an authorised person in the exercise of their powers conferred by Regulation 12. Finally under the Scottish Regulation is an offence for a keeper of a dog to fail to comply with a notice served under Regulation 12(1) (b).

Regulation 12(1) (b), from 6th April 2016, on producing (if required to do so) the written authorisation mentioned OR other official identity document in the case of a constable, an authorised person may serve on the keeper of a dog a notice requiring the keeper to have the dog microchipped where the it has not been microchipped. The keeper of the dog will commit the offence if they refused to have the dog implanted with a compliant microchip that can transmit the number encoded in it when scanned by an appropriate transceiver in cases where the dog keeper notes a failure of a compliant microchip implanted in the dog. The dog keeper will also be held to have committed the offence in Regulation 13 of the Scottish Regulation where there has been a failure on their part to comply with Regulation 6(7) within 21 days beginning with the day on which the notice is served.

Regulation in Wales and offences to the keeper ("ceidwad")

In contrast, the Regulation in Wales have some offences in Regulation 13 related to dog keepers that commenced from April 2016. These Regulations state that;

From 6 April 2016 the keeper ("ceidwad") of a dog in Wales has committed an offence if they transfer a dog to a new keeper without having that dog microchipped in accordance with Regulation 7 (1) (a) of the Microchipping of Dogs (Wales) Regulations 2015. The defence to this offence is the presentation of a certificate issued under Regulation 3(2) or 3(3) stating that microchipping would significantly compromise a dog's health. It is imperative to note that the offence under Regulation 13 in Wales has the retrospective characteristics of criminal law. In other wards under the Regulations in Wales, a keeper ("ceidwad") will not be held liable for any transfers of the dog that happened in January 2016 since by that time it was lawful to transfer the dog without having it microchipped. However, such transfer only become unlawful after being criminalised from April 2016. There is hardly evidence of this retrospective aspect explicitly exemplified in the work of the Regulation of Scotland.

Unlike the Scottish Regulation that specifies that the counting of the 21 days start, when the day after the keeper ("ceidwad") is served, the offence in relation to Wales there is silence on this counting of the 21 days start. That silence could lead to a lack of clarity in terms of the law in Wales as to the tie when the counting is expected to start.

Offences against third parties based on omission of duty to act

According to Regulation 13 (3) in conjunction with Regulation 13 (7) of the Microchipping of Dogs (Scotland) Regulations 2016, a failure to report an adverse reaction or the failure of a microchip in accordance with Regulation 10(1) is an offence committed by the person who has known of that adverse reaction, failure or migration in the implanted microchip but chooses to hardly consider reporting it. This hence punishable on summary conviction by a fine not exceeding level 2 on the standard scale.

Unauthorised third parties that implant the microchip in any dog are held to have committed the under the Scottish regulation, and that offence this is punishable under the Regulation 13. In the same accords an implanter must not hold out to the keeper of a dog that a microchip is a compliant microchip where they implant a noncompliant microchip knowing in cases where they could reasonably be expected to know, that such a microchip is none complaint in relation to Regulation 3 (2) and Regulation 13 (4) and (7). It is imperative to note that the above offence is based on the actual act of implanting of the microchip inside the body of the dog as opposed to acts of attempted acts of implanting. This is key in the understanding of the flaws and limitation of this law in the real world of criminal evidence for the act of the implanting.

The law in England and Wales has a similar offences, which are evident in relation to third party individuals that refuse reporting the adverse reactions ("adwaithanffafriol") as per the Microchipping of Dogs (Wales) Regulations 2015, including Regulation 10 (1) in conjunction with Regulation 13 (2) (d). There is a difference in terms of offence of authorised persons between Wales and Scotland. Offence are implied in Wales where an individual commits a crime when they obstruct the authorised persons ("person awdurdodedig") in terms of Regulation 13 (2) in conjunction with Regulation 12(b) or 12(c). Whereas in Scotland an individual committee a crime when they pretends to be authorised persons ("person awdurdodedig") and yet they are unauthorised for purposes implanting microchip in dogs in terms of Regulation 3 (1) in conjunction Regulation 13 (4) (7) of the Microchipping of Dogs (Scotland) Regulations 2016. More discrepancies relate to offences applied to an authorised persons that implants a noncompliant chip knowing that it falls short of the expect standards as per Regulation 3 (2) and Regulation 13 (4) and (7).

Challenges for the 2016 UK law on microchipping

The definition of ownership and possession might be rather challenging. In this case, the legal concept of bailment can be used to explain issues of liability in these cases. In most of the case law, the language used is that of the dog owner but not dog keeper. That is exemplified in Russell v. The Crown Prosecution Service [2015] EWHC 2065 (Admin), 2015 WL 4275095 where the dangerous dog escaped from its owner attacking the complaint. The term dog owner was used in the summary trial and at the appeal. Similarly, in Reid v Murphy [2015] HCJAC 60, 2015 S.C.L. 772 among other cases, courts apply the term dog owner as opposed to dog keeper. Moreover, in terms of assistance dogs it is common for these to be take care of by another person that provides disability support to an individual with disabilities as per section 173 of the Equality Act 2010. The inconsistence in legal language appears to red flag confusion and can be problematic and might in some cases create ambiguities where the day-to-day dog keepers that are occasional caretakers of the dog fail to take their responsibility in which the registered keeper is held accountable.

The issues of less clarity on the role of Data Protection Act in regulating activities of (a) Dog owners or dog keepers as data subjects and data controllers' microchip. The database obligations and standards are provided in *Regulation 6*. The duties are several and they include storing, providing, informing, identifying, communicating, data regarding the dog to either its keeper or any other authorised person. Additionally, according to Regulation 7, the Welsh Ministers' powers have the discretionary powers to monitors microchip databases. Conversely from 6 April 2016 the Welsh Ministers may, as a result of The Microchipping of Dogs (Wales) Regulations 2015, serve a notice on a database operator requiring it to provide to them any information recorded on the database, any information relating to the functioning of the regulatory regime established by these Regulations under Regulation 7 (1) (b), any information necessary to demonstrate that it is meeting the conditions in *Regulation 6* as per Regulation 7 (1) (c).

Secondly, where the Welsh Ministers are satisfied that a database operator does not meet the conditions in regulation 6, the Welsh Ministers may serve a notice requiring the operator to cease holding itself out as meeting the conditions in Regulation 6 as per Regulation 7 (2) (a). That notice could also request the operator to provide the Welsh Ministers or another database operator with an electronic copy of all the data recorded on its database pursuant to *Regulation 3(5) (b)* as Regulation 7 (2) (b). There is also a penalty as a consequence of acting with contempt to served notices on microchip data base operator. Subsequently the law in Wales provides that, it is an offence, punishable on summary conviction by a fine not exceeding level 4 on the standard scale, to fail to comply with a notice served under *Regulation 7* (see Regulation 13(1)). This approach of data from microchip implanting in Wales is different from that of Western Australian under the law on microchipping Cats. See the Cat Act 2011, sec. 15-16 Cat Regulations 2012.

"Microchip implanter to give information to microchip database company A microchip implanter who implants a microchip in a cat must, within 7 days after the microchip is implanted, give notice in writing in the

form, if any, prescribed of the information prescribed to the microchip database company for that cat. Penalty: a fine of $5 000.”

There is hardly specification of period win that the implanter pass on the information to the database company. In the legislation of Wales, regarding compulsory microchipping might encounter enforcement challenges in the practical sense (Hirby, Eckham & MacFarlane, 2014). Especially if compared with the seemingly better-regulated system of Western Australian.[67]

Cost and funding of microchipping expenses

There is need to acknowledge that in some cases a single dog owner might have more than 10 dogs. Such an incident is exemplified the case of *Myatt -v- Teignbridge* D.C. [1995] Env. L.R.78. In this case the complaints were neighbours of the defendant who owned more than 15 dogs and lived in two cottages. Leaving in cottage resonates a possibility of the person being an average or even a low-income earner. The compliant filed a case of public nuisance against the defendant. The other details might of less important for this argument. It is imperative to mention that even though such cases might be exceptionally rare that certainly case demonstrates this is a likely possibility. That implies each of the 15 dogs if they belonged to the same dog owner or if they were passed on for their lifetime keeping by their owners, then microchipping can be expensive in such cases. Numerically this law seems to have been based on the presumption that households have few dogs that might hardly be the case. Thus, the cost might increase with the increase in the number of dogs. The costing element must be taken seriously in view of the likely income inequalities in certain parts of Wales, England and Scotland. Thence microchipping costs might have an effect of discouraging low-income earners individuals from having many dogs.

Responsibility in the event of divorce for jointly owned pets in family law.

The tightened regimes of microchipping might make dogs part of the disputed issues in cases of divorce. Of course, it mattered less in absence, of the microchip databases that retains the pet in the event of divorce, especially where it was jointly perceived as a family pet. In the new regime that might increase, tracing and linking ownership with legal liability that could make pet another complex family issue in some cases. Similarly, it is unclear whether joint ownership or co-ownership of dogs by couples shall be accepted for registration on the same microchip. This is vital in cases where one of the partners works abroad but leaves the dog in custody of their spouse.

Recommended changes to the government departments in the UK following this study

Harmonization of the differences

Difference in adverse reaction and microchip failures are made. Hypothetically there might possibility that having to make reports to different public offices could raise questions as to whether those offices have the same approaches in terms of their competency and capacity in responding the matters of adverse reactions and failures in microchips. That would need further empirical based research as to whether those offices are responding to issues of microchips differently. If so how and possibly the effect this might have on public confidence. The historical evolvement of the law on microchipped data could be used to regulate the conduct of dog breeders and dog keepers by using powers of administrative law to control of data base operators or monitor activities of authorized persons. This trend of events raises questions of clarity in the event of clashes or divergences that might arise and hence increasing the likelihood of conflict in laws.

Factoring in the health of animals

Furthermore, the law of microchipping of dogs in the UK is generally limiting the exemptions of microchipping to dogs whose health could be detrimentally affected. It remains unclear of the legitimacy of microchipping dogs that might be eventually used for festival presents. This makes the offences in this law to concentrate on omissions by dog owners to microchip dogs, but it should also create offences based to acts such as microchipping or conspiring by aiding, betting to microchip dogs to subject them ethically and morally contested activities. Such a law would adopt ideas of a criminal model that could be collaborative or complementary in punishing committed acts or attempted acts of misusing the position of microchipping for stolen dogs or microchipping dogs for commercializing the as Christmas pet presents.

Control of Database operators

Additionally, the issue of data base operators destroying or deleting the data concerning a dog before a minimum of 30 years from its time of birth. Given that, this 30-year period is not applicable in the context of Wales and England, it is worth mentioning that the law on retention period for the dog's microchipped data in needs to be clarified in both of those localized regions or jurisdictions. Consistence in the period of data retention must be a vital benchmark these regions to ensure that there is some degree of the uniformity in the developing the law in this area.

In the UK the manner in which microchips laws is developing is a practical application of legislative powers through devolution, reserved power models as well as the regionalization or delegation. In relation to the 21 days period of in Scotland's reporting of adverse reactions, that seems to appear that the Scottish Regulations, a condition which remains absent in England and Wales regulation. That 21 period within which adverse reaction must reported could be a good policy since it creates the time within which the person is to take necessary action. However even this condition might need more clarity some respects. For example, it seems there is a likelihood of ambiguities related to questions of the nature of evidence and standard of required proof for ascertaining with accuracy when the persons held responsible had omitted their duty to take necessary reporting measures in relation to this duty.

Discussion

In summary, this work has explored a complex and controversial debate on the credibility, legality, necessity of having a law providing for compulsory microchipping. It is true that this discussion has hardly been exhaustive of the numerous legal developments across the global spectrum in this regard. However, the following observations have been reached. The need for legalising the compulsory microchipping of animals has been driven by a number social-legal factors as well as scientific applications in improving aspects of animal management (Simon,) It is also true that based liability regimes are most likely to benefit from aspects of microchipping developments. In this case, the stakeholder must only be identified but also aim at working as a team if the meritorious attributes of this law are to ever the realised. This study has overlooked neither looked nor entirely conceded with critics on the law of microchipping. The views regarding health effects are worthwhile considering, although these are barely convincing outweigh to benefits of using microchipping to manage the owner-animal relationships. It might be finally mentioned that this study has hardly explored the future use of microchips on the body of mankind but it that must be a discussion to yet another time.

References

Hirby, Elly; Eckham, Harry & MacFarlane, Ian (2014). Cat population management. In: Dennis C. Turner, (ed.) The Domestic Cat: The Biology of its Behaviour, Cambridge University Press, 2nd Ed., (Page 224)

Harding, Simon (2014). Unleashed: The Phenomena of Status Dogs and Weapon Dogs, policy Press (Pages 261-263)

Legislation and Cases

Myatt -v- Teignbridge D.C. [1995] Env. L.R.78

Cat Act 2011 (Western Australia)

Cat Regulations 2012 (Western Australia)

Dangerous Dogs Act 1991 c. 65 sec. 3 (England & Wales)

Data Protection Acts 1998, 2018 (England & Wales)

Dogs (Amendment) Act (Northern Ireland) 2011 c. 9 sec.2

The Dog Act 1976 (Western Australia)

The Microchipping of Dogs (England) Regulations 2015/108,

The Microchipping of Dogs (England) Regulations 2015/108,

The Microchipping of Dogs (Scotland) Regulations 2016 Regulations

The Microchipping of Dogs (Wales) Regulations 2015, Regulation

Western Australia Sec. 14 Cats to be microchipped As at 01 Nov 2013 and Western Australian

Reid v Murphy [2015] HCJAC 60, 2015 S.C.L. 772

Russell v. The Crown Prosecution Service [2015] EWHC 2065 (Admin),

2015 WL 4275095

Veterinary Surgeons Act 1966

Documentation

Petlog; A veterinary guide to compulsory microchipping for dogs. URL:

https://www.thekennelclub.org.uk/media/623648/kc_petlog_8pp_a4_br

ochure_update_vets_final.com pressed.pdf. Accessed 27 January 2016.

Transforming the UK Home Office into a Department for Homeland Security: Reflecting on an Interview with a Litigant Defending Against Online Retaliatory Feedback in the US

Jonathan Bishop

Abstract

Retaliatory feedback is a significant problem on the Internet, which is not just confined to online auction websites, but other online environments dependent on reputation systems. Explored in this paper are the acts of an Internet troller who spread malicious and false allegations that the series of conferences called WORLDCOMP are "fake." This paper interviews one of the organisers of this conference to ask how they went about dealing with the retaliatory feed- back, and in particular their engagement with law enforcement agencies, such as from the FBI to the US Department of Homeland Security. To reform the UK Home Office to learn lessons from this, the paper proposes making greater use of National Crime Agency and Police and Crime Commissioners to provide a better strategic set-up for law enforcement under the UK Home Office. It also suggests using publicly funded solicitors and community wardens, as opposed to the current set-up of police constables, to deal with community policing.

Introduction

To date the UK has shied away from the concept of creating a department for homeland security. In some cases, this has been because the Home Office (i.e. the Home Department) has been of a substantial size that to introduce such a remit would be too overbearing. Since the creation of the Ministry of Justice by the New Labour Government, many of the functions of the Home Department have been transferred. Using an interview of a victim of retaliatory feedback against their academic conference, this paper reviews the effectiveness of the US Department for Homeland Security and federal law in dealing with cybercrime, as well as looking at what lessons can be learned for an enhanced Home Office in the UK, which would be a department of homeland security in all but name. The paper suggests that by military personnel being part of the Home Office when they are at home, and the Ministry of Defence (MoD) when they are away, a greater amount of law enforcement time currently carried out by police constables can instead be spend on issues like cybercrime, such as through the newly created National Crime Agency (NCA). Military personnel would only need to change their uniforms to look like police officers, yet have the necessary powers, meaning the existence of a standing army could be reduced. It would also allow the Department of International Development to merge with the MoD to focus on peace keeping and overseas development. By moving mainstream public-facing police constables onto crime solving duties like cybercrime, within the NCA, such as dealing with retaliatory feedback, could make online faults more effectively dealt with. This could then lead to conferring the duties for community policing onto local authorities, who would engage more affordable community wardens, who could be accountable to Police and Crime Commissioners.

Retaliatory Feedback as a Homeland Security Issue

Retaliatory feedback has been a major problem in terms of online auction sites, where reputation systems designed to allow users to decide whether to trust a buyer or seller, are either misused or misunderstood (Malaga 2013). Retaliatory feedback can take the form of providing negative feedback in response to another person's negative feedback, or "feedback extortion" where a user threatens to leave bad feedback if one party does not accede to a request that did not form part of the original contract (Malaga 2013). In terms of eBay it has been argued that retaliatory feedback is not as widespread as one might think, because reciprocating to positive feedback is around 50%, which is higher than the retaliation figure, but significantly less than a default positive response (Beyene et al. 2008). Whilst it might not be immediately obvious that retaliatory feedback is a homeland security issue, one needs to understand the cultural differences in how homeland security is measured. In the UK, the Home Office is responsible for dealing with cybercrime, including cyber-terrorism, meaning retaliatory feedback is already within its remit. It was the Home Office that brought in the UK's privacy laws embodied in the Data Protection Act 1998 (repealing the 1984 Act). Many may also not see retaliatory feedback beyond the leaving of bad reviews by those who were left bad reviews. However, if one considers the existence of Operation Viral Peace, where the US Government are actively trolling Jihadists online, then it can be seen that it is as much a national security issue as any other form of cybercrime (Mali 2014). The Arab Spring Uprisings showed that the posting of provocative and intentionally damaging images, videos and other electronic communications, are effective in creating propaganda. The recording of the killing of US-journal- ist James Foley, was likely to have been an edit of a knife being put to his throat with no impact (there was no dripping blood), along with an audio dubbing of an English accent, fully staged for mass impact. Equally, the abusive message was not likely to be the person speaking in the video, because the email was more of a rant with only one word being emphasised, whereas the video voice-over was eloquent, almost like an actor, with more moments of emphasis throughout. With social and mass media playing an important role in international terrorism, it is no longer suitable for electronic communications laws to sit alongside culture and sport, as they do in the UK at present. Such laws and other measures should be placed firmly within the remit of homeland security, as what may seem minor issues in relation to petty every-day acts of abuse, such as Olympic diver Tom Daley being told on Twitter he left his late father down after not winning a medal, can have huge economic and security consequences for businesses and government alike.

The UK and US Legal Systems and Governmental Framework

The US legal system is based around the existence of federal law, state law and regulatory authorities. The UK's legal systems are similar in that there is UK law, which like US federal law can affect all the regions within the country, and then there are the separate legal systems in the respective regions and jurisdictions (i.e., England & Wales, Wales, Scotland and Northern Ireland), which operate similarly to US state law. At the time of going to press there was talk of creating a jurisdiction for England, which might result in the discontinuance of the "England & Wales" one. The main difference is that unlike the US, where there are courts for the federal, state and regulatory levels, there is near enough a common court structure in the UK with regional variations, with the Supreme Court in London being the highest court in the land. In addition the UK is subject to rulings from the Court of Justice of the European Union (CJEU), which has direct effect, and also from the European Court of Human Rights (ECtHR), whose decisions are not automatically binding. These similarities thus make it easier to conduct a comparative analysis of how the US and UK legal systems do and can respond to retaliatory feedback, for the purposes of reforming the way the UK handles the problem. There have been discussions on reforming the UK's relationship with the EU and ECtHR.

Comparing the Effectiveness of US Federal and State Law and UK Law in Relation to Cybercrime in the Backdrop of the US Department for Homeland Security

The methodology chosen for this investigation was based around an interview with a victim of retaliatory feedback. The interviewee is part of the WORLDCOMP series of conferences, which was targeted with an online hate campaign following rejecting a proposal for a workshop session from the troller. The troller took part in acts where they were essentially saying that WORLDCOMP was a fake conference and that people should not submit to it. The interview aided in exploring the effectiveness of US federal laws and to a minor extent the state laws of Florida, where the troll conducting the retaliatory feedback was based, through an online interviewing approach. Some approaches to online interviewing involve observing participants posting messages and then responding to them (James and Busher 2009). After attempting this with the JISC-hosted academic discussion lists of Support Vector Machines (SUPPORT-VECTOR-MACHINES), PhD Design (PHD-DESIGN) and Operational Research (ORNET), it proved to perpetuate the problem rather than understand and deal with it, as can be seen from Figure 1.

Conducting an interview with the party affected by the retaliatory feedback thus seemed most appropriate. Those affecting by online interactions often develop their own social order to cope with the different experiences thrown at them (James and Busher 2009: p. 27), so interviewing the participant directly avoided any conflict with administrators as was the case when attempts were made to discuss the matter on the JISC mailing lists, as the example presented in Figure 1. The interview took place by email using the processes proposed by (James and Busher 2009: pp. 12–15, p. 22). In addition to the interview the laws are discussed in relation to how they are placed within the literature in order to provide context to the interview.

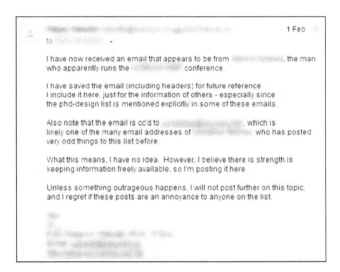

Figure 1 Examples of Outcomes of Trying to Research Retaliatory Feedback

on the PHD Design Discussion Group.

Malicious Communications Laws in the US and UK

The Malicious Communications Act 1988 (MCA) in the UK prohibits the sending of a letter or an article, whether electronic or otherwise, that is indecent, offensive, or threatening with the intention of causing distress or anxiety to the recipient (Bishop 2013; Gowland 2013; Tarapdar and Kellett 2013). A related law in the UK is the Communications Act 2003, which in Section 127 introduced two offences of sending or causing to be sent "a message or other matter that is grossly offensive or of an indecent, obscene or menacing character" via a public communications network as well as an offence of causing "annoyance, inconvenience or needless anxiety to another" in the same manner. The equivalent federal law in the US to these is 47 U.S. Code § 223 on "Obscene or harassing telephone calls in the District of Columbia or in interstate or foreign communications" (Cannon 1996). The MCA was made in 1988 and 47 U.S. Code § 223 was made in 1996. These were made in the early days of the Internet's adoption and in the case of the MCA it required an amendment in order to explicitly cover electronic materials (Bishop 2013). This problem of legislation often being out of date was raised by the interviewee.

"The ultimate problem is that changes in technology occur much faster than changes in the law. As such, the law is 'behind on the times' when it comes to cyber-related crimes," with her concluding that "Enforcement of the law is also a huge obstacle because many agencies are uncomfortable dealing with this sort of thing without much (or any) precedent – and they do not want to spend the time and money to do so."

Defamation and False Personation Laws in the US and UK

In the US, the federal law of 18 USC Chapter 43 § 911 prohibits the false personation of a citizen of the US. In the UK false personation is covered by the Protection from Harassment Act 1997 through Section 2A(3) which prohibits "publishing any statement or other material (i) relating or purporting to relate to a person, or (ii) purporting to originate from a person." As can be seen from Figure 3, this was a major issue for the interviewee, whose colleague had been a victim of personation.

"[An FBI Agent] indicated that because the conduct (of false personation) does not target the government or a large group of people, that he could not do anything about it," she said. "Another agent indicated that because no federal identifying documents were used to impersonate (a colleague) and others, and instead, the individual simply sent emails using a colleague's and other's names, the FBI could not do any- thing."

Such issues are not necessarily present in the UK as the Protection from Harassment Act 1997 allows for both action by the police authorities and the individual to take action through the civil courts. Asked about the effectiveness of the courts procedure the interviewee's position was clear.

"As far as due process of the respondent in these cases – clearly they get more than enough notice and opportunity to be heard," she

said. "The due process aspect of the law is sufficient," but stated; "It is

the protection of the rights of complainants part, both on a criminal and

civil level, that needs improvement in cyber/internet related matters."

In terms of defamation the laws of the UK have lagged behind the US for decades at a time. The Communications Decency Act of 1996 introduced the federal law 47 U.S.C. § 230 on "the protection for private blocking and screening of offensive material." This gave publishers immunity from prosecution for information carried on their platform written by someone other than them. In the UK by comparison, the Defamation Act 1996 provided that a publisher is as liable for any defamatory content as the person posting it via their service. This has led to information society service providers in the UK, such as Heart Internet Limited, to have blanket policies of requesting the removal of content believed to be defamatory or in breach of copyright, which has seen them issued with court proceedings on at least two occasions. Heart Internet Limited's actions were challenged under the Electronic Commerce (EC Directive) Regulations 2002 which prohibits information society service providers from allowing or carrying out any unlawful acts. The Digital Economy Act 2010 in the UK put in place arrangements for copyright disputes to be resolved without the involvement of information society service providers and The Defamation Act 2013 reduced the liability to them for alleged defamation if they provided the contact details of the person who is alleged to have committed defamation. Such policies if they existed in the US might have helped the organisers of

WORLDCOMP in collecting evidence that the person who is believed to be posting the unlawful content was responsible. In terms of civil litigation, the Electronic Commerce (EC Directive) Regulations 2002 provide an effective means for either the person who is a victim of defamation or a victim of false allegations of defamation, or indeed any other fault, to bring legal action against an information society service provider.

Harassment and Stalking Laws in the US and UK

In the UK the Protection from Harassment Act 1997 prohibits a course of conduct that "amounts to harassment of another, and which (a person) knows or ought to know amounts to harassment of the other."

The equivalent laws in the US are 18 USC § 2261A on "stalking" and 18 USC § 875 on "interstate communications." To prove that a person has been a victim of harassment in the UK it needs to be shown that there was a "course of conduct" of at least two connected incidents that could be perceived by a reasonable person to amount to harassment. The advantage of the UK system is that legal action can be brought under the same legislation in both the civil courts and the criminal courts. Even so, as the interviewee explained, the civil route is not always easy.

"Civil remedies are a little more effective (than criminal ones)

simply because the burden of proof is lower."

"However, the frustration with pursuing on a civil matter is that it moves very slow, it is expensive, and we are limited as to what we can do/request"

"We would be able to do more with a criminal charge. It is also very easy for the respondent in a civil case to delay matters over and over again."

In the UK and US there are strong principles in terms of allowing injunctions to prohibit a particular action or mandate a specific act. In the case of harassment, the Protection from Harassment Act 1997 provides for special "restraining orders" to prevent "future courses of conduct." The disadvantage to this for the person subject to it is that the injunction is marked "future courses of conduct," even if the injunction was agreed on a no-blame or non-conviction basis. Another difficulty is that an injunction has to be directed at a legal or natural person, meaning it is not as easy to prevent specific postings via specific information society service providers as the interviewee explains:

"In a civil case, we can theoretically ask for a temporary injunction for the postings and attacks to stop," she said. "[H]owever, if the individual respondent is denying that he/she is the one making the postings, or if he/she asks someone else to, it defeats the purpose and the injunction essentially does nothing without a final judgment."

This shows the importance of making it easier for those bringing civil cases to be allowed to easily obtain the identity of the person posting malicious content about them so that the injunction can be made against them directly, which makes it applicable to all arenas.

Incitement, Interference and Public Order Laws in the US and UK

There are two major laws in the UK affecting public order that have been used to tackle Internet trolling. These are the Serious Crimes Act 2007 and the Public Order Act 1986. The first was used in the aftermath of the 2011 UK riots to prosecute a number of people for setting up Facebook pages to encourage riots in their locality, including in the case of Anthony Gristock and Jamie Counsel (Mugabi and Bishop In Press; Newburn 2012; Bishop 2014a). The second has been used in the case of Liam Stacey, who was a student at Swansea University that posted racist remarks on Twitter in the aftermath of the cardiac arrest of footballer Fabrice Muamba. One of the most relevant US laws similar to these is the federal law 18 USC § 1951 on "interference with commerce by threats or violence," also called the Hobbs Act 1988. But for the interviewee it appeared the existence of such laws, including ones at state level that were more specific, offered little to assist them. "*[W]e have not received much help on a state law level either*," they said. "*Many state law enforcement agencies do not want to deal with this kind of situation because they simply do not know how – so, we initially had to deal with a fight back and forth as to which agency had proper jurisdiction to handle the matter.*" In the circumstances where they did get state authorities involved, little progress was made for the interviewee. "*After weeks of 'investigating' and having one simple conversation with the individual who denied his involvement, the state law enforcement agency indicated that they had to close the case,*" they said. "*It was explained that although the conduct does fit the definition of a statutory crime in this state, that it would only be a misdemeanour and the case would involve too much time and money to investigate for them to move forward because it will be difficult to prove that the individual was the individual behind a certain computer at a certain time in order to meet the 'beyond reasonable doubt' standard of proof that is required for a crime to stand,*" concluding that "*[i]f it was considered a felony, they would be more inclined to investigate further, but that it would still be difficult to prove the standard required.*"

Anti-Terrorism and Surveillance Laws in the US and UK

In the US, the Communications Assistance for Law Enforcement Act 1994 (47 USC §§ 1001–1010) on "*interception of digital and other communications*" is intended to preserve the ability of law enforcement officials to conduct electronic surveillance effectively and efficiently, despite the deployment of new digital technologies and wireless services that have altered the character of electronic surveillance (Moloney Figliola 2005). CALEA requires telecommunications carriers to modify their equipment, facilities, and services, wherever reasonably achievable, to ensure that they are able to comply with authorized electronic surveillance actions (Moloney Figliola 2005). Similar legislation has existed in the UK since the 1980s, namely with the Interception of Communications Act 1981 and the Regulation of Investigatory Powers Act 2000. The UK's Terrorism Act 2006 provides remedies for offences that involve promoting acts of terror and the US's PATRIOT Act provides the same there.

As the interviewee explained, however, making use of these pieces of legislation can be difficult. "I spoke to a few FBI agents who indicated that there is nothing they could do," they said. "As such, I did some research and sent them the statutes that I found that could apply for them to review and let me know if they can help," they continued. "Basically, we are dealing with an individual whose conduct is falling through the cracks of what the federal agencies are willing to do," they said. "With that said, the last FBI agent that I just referred to still wants to help and indicates that he tries to talk to people within his agency to see if there is anything that can be done. However, we have yet to hear anything."

These laws, in both the UK and the US, could be effective for allowing those bringing legal cases to access the identity of their abuser, but as the interviewee explains, the system is not fit for purpose. "*Although there are more 'remedies' in a civil case for cyber-attacks such as this, there are still too many loopholes in the law as it is now for cyber- attacks and internet conduct in order for those remedies to effectively serve their intended purpose,"* they said.

Reforming the UK's Home Department into a Department for Homeland Security

The Home Department has undergone a significant amount of restructuring over the period of its existence. Under the New Labour Government of 1997 to 2010 this mammoth of a department was split with responsibility for the constitutional and administrative law being transferred to a newly created Ministry of Justice. Furthermore, under the Coalition Government that came to power in 2010 a new National Crime Agency was created, as well as Police and Crime Commissioners. The benefit of this is that it now creates an opportunity for the Home Department to take on duties found in the US Department of Homeland Security. The realization of the US's Department of Homeland Security included creating a new unified military command and a fundamental reorganising of the FBI was also required in order to secure the homeland in a way that encompasses every level of government and the cooperation of the public and the private sector (Bush 2002).

Reforming Legal Principles

In UK law and many common law jurisdictions like the US, there are core principles needed to prove most criminal offences, namely actus reus and mens rea. In terms of mens rea, this is becoming less important in the UK legal system in relation to trolling, with its merits being questioned by academics in this regard (Bishop 2010; Edwards 2012; Edwards et al. 2013) as well as judges, such as in the case of DPP v Chambers. It has been argued that in terms of cyberattacks, it is more difficult to understand whether mens rea would be satisfied in most cases, and that to do so would require supervisory control over national cyber- security efforts to be transferred from the Department of Homeland Security (Miller 2014). This section will therefore explore not only actus reus, but two tests that could replace mens rea, namely "malum reus" and "pertinax reus" (Bishop 2012; Bishop 2013). The section explains why further use of these terms in a wider application of them to the law is founded on essential concepts for legal justice.

No Fault No Crime – The Concept of Actus Reus

There is a long-established principle that one should not be able to be prosecuted for an action that was not a criminal or civil fault at the time that act was committed, which is embodied in the legal test of actus reus. This is enshrined in UK law through the Human Rights Act 1998, which implemented the European Convention on Human Rights (ECHR). This is based on the UN

Universal Declaration of Human Rights, which the US have also agreed to. The ECHR in gives room for maneuver as it could be interpreted to mean that if a person thought an act committed against them was a "crime" that even if it was not an "offence" that it could be prosecuted. This is what happens with the law of tort, where a person can be found to have breached someone's civil rights for an act that might not have previously existed but falls within an established set of wrongs (i.e., torts). It has been strongly argued that the legal system should be based on dualism (Bishop 2014a; Mugabi and Bishop In Press), which is where a legal system puts both the complainant and the respondent on trial at the same time, and both the civil and criminal faults, torts and offences respectively, are considered at the same hearing. In the case of retaliatory feedback, this would mean that the police authorities could bring a case with less risk as even if they did not meet the threshold for beyond reasonable doubt, a case could still be won on the balance of probabilities. Examples of evidence that could show actus reus are presented in Figure 2, which includes websites showing "WORLDCOMP, FAKE" in large text (a) and the results of Google Scholar, showing 815 results for papers that appeared in WORLDCOMP proceedings (b).

No Injury No Crime – The Concept of Malum Reus

One of the major problems in the treatment of Internet trolls is the unequal application of the law to the same circumstances, and worse still the prosecution of people for offences where there was no clear victim, or where the comments made could not be considered to go beyond the discourses expected in a democratic society. The concept of malum reus has therefore been defined as a means to determine whether someone (i.e., the complainant or respondent) has actually been harmed by a specific action. Posting a message to one's friends and not intending it for wide distribution exempts one from prosecution in the UK, as are posts deleted soon after they are created (Starmer 2013). In terms of the interviewee's WORLDCOMP conference it is quite easy to see the damage done by them. The malicious comments by their troll led to many people wrongly thinking the conference was fake, as the troll has search engine optimised a series of websites making the allegations. WORLDCOMP is not a fake conference, but the fact the mistruths were propagated, including between fellow academics, gave the allegations credibility through the concept of social proof, which is where if a person one knows says something it is more believable (Bishop 2014b). Even so, this fact did nothing to help bring prosecution against the person trolling the organisers of WORLDCOMP with retaliatory feedback as the authorities were not interested.

The alternative therefore was to use the civil courts at state level, but the lack of access to investigatory powers using this route hampers such action in terms of getting absolute proof. In the UK, it has been argued that the Police Information Technology Office (PITO), the Association of Chief Police Officers (ACPO) and the Home Office must share responsibility for the fact that there is still no national intelligence IT system, nor even a system which flags up to police forces that there is intelligence held on an individual by another police force, beyond those added to the Police National Computer by local police (Bichard 2004).

It has been recommended that surveillance should be collected by the new National Crime Agency and made available to solicitors who want to bring action on behalf of their clients (Bishop 2014a). This would mean that those who are victims of crime could have the benefits available to major cases that the FBI and other agencies like the US Department for Homeland Security has without needing to navigate the criminal law system, which has been so fruitless for the organisers of WORLDCOMP trying to defend against false accusations claiming they are a fake conference.

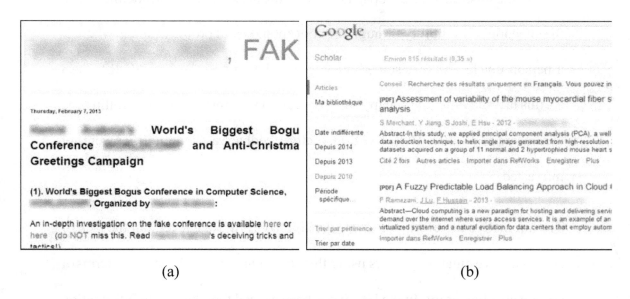

(a)   (b)

Figure 2 False Allegations WORLDCOMP is Fake (a), Evidence of 815

WORLCOMP Papers Since 2010 (b).

No History No Crime – The Concept of Pertinax Reus

An emerging feature in relation to Internet trolling laws in and the guidance around their use is the concept that a person should not be prosecuted for a single one-off act of Internet trolling (Starmer 2013). The UK's Protection from Harassment Act 1997 states that a person must *"not pursue a course of conduct which amounts to harassment of another and is intended to amount to harassment of that person; or occurs in circumstances where it would appear to a reasonable person that it would amount to harassment of that person."* And its Communications Act 2003 says a person commits a fault if *"for the purpose of causing annoyance, inconvenience or needless anxiety to another they persistently make use of a public electronic communications network."* The US federal law, 18 USC § 2265A, on "repeat offenders" pro- vides that prior domestic violence or stalking convictions doubles the maximum sentence allowed under federal law for such an offence (Kapley and Cooke 2007). In the UK, offences that involve content of a homophobic or disabilist nature can have sentences extended by section 146 of the Criminal Justice Act 2003 and section 145 of that act provides for extended sentences where an offence is aggravated by racial or religious characteristics. Amendments to the Malicious Communications Act 1988 are likely to mean trolling cases can result in jail terms of 2 years.

Perspectives on the Information Society

Figure 3   The Effects of False Personation on WORLDCOMP.

The concept of pertinax reus states that a person needs to have been proven to have committed an unlawful act on more than one occasion for there to be significant evidence to show that it is in the public interest to try someone for a fault. Some faults might be superfluous in nature, especially where a person is of good character and are being brought to trial for reasons other than judicial ones, such as where the aim is to censor someone from posting legitimate criticisms of public figures online or about those who are members of public authorities with law enforcement powers. This is especially true in the case of mistreatment of journalists, who face regular allegations of harassment for investigating wrongdoings, who are supposed to be protected by the Human Rights Act 1998 in the UK, but that has not stopped its police from issuing "police information notices" warning of potential criminal action if the journalist does not cease a course of conduct the police consider harassment. This, however, shows the difficulty in establishing pertinax reus, as it would be unfair for unproven allegations of harassment or similar to be used as an example of past form when their merits have not been considered by an impartial tribunal. Reforming the law so that the law enforcement authorities have to prove that a person met the test of malum reus in relation to their alleged course of conduct for the same fault on more than one occasion might be appropriate for summary offences (misdemeanours in the US). In other words, it might be that a person would have to be proven to be a repeat offender on their first hearing, rather than at a succession of hearings, before pertinax reus can be proven, as is the case with conditional discharges. Clearly, indictable offences (felonies in the US) would result in pertinax reus being based on the likelihood of the person to reoffend and the magnitude of the malum reus caused, with homicide being at the top end of the scale and name-calling at the bottom end.

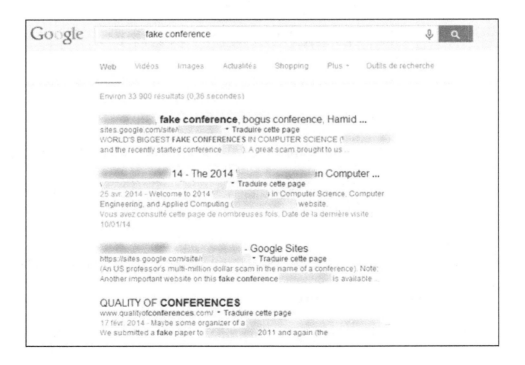

Figure 4   Evidence that Repeated Attempts have been made to Damage WORLDCOMP.

As can be seen in Figure 4, there is a clear and concerted effort to damage the reputation of the WORLDCOMP series of conferences with false allegations that they are fake. Under UK law it might be simple to prove that this amounts to a "course of conduct" within the meaning of the Protection from Harassment Act 1997. If as the interviewee suggested that the person making these posts did so out of retaliation for being denied the right to run a conference session, then the actions are related within the meaning of DPP v Lau and as there are at least two of them then a course of conduct exists, meaning action can be brought through either the criminal or civil courts.

Integrating the Home Department with the Armed Forces and Security Services

Reducing the size of standing armies would appear to be consigned to the early 20th century, with few discussing the issue in recent time (Boynton 1929; Binnendijk and Kugler 2006; Brown 2006). Reducing the size of the UK's standing army was part of the UK Government's agenda in the 2010s, but this was solely because of its ideology around public spending cuts, as opposed to any peace agenda. One might wish to argue that this was short-sighted, as in the Winter Storms of 2013 and 2014, the government needed to draft in the military to deal with the near disaster situation. It has been proposed that Army Reserves become part of the National Crime Agency (Bishop 2014a), and this section goes further to argue that when the military are at home they should be part of the NCA and when they are part of operations abroad they should be part of the Ministry of Defence (MoD). Ideally the UK Government's Department for International Development could then become part of MoD to focus on peace keeping as much as military engagements in general. On this basis, it would appear that integrating the Home Department with the aspects of the armed forces based on the UK mainland could offer benefits for both strategic and financial reasons. Indeed, it has been argued that the Home Office must demonstrate a "tight ship," with consistency between resource allocation and objectives, as well as the monitoring of resource use and effectiveness (Stockdale et al. 1999). One might debate whether this enhanced Home Department with the strategic resources currently available to the Ministry of Defence should be renamed from "The Home Office" to "The Department for Homeland Security," but such a decision would need to consider the political factors at the time. There is generally a mood in the UK against the armed forces being on the streets of the UK, meaning the use of the word "Homeland Security" would give weight to the fact that those members of the armed forces are not involved in "military operations" at home, especially as they could be uniformed according to the duties they are engaged in – such as police uniforms when they are seeking to quell any riots. Recent killings by the police of members of the public displaying suicidal tendencies might suggest that the role the military play in policing would be best confined to rioting and other areas where incident management skills for defusing situations are not an essential requirement

Towards a "Community Command"

The concept of a community command has been proposed following the introduction of Police Crime Commissioners (PCCs) and the National Crime Agency (Bishop 2014a). Such a system introduces PCCs as the intermediary between national agencies and community response teams, as can be seen in Figure 5. Any actions that need to be taken by the NCA at community level would need the attention of the local Police and Crime Commissioner in the first instance. Indeed, it has been argued that the Home Office must also help reduce reoffending and ensure that chief officers (or perhaps PCCs) have access to the right level of physical, mental and forensic services for those who come into contact with the policy (Fowles and Wilson 2009). The role of the NCA in assisting the bringing of civil claims through allowing registered legal service providers like solicitors and direct access barristers to access evidence stored securely by the NCS, which could include CCTV, would better provide for justice without the involvement of criminal law and make brining civil claims less fruitless. Other academics have different views for related purposes, such as arguing that the Home Office needs to drop data retention and start again, perhaps with a targeted preservation scheme such as is used in the US (Munir and Yasin 2003).

This might be satisfied through the time stamping of CCTV in an encrypted format that is only decrypted when a complaint is made. Figure 5 shows a setup of how the NCA, PCCs, local authorities, the court and tri- bunals, solicitors and members of the public could cooperate to resolve disputes amicably outside of the criminal justice system where possible.

It has been argued that IT across the police service as a whole is not fit for purpose, to the detriment of the police's ability to fulfil their basic mission of preventing crime and disorder and that the Home Office must make revolutionising police through IT a top priority (Fowles and Wilson 2012). It has also been argued that the Home Office needs to make use of modern communication methods to develop a strategy for providing local crime information that is useful and relevant (Buchanan and Coulson 2007). Furthermore, some have suggested that Home Office could more readily involve other Government Departments, local authorities, and agencies outside government in the crime prevention field (Gilling 2000).

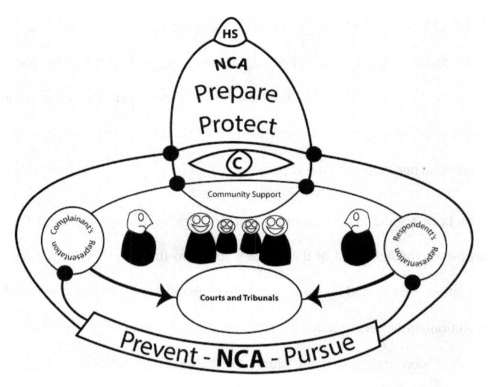

Figure 5 A Dualist Model of Law Enforcement Linking Agencies Through a

"Community Command."

The dualist approach presented in Figure 5 to enable such cooperation to prepare and protect communities and at the prevent crime and pursue those committing faults might be the solution. Police officers are now deemed to be expensive and the Home Office must be satisfied that as far as is practicable, any increases in police numbers are likely to be cost-effective (Loveday 1990). As since the coming to power of the Coalition Government there have been reduction in police numbers, then the dualist system in Figure 5 depending on more affordable "community wardens" with investigation of offences carried out by legal aid funded solicitors and related teams could offer better value for money than police constables who have more powers than they are able to use in a fair and consistent manner.

Increasing Community Cohesion and Social Integration

It has been argued that the Home Office needs to stand back from its dominance of governance once it strengthens the role of police authorities as an equal partner in governance (Collier and Hartley 2008), which may be more possible now with the introduction of Police and Crime Commissioners (PCCs). These PCCs could provide for this if enhanced through greater collaboration with other government agencies including local authorities and the NCA.

The New Labour Government said they would be "tough on crime and tough on the causes of crime," but as has been argued elsewhere, all that happened was they were tough on crime through the introduction of new offences, but soft on the causes. For instance, it has been argued for decades that the Home Office need to combat illiteracy among adult prisoners and in so doing contribute to the raising of reading standards among the general public (Palfrey 1974), yet the Coalition Government that came to power in 2010 has sought to reduce the opportunities for prisoners to engage with literary works such as books, reducing opportunities for the education and rehabilitation of offenders, who would otherwise have the opportunity to have discussions of a more accept-able fashion common among those with wealth, who are often in their minds worthy art critics. It has been argued for a lengthy period also that if probation services are to become more effective in reducing the use of custody for punishment as opposed to rehabilitation, such as by effectively containing offenders in the community, then the Home Office must give the lead and develop a coherent criminal justice philosophy which is applied consistently (Gadd 1989). The encouragement of greater dialogue between communities and former convicts as a means to build trust cannot be underestimated. The fact that so many prisoners are released without state benefits or housing in place means the opportunity for integration of them into communities is reduced. Therefore it may be that the introduction of a "Community Command" that allows for a partnership between the Home Office, the NCA and community organisations such as local authorities, as argued by others (Collier and Hartley 2008), which will mean it will be possible to be both tough on crime and tough on the causes of crime.

Discussion

Retaliatory feedback is a major problem on the Internet, especially since the ability to post content to the Internet without being caught is easily done. As shown in this paper, even in environments like academia, retaliation is likely to follow any kind of rejection. As explored in this paper, the Internet troller posted malicious articles online to try to damage the reputation of the organiser of a series of conferences called WORLDCOMP. His allegations state they WORLD-

COMP is a fake conference, which are false. Such untrue claims were made when the troller had a conference session rejected by the organisers. This paper interviewed one of the organizers to ask how they went about dealing with retaliatory feedback, and especially their involvement with law enforcement agencies such as the FBI, which now works closely with the US Department of Homeland Security.

Through this interview it has been shown that the laws and technologies exist to identify those involved in such abuses, but that the legal system as it stands is too focused on the use of state-run law enforcement agencies and not providing equal opportunity to obtain evidence to civil litigants, who are struggling to protect their name and brand. The paper has examined the various laws that exist in the UK and US for dealing with retaliatory feedback. These have included not only dedicated Internet trolling laws, but some more general harassment, incitement, defamation and anti-terrorism. Having investigated the way that the FBI, military and other agencies are working with the Department of Homeland Security in the US, it would seem to make sense that the new National Crime Agency (NCA) in the UK, if put together with the military when they are operating at home and work with the new Police and Crime Commissioners, could create a "Community Command" to enable better responses to cyber-crime. In particular, it could do this by enabling not only the law enforcement agencies in the public sector to have access to its surveillance evidence, but also those members of the public trying to gain evidence for civil litigation. Military personnel should be part of the Home Office when they are at home, and the Ministry of Defence when away. The Ministry of Defence should merge with the Department for International Development after losing this responsibility, in order to focus on peace keeping and overseas development, becoming the Ministry of Overseas Development. The amount of law enforcement time spent on issues such as cybercrime, as opposed to public order could be increased, such as through the expansion of the NCA. Military personnel need only change their uniforms to look like police officers and have the necessary powers also. This would mean the existence of a standing army could be reduced. By moving police detectives from community focused units to global crime-solving duties such as cybercrime, within the NCA, would enable them to more effective dealing with retaliatory feedback. This could then lead to community policing duties being part of local authorities, who by replacing constables with community wardens, made up of street care wardens and civil enforcement wards, could more affordably act as "bobbies on the beat," and could be accountable to Police and Crime Commissioners. It is clear that the new agencies introduced by the Coalition Government need to be conserved and have their remit extended in order to achieve the aim of being tough on crime and tough on the causes of crime, which was envisaged by the previous New Labour Government. In parts of the country where PCCs have been replaced with mayors, PCCs could be reintroduced on the same basis as London – a policing expert appointed by the Mayor or First Minister.

References

Beyene, Y., M. Faloutsos, D. H. Chau and C. Faloutsos (2008) *The eBay Graph: How do Online Auction Users Interact?* Paper Presented at the INFOCOM Workshops 2008, IEEE, pp. 1–6.

Bichard, M. (2004) Return to an Address of the Honourable the House of Commons Dated 22nd June 2004 for the Bichard Inquiry Report.

Binnendijk, H. and R. L. Kugler (2006) *Seeing the Elephant: The US Role in Global Security.* Potomac Books, Inc.

Bishop, J. (2010) Tough on Data Misuse, Tough on the Causes of Data Misuse: A Review of New Labour's Approach to Information Security and Regulating the Misuse of Digital Information (1997–2010), International Review of Law, Computers & Technology, 24(3):299–303.

Bishop, J. (2012) *Tackling Internet Abuse in Great Britain: Towards a Framework for Classifying Severities of 'Flame Trolling'.* The 11th International Conference on Security and Management (SAM'12), Las Vegas, NV.

Bishop, J. (2013) The Art of Trolling Law Enforcement: A Review and Model for Implementing 'Flame Trolling' Legislation Enacted in Great Britain (1981–2012), International Review of Law, Computers & Technology, 27(3):301–318.

Bishop, J. (2014a). Internet Trolling and the 2011 UK Riots: The Need for a Dualist Reform of the Constitutional, Administrative and Security

Frameworks in Great Britain, European Journal of Law Reform, 16(1):154–167.

Bishop, J. (2014b). My Click is My Bond: The Role of Contracts, Social Proof, and Gamification for Sysops to Reduce Pseudo-Activism and Internet Trolling. In: (J. Bishop, ed.) Gamification for Human Factors Integration: Social, Educational, and Psychological Issues. Hershey, PA: IGI Global (1–6).

Boynton, F. D. (1929). Education: What Program? What Price? Music Supervisors' Journal, 15(4):9–19.

Brown, G. W. (2006). Kantian Cosmopolitan Law and the Idea of a Cosmopolitan Constitution. History of Political Thought, 27(4):661.

Buchanan, H. and N. S. Coulson (2007). Accessing Dental Anxiety Online Support Groups: An Exploratory Qualitative Study of Motives and Experiences. Patient Education and Counseling, 66(3):263–269.

Bush, G. W. (2002). The National Security Strategy of the United States of America. Washington, DC: The White House.

Cannon, R. (1996). Legislative History of Senator Exon's Communications Decency Act: Regulating Barbarians on the Information Superhighway. The Federal Communications Law Journal 49 (51).

Collier, P. M. and J. Hartley (2008). *Performativity, Management and Governance*. Managing to Improve Public Services, 46–54.

Edwards, L. (2012). Section 127 of the Communications Act 2003: Threat or Menace? SCL Journal, 23(4).

Edwards, L., J. Rauhofer and M. Yar (2013). *Recent Developments in UK Cybercrime Law*. Handbook of Internet Crime, 413–436.

Fowles, T. and D. Wilson (2009). Penal Policy File No. 118. The Howard Journal of Criminal Justice, 48(1):92–104.

Fowles, T. and D. Wilson (2012). Penal Policy File No. 133. The Howard Journal of Criminal Justice, 51(1):100–104.

Gadd, B. (1989). *The Probation Service: Blueprint for Change?* Public Money & Management 9(4):49–52.

Gilling, D. (2000). Policing, Crime Prevention and Partnerships. Core Issues in Policing, 124–138.

Gowland, J. (2013) "Protection from Harassment Act 1997: The 'New' Stalking Offences. The Journal of Criminal Law 77(5), 387–398.

James, N. and H. Busher (2009) *Online Interviewing*. London, UK: Sage Publications.

Kapley, D. J. & Cooke, J.R. (2007) Trends in Antistalking Legislation. In: D. A. Pinals (ed.). Stalking: Psychiatric Perspectives and Practical Approaches. Oxford, GB: Oxford University Press, pp. 141–163.

Loveday, B. (1990). Joint Boards and the Local Accountability of Police in the Metropolitan Areas. Local Government Studies 16(2):37–53.

Malaga, R. A. (2013). The Retaliatory Feedback Problem: Evidence from eBay and a Proposed Solution. Hershey, PA: IGI Global (Pages 246–253).

Mali, P. (2014). *Cyber Law & Cyber Crimes Simplified* (1st ed.). Pune, Mumbai: Aarti Publication.

Miller, K. L. (2014). The Kampala Compromise and Cyberattacks: Can there be an International Crime of Cyber-Aggression? Southern California Interdisciplinary Law Journal 23, 217–409.

Moloney Figliola, P. (2005). *Digital Surveillance: The Communications Assistance for Law Enforcement* (Act No. RL30677). Fort Belvoir, VA: Defense Acquisition University.

Mugabi, I. and J. Bishop (2015). The Need for a Dualist Application of Public and Private Law in Great Britain Following the Use of 'Flame Trolling' During the 2011 UK Riots: A Review and Model. In: (M. Dawson and M. Omar, eds.) Handbook of Research on New Threats and Countermeasures in Digital Crime and Cyber Terrorism. Hershey, PA: IGI Global. (Page 195)

Munir, A. B. and S. H. M. Yasin (2003). *Retention of Communications Data: A Bumpy Road Ahead.* J Marshall J Computer & Info L, 22:731.

Newburn, T. (2012). *Counterblast: Young People and the August 2011 Riots.* The Howard Journal of Criminal Justice 51(3), 331–335.

Palfrey, C. (1974). *Remedial Education and the Adult Offender.* The Howard Journal of Criminal Justice 14(1), 78–85.

Starmer, K. (2013) Guidelines on Prosecuting Cases Involving Communications Sent Via Social Media. London, GB: Crown Prosecution Service.

Stockdale, J. E., C. M. Whitehead, P. J. Gresham (1999). *Applying Economic Evaluation to Policing Activity*. Home Office, Policing and Reducing Crime Unit, Research, Development and Statistics Directorate.

Tarapdar, S. and M. Kellett (2013). Cyberbullying: Insights and Age-Comparison Indicators from a Youth-Led Study in England. Child Indicators Research 6(3), 461–477.

An African Perspective

Social Media and the Freedom of Expression in Nigeria: Posting the mind of a Nation

Joseph Wilson, Nuhu Gapsiso

Abstract

Nigerians cherish the freedom they are guaranteed under the United Nations Declaration of Human Rights and other international human rights Instruments and the constitution especially section 39(1) of the 1999 constitution of Nigeria which guarantees freedom of expression as a fundamental right. But the collective commitment to freedom of expression in Nigeria is often tested when these expressions are conveyed via popular conventional channels. Nigerians rights to free expression has over the years been characterised by numerous attempts by state and non-state actors to suppress or bully them into silence. However, the emergence of social media platform and the overwhelming embrace by Nigerians have changed the status quo, as more Nigerians take to social media to express their views on all issues and the perceived use by political and other elites to reach out to supporters. For example the incumbent President of Nigeria has from time to time used his Facebook platform to address Nigerians on some important government decisions and policies that elicits response from Nigerians via same platform. Media organizations have also used the same platform to generate comments on some issues of national interest (eg Removal of fuel subsidy, corruption in Nigeria etc. This paper explores people's posts on the Facebook site of selected media organizations on the popular Nigeria's aviation ministry armoured car scandal. The analysis would look at the tone of the posts (positive or negative, sectional based on regional and ethnic affiliation) and the overriding position.

Introduction

Nigerians are passionate about expressing their minds on issues of national importance. These expressions cut across all spheres of national endeavours-politics, religion, family, economy, culture, corruption, government policies, sports etc and the media serve as channels. The social media platform has emerged in recent years to be widely explored and utilized by Nigerians to post comments that, to a large extent represent the opinions of many Nigerians. Conventional Media organizations in Nigeria and diaspora have cashed-in on the popularity of these social media by sharing news stories on their social media accounts, which often times attract speedy comments from Nigerians. However, these comments are often not devoid of showcasing Nigeria's diversity in terms of ethnicity, religion, political ideology etc. They could sometimes be offensive in nature. This paper explores people's comments on the Facebook accounts of two popular media organizations (Premium Times and *Sahara Reporter*s) on national issues that have attracted a lot of comments from Nigerians. The Nigeria´s Ministry of Aviation armoured car scandal has continued to attract comments from Nigerians. The paper looks at the tone of the comments (positive or negative, sectional based on regional and ethnic affiliation) and the popular position.

Freedom of expression is an important component of national and individual development.it is a key to dignity and fulfilment at both nation and individual levels. Free expression enables individual to gain an understanding of his surroundings and the wider world by exchanging ideas and information freely with others. It also influences and promotes positively, good governance by enabling citizens to voice their concerns and opinions on issues of probity and accountability with the Authorities. If people can express their views without intimidation and the media are allowed to report what is being said, the government can be kept abreast of people´s concerns and address them (article19.org, 2014). It is therefore not surprising that people worldwide uphold the freedom they are guaranteed under the United Nations Declaration of Human Rights and other international human rights Instruments. Unfortunately, the collective commitment to freedom of expression globally is often tested when these expressions conveyed via popular conventional channels such as newspapers, television are suppressed directly or indirectly by state or non-state actors.

Interestingly, the emergence of social media platform especially, Facebook and twitter etc has transformed the exercise of freedom of expression especially in societies like Nigeria where significant constraints over traditional media and participation still exist. Individuals now have the opportunity to freely express their minds on any issue of human interest and most interesting is citizen's ability to use the social media to express their positions on issues of national interest.

Social Media

Social media web- based and mobile technologies used for interactive communication Social media comprise the internet and mobile phone based tools for sharing and discussing information. It is a blend of computing, telecommunications, and interactivity through a platform to communicate via words, videos, audio and visual (Paranjoy, 2012). Social media also refers to web or mobile based platform that enables an individual or agency to communicate interactively and enables exchange of user generated content (Tiwari and Gosh, 2013). Kaplan and Haenlein (2010) see social media as internet-based application that centres on the web 2.0 (interactive platform) technological ideology that allow the creation and exchange of user-generated content.

Types of Social Media

There are several classifications of the social media with overlaps among various services. One social media service can carry features of another service. For instance, Facebook has micro blogging features with their 'status update'. Also, Flickr and YouTube have comment systems similar to that of blogs (Grahl, 2014). Grahl (2014) notes that as you think through all the options for engaging social media, they all fall into 6 broad categories (social network, book marking sites, social news, media sharing, micro bogging, blog comments and forums). Similarly, Kaplan and Haenlein (2010) outlined 8 broad categories of Social Media. They include:

Social networks

Social networks are online services that enables users connect with other people of similar interest or background. It involves creating virtual networks by likeminded people. It proffers facilities such as chat, instant messaging, photo sharing, video sharing, updates etc. For example Facebook and LinkedIn.

Blog

Blog is a shared online journal where individuals or a group post diary entries about their experiences, opinions, hobbies and may contain text, photos and links to other websites. Blog ordinarily are interactive in nature, which enables of readers to leave comments and the comment trail can be followed.

Micro blogs

Micro blogs are similar to blogs. However, micro blogs focus on short updates that are sent to subscribers. For example twitter (is a micro blogging site that enables its users to send and read 'tweets'.). Micro blogs are typically restricted of 140 characters or less.

Wikis

Wiki is a collaborative website service that allows multiple users to create and update pages on particular or interlinked subjects. These multiple pages are linked through hyperlinks and allow users to interact in a complex and non-linear manner. A single page is referred to as 'wiki page'; the entire related content on that topic is called a 'Wiki'. The most popular is Wikipedia. (other examples are Library Blog Wikis,Charles Sturt Library Wiki, Tolkien Wiki etc)

Vlogs and Video Sharing sites

Video blogs (Vlogs) are blogging sites that primarily use video as the major form of content and in some cases supported by text. For example you Tube. It is one of the most popular video sharing sites. It is a video live casting and video sharing site where users can upload, share, view videos and leave comments.

Social Bookmarking

These services allow users to save, organize and manage links to various websites and internet resources. Links are tagged (labelled) to allow for easy search and sharing .The most popular are Stumble Upon and Delicious.

Social News

These services allow users to post various news items or links to outside articles and allow them to vote and comment on the items. Voting is the major social aspect, as the items that get the most votes are displayed as the most prominent. Popular examples of Social News are Digg, Propeller and Reddit.

Media Sharing

These services allow users to upload and share various media such as photos or videos. Users also have the opportunity of commenting on the shared media. The most popular are Flickr and YouTube.

Freedom of Expression

The concept freedom of expression dates back to ancient times of the Greek Athenian era more than 2400 years. The widely used international definitions of freedom of expression is provided in article 19 of The Universal Declaration on Human Rights (UDHR) and the International Covenant on Civil and Political Rights (ICCPR) ,summarised as the freedom to freely express ones opinion without interference:

"Everyone has the right to freedom of opinion and expression; this right includes freedom to hold opinions without interference and to seek, receive and impart information and ideas through any media and regardless of frontiers." (Article 19, Universal Declaration of Human Rights, 1948 (UDHR))

"Everyone shall have the right to hold opinions without interference. Everyone shall have the right to freedom of expression; this right shall include freedom to seek, receive and impart information and ideas of all kinds, regardless of frontiers, either orally, in writing or in print, in the form of art, or through any other media of his choice." (Article 19 (2), International Covenant on Civil and Political Rights, 1966 (ICCPR))

Freedom of expression is not only important in its own right but is also essential if other human rights are to be achieved .It is globally seen as underpinning human rights and democratic freedoms in that it guarantees the exchange of views and opinions necessary to inform and stimulate public debate as well as supporting freedom of association, the questioning and challenging of public officials etc. It has long been valued as a foundation right in all democratic societies (Puddephatt and Oesterlund, 2012). At an individual and national levels, freedom of expression is key to the development, dignity and fulfilment of every person wishes and for good government and therefore for economic and social progress respectively.

Freedom of speech and expression centres on the notion that people have the right to freely expressed themselves through any media and frontier without interference, such as censorship, and without fear of reprisal or molestation, threats and persecutions. However, it is important to note that, freedom of expression is not absolute, as it carries with it special duties and responsibilities therefore it may be subject to certain restrictions provided by law (Tiwari and Gosh, 2013).

In the same vein Nigeria like any nation of the world is guaranteed freedom expression under its constitution especially Chapter 4 section 39 (1) of the 1999 constitution of Nigeria which guarantees freedom of expression as a fundamental right. It states that:

39(1) Every person shall be entitled to freedom of expression,
including freedom to hold and to receive and impart ideas and information
without interference.

This can only be achieved through access to accurate, fair and unbiased information, representing a plurality of opinions, and the means to actively communicate vertically and horizontally, thereby participating in the active life of the community (Wakawa, 2013). But the collective commitment to freedom of expression in Nigeria is often tested when these expressions are conveyed via popular conventional channels. Nigerians rights to free expression has over the years been characterised by numerous attempts by state and non-state actors to suppress or intimidate Nigerians into silence. However, the emergence of social media platform and the overwhelming embrace by Nigerians have changed the status quo, as more Nigerians take to social media to post their views on all issues and its use by politicians and other elites to reach out to supporters. Nigerians, do not hesitate in taking to social media to "dish out" opinions on any issue. Nigerians embrace of the social media is so profound that even public officials as high as the President and members of his cabinet and State Governors all have viable social media accounts especially Facebook which they use periodically to comment on issues of national importance.

As Nigerians explore this new found "citizen-social media romance as means of expressing their views on issues that concerns the nation, these expressions are often characterised by the diversity of a nation in terms of religion, political interest, ethnic and regional affiliations etc. These comments are sometimes offensive.

Freedom of Expression and Social Media in Nigeria

According to Erjavec and Kovačič (2013), an important turning point in the history of audience participation in news is connected to the development of new technologies. Chung (2007) notes that with the use of the internet and its components such as the social media participatory journalism has changed from the top-down journalistic model to a bottom-up phenomenon of information distribution, with the news audience having the possibility of increased control over, and greater involvement in, the news consumption process. The development of new media technology has meant a change from the old way of writing letters to editors: the editorial staffs are more accessible and the former barriers of time and space are considerably lower with new technology (Bergström, 2008).

Audience are now able to instantly interact with traditional content providers through interactive facilities such as comments on news sites and social media (Bergström, 2008).

The Social Media has become a vital communication tool through which individuals can exercise their rights to freedom of expression and exchange information and ideas. In recent times the greater number of individuals and groups have taken to the social media to mobilize support and challenge inequality, corruption and advocate for change in government policies and accountability. The social media has often played an important role in this regard (OHCHR, 201). In such movements, the Internet and Social Media has often played a key role by enabling people to connect and exchange information instantly and by creating a sense of solidarity. Recent examples include: the Arab Spring that changed the history of the North African countries of Egypt. Tunisia and Libya

In Nigeria, Occupy Nigeria was a socio-political protest movement that began in Nigeria on Monday, 2 January 2012 in response to the fuel subsidy removal by the Federal Government of President Goodluck Jonathan on Sunday, 1 January 2012. Protests took place across the country and at the Nigerian High Commission in London. At least the use of social media services such as Twitter and Facebook was a prominent feature of the protest. Facebook group pages were created to spur Nigerians globally against the fuel-subsidy removal regime. An example is "Nationwide Anti-Fuel Subsidy Removal: Strategies & Protests" which was created on 2 January 2012 had over 20,000 members by 9 January 2012. Student websites in universities and blogs were used to report the Occupy Nigeria protests .Twitter was also extensively used as a connecting platform for the protesters across the nation.

The scenario was different before the emergence of the Internet and the social media as a platform for citizen engagement in freely expressing their various opinion on national issues. Nigeria spend greater part of its existence since independence under military rule which spanned 30 years. Between 1966–1979 and 1983– May1999, there were several decrees and laws that infringed upon the rights of Nigerians including their freedom of expression. The media being the major channels of expression for Nigerians were restricted in various ways especially access, ownership control and manipulation. Not a few journalists and citizens have suffered humiliations, threats, arrests and even untimely deaths in the hands of politicians and law enforcement agencies over reports, opinion and expressions the authorities and highly placed individuals found unpleasant even when such views are correct (Akingbolu, 2013).

In recent times, governments across the globe have tried to withhold information from the common man under one pretext or another. But, with the advent of social media vested with the immense power of delivering information to the masses and enabling them to make comments and share opinion against or for such information. Although attempts were made by Governments to carefully regulate internet, its impact on information sharing is still unimaginable high compared to conventional media platform (Television, Newspapers etc). Facebook has for a long time been a popular destination for Nigerians online with many Nigerians setting up their first Internet accounts on the platform. The number of Nigerians that have signed up to Facebook, as a means of communication and interactions, has continued to increase over the years.

For example from 400, 000 between 2008 and 2010 to 4.3 million mark at the end of December, 2011 (Elebeke, 2012).

In 2012 Nigeria became Africa's second largest country on Facebook, after Egypt with over 6 million users (TechLoy, 2012). It was reported in 2013 that Nigeria has overtaken South Africa to become Facebook's largest user base in Sub Saharan Africa with over 11 million users (CP-Africa.com, 2013). With this enormous number of users, it is obvious that there is hardly a moment of each day that you don't find Nigerian Facebook users Online. Their online presence on Facebook is often characterised by several activities such as, chat, discussion, comments, visual/audio uploads, updates about daily routine of subscribers, news update from various organizations etc. It is a handy platform for quickly measuring opinions of millions of Nigerian users on several personal, national and international issues, which usually cuts across all subject (sports, family, crime, education, corruption etc). For example, corruption allegations against government officials always attract huge discourse among Nigerians. This paper centres on one of such issues.

Facebook and Nigeria's Minister of Aviation Armoured BMW Car Scandal

Recently Nigerians took to Facebook to freely express their views on a national issues that centred on the Nigeria's Ministry of Aviation officials over an inflated price of two BMW armoured cars. Popularly referred to by most media organizations as "Nigeria's Minister of Aviation Armoured BMW Car Scandal "generated a lot of comments from Nigerians.

On 16 October, 2013 a web-based News media (*Sahara Reporters*) reported that:

a cash-strapped agency of the Ministry of Aviation purchased two armoured BMW 760 Li cars for the private use of Aviation Minister Stella

Oduah, several automobile sales companies have indicated that the cars were massively overpriced.

Our report yesterday disclosed that the Nigerian Civil Aviation Authority (NCAA) paid

approximately $1.6 million to buy the two cars from Coscharis Motors Limited in Lagos, meaning that each car cost close to $800,000. But our investigations with car sale companies revealed that the NCAA could have got eight, not two, BMW armoured cars for their money……..at each of the BMW cars could have been provided to the NCAA for $200,000 plus the cost of shipping to Nigeria (Sahara Reporters, 2013)

Premium Times, another popular web based newspaper reported the story and gave updates on the report. Most recent was its headline:

BREAKING: Jonathan drops corrupt Aviation Minister, Stella Oduah, 3 others.

President Goodluck Jonathan has accepted the resignation of four cabinet ministers.

They are Minister of Aviation, Stella Oduah; Minister of Police Affairs, Caleb Olubolade; Minister of Niger Delta Affairs, Godsday Orubebe; and Minister of State for Finance, Yerima Ngama. They were asked to resign to save them the humiliation of being sacked. It is not immediately clear why Messrs Olubolade, Orubebe and Ngama were asked

to leave. But Mrs Oduah was sent packing over corruption-related

offences. She was indicted by both the House of Representatives and a

presidential committee for compelling an agency under her supervision,

the Nigerian Civil Aviation Authority, NCAA, to buy her two exotic

armoured cars in violation of Nigeria's public procurement laws.

(Premium Times, 2014)

These and other related reports were also shared on the Facebook accounts of the two popular online news media and afforded Nigerians the opportunity to freely express their positions on the issue. What are the discourse characteristics of these comments on the Facebook sites of the two news media (Sahara Reporters and Premium Times)? Are the comments positive (in favour of the Minister) or negative (against the Minister), sectional based on regional and ethnic affiliation (are the comment based on her ethnic and regional affiliation? What is the overriding position (More in favour or more against the Minister) Are there offensive or abusive comments?

Method

Critical Discourse Analysis (CDA) and Discursive Psychology approaches were used to address the research questions. Critical discourse analysis provides theories and methods for the empirical study of the relations between discourse and sociocultural developments in various social domains (Jorgensen and

Phillips, 2002) .Discourse analysis is a useful method for uncovering discrimination or nature of discourses in news items (Van Dijk, 1988; Richardson, 2007). Critical discourse analysis is an interdisciplinary approach to the study of discourse that views language as a form of social practice and focuses on the ways social and political domination are reproduced in text and talk (Norman and Holes, 1995). CDA does not limit its analysis to specific structures of text or talk, but systematically relates these to structures of the socio-political context. The aim of critical discourse analysis is to shed light on the linguistic discursive dimension of social and cultural phenomena and processes of change in late modernity. It is also designed to contribute to social change along the lines of more equal power relations in communication processes and society in general.

According to Jorgensen and Phillips (2002), Discursive Psychology centres on language use in everyday text and talk – is a dynamic form of social practice which constructs the social world, individual selves and identity. Discursive psychology deploys many of the same methods as other qualitative approaches. As in other qualitative approaches, research questions in discursive psychology point in the direction of analyses of the production of meaning. But discursive psychology differs from other qualitative approaches in being interested in how meanings are produced within the discourses or repertoires that people draw on as resources in order to talk about aspects of the world (Jorgensen and Phillips,

2002). Discursive Psychology deploys many of the same methods (coding, transcription, interview etc) as other qualitative approaches.

Procedure

Two news media were purposively selected for this study. The choice of the two news media was purposive because they first broke the news on the armoured car and followed and gave an update on the scandal to the point of the Minister´s resignation. They are also news media that have a large followership among Nigerian due to their investigative journalism qualities and proactive posture against corruption in governance and also coverage of issues of national importance that often times are overlooked by conventional news media organizations especially in Nigeria. *Sahara Reporters* is a Nigeria online news media in the diaspora while *Premium Times* is a home-based online newspaper.

To effectively analyse the discourse, reader's comments under the news item posted on Facebook walls of the selected online news media, themes were drawn based on the objectives of the study. Comments posted on the walls of the two news media were read and reread in order to identify and place them in the relevant themes or categories. The themes included: comments considered to be offensive, abusive, comment with ethnic or regionally inclination, comments that are positive and negative. Comments that attacked the dignity of the subject, comments based on the political orientation or affiliation of the subject and comments that centred on the news media instead of the subject.

To identify the key messages in comments which included offensive speech, we conducted an analysis of macro propositions. According to Van Dijk (1980), macro propositions analysis is based on an identification of the most relevant collection of information in a text, derived from the local meanings of words and sentences by macro rules, such as deletion, generalisation and construction. Such rules combine similar meanings with construct different meaning constituents in higher-level events or social concepts, which enable one to identify the main idea news item or even multiple news items or comments. The study also included an analysis of keywords which constituted a particular discourse. Keywords direct discursive attention towards a specific segment of the society (Fowler, 1991). In this case the study looked at the comments that tilted towards to regional or ethnic affiliation, political affiliation and orientation. The findings were quantitatively and qualitatively presented.

Results

A total of 250 comments were identified and analysed based on the various themes.

Positive Comments (in favour of the Minister) under News Items on Facebook Accounts of The selected Media

The critical discourse analysis showed that there were positive comments. The positive comments were negligible when compared to the negative comments. From the 250 comments analysed only 23 were in favour of the Minister. Some of the examples are:

"Stella actually made a great difference in Aviation, she was a hardworking minister. She did well in the face lift of Airport facilities across the country"

"Aviation Minister So Far....your criticisms will not change that fact....he without sin should cast the first stone"

"PRINCESS STELLA ODUAH the great daughter of NDI IGBO, your good works and excellent performances in the time u spent as aviation minister speaks for itself, u are the best aviation minister so far, history will judge…….."

"As a matter of d records Adewumi Adesina & Stella r d best minister prior to her sack in dis country we sacrifise excellence on d alter of personal interest"

Negative Comments (Against of the Minister) under News Items on Facebook Accounts of the selected Media

The negative comments were overwhelming. Out of the 250 comments analysed from both news media only 23 where in favour of the minister. 227 comments were not in favour of the minister. The negative comments were a combination of attack on her personality, abusive and offensive. Some of the abusive or negative comments were even extended to her political affiliation and the President of the country. Examples of such comments include:

"shameless criminal woman"

"She Must be Persecuted by d Laws of Nigeria, otherwise, all Robbers in jails Deserve Freedom 2!"

"yeah i agree with u she is the best aviator and the best thief"

"You don't fire thieves, you jail them."

"Oduah has ruined her own career in Nigeria polity. Corrupt female minister for that matter."

"Mrs BMW."

"Finally,the chiken(thief)has come home 2 roast"

Comments based on Regionally and ethnic affiliation of the Minister under News Items on Facebook Accounts of The selected Media

Some of the comments were tilted towards regional and ethnic affiliation. Some of the comment were in favour of the minister and praised her for being a worthy ambassador of her kinsmen. While some saw her action as an embarrassment to her ethnic group (Igbo people). Some of the crucial macro propositions were the following:

"u pple shul live that woman alone, the car belong to ministry and not her, those enemy of progress that call for her sack is becos she has build international airport in igbo land that diverted igbo businessmen to igboland.."

"Anti-North Minister is Out."

"Are those cars registered in her name? Why the noise? Is it because she gave the igbos what Nigeria thought the igbos will never get"

"Ojoro, we the igbos are proud of her"

"I don't even know why all these igbos ar supporting this woman, anyway, they ar all d same......greedy people"

"PRINCESS STELLA ODUAH the great daughter of NDI IGBO, your good works and excellent performances in the time u spent as aviation

minister speaks for itself, u are the best aviation minister so far, history will judge"

"How abt d stolen money or must we be quite bcz she z so called thief ndi igbo?"

"am so ashame of some comments by some of my Igbo brothers.must ethnicity n tribal colouration be introduced in every discussion?...udua 's action must be condemned by any sane person"

These comments either tried to portray the minister as a worthy ambassador of the Igbo people (The igbo people are one of the major ethnic groups in Nigeria living in the South East of Nigeria) while some of the comments criticised the ethnic group for producing a leader that has brought shame to her kinsmen. Others focussed on the issue rather than the ethnic or regional background of the Minister. They condemned the action of the minister.

Offensive/Abusive Comments under News Items

Our critical discourse analysis showed that writers made different kinds of offensive and abusive comments. A notable common feature was that writers criticise the personality involved and also attacked the news media . Some few selected comments are as follows:

"Is she married mi I want to marry her as second wife so that we enjoy BMWssss"

"shameless criminal woman"

"Cary go,olee (Thief)"

"USELESS SAHARA REPORTER....."

General Attacks on Dignity of the Minister

The analysis revealed that there were comments that attacked the personality of the minister mostly labelling her as "thief". Some of the posts or comments include

"Thieves ole carry am go"

"oh GOD save our country from the evil and useless leaders"

"shameless criminal woman"

"Ashawo (prostitute) dis is jst b4 u go to hell fire if u die as u r now"

"she's Jezebel witch.....bitch minister"

"A rogue is a rogue; can she spend her stolen loots on those cars???"God is watching".

The attack on her personality focused on her being dishonest and the act was unlawful

"This woman is just a common criminal"

Comments Based on the Supposed Political Orientation of the minister

There were also comments that touched on her political affiliation. The minister belonged to the People Democratic Party (the ruling party in Nigeria). The comments generalised attack on the Ministers political affiliation. One of the comments was calling for protection against the main opposition party (All People's Congress): Some examples are:

"She should be protected against apc and boko haram"

"Stella Oduah is a certified pen-robber, working in tandem with Jonathan led PDP anti-masses and most corrupt-ridden government in Nigeria history"

Comments on the online newspaper

Some of the comments were direct attack on the news media organization for being biased and over blotting the issue and overlooking other public office holders who have don worst. They tried to discredit journalists by presenting them as biased because of their dislike of the minister. However some of the comments commended the effort of the news media for fighting corruption. Some examples are:

"At the end of the day the devil premium times and Sahara reporters will be disappointed. Ganging up against our dear princess will never succeed"

"its not news again, hip hip Sahara Reporter,dont fool ur self, why not we report the good side of that woman also."

"Is obviously that there's an issue between sahara Report and stella Odoah when it comes to her issue of report"

"USELESS SAHARA REPORTER....."

Overriding position (are more comments in favour or against the Minister)

The overriding position was the negative or comment not in favour of the minister. A total 250 comments from the two news media were analysed out of which only 23 where in favour of the minister. The other 227 comments were against the minister's action a number of which were abusive.

Discussion and Conclusion

Conventional journalism mostly enabled audience participation through letters to editors or writing complaints, which journalists either took into consideration for future

reference, or immediately published as corrections. But the major challenge with this form of audience participation in journalism process is that it does not guarantee the publishing or broadcast of such contributions. This obviously hinders freedom of expression. It is often the case that comments, articles, opinion from audience that does not meet the interest of media owners, relations and friend of media owners are often left unpublished, whether the opinion is in the interest of the nation. This is not the case at the moment, as the emergence of the internet has greatly enhanced audience participation or engagement in news process.

Audience now have the opportunity of posting comments under news items with little or no hindrance. The social media have emerged to be a viable tool for realising freedom expression as people take to social media of their choices to express their opinions freely on any issue.   Although there is the major challenge of abusing the opportunity of participatory online journalism by using offensive speech (Karlsson, 2008).

Nigerians prolonged military rule and the problem of poor access to conventional media has for several years deprived them of freely expressing themselves on important issues. The Social media now gives them the opportunity to freely express their views on any issue and as it pleases them. The Minister of Aviation BMW car scandal has shown that Nigerians are waiting for any breaking news to take to social media accounts to express their minds

The main finding from the critical discourse analysis was that comments included more negative comments (against the action of the Minister) than positive comment (in favour of the minister). There were also comments that were general attacks on human dignity, attacks based on supposed political affiliation, attacks based on supposed regional and ethnic affiliation. There were also attacks on the news media organization.

The conclusion of this study is that the social media platform has actually improved Nigerians rights to free expression. However, there is a clear abuse of the idea of participatory journalism. According to Erjavec and Kovačič (2013), "with the excuse of audience participation, personal attacks on personalities in comments under news items are tolerated. According to Tiwari and Gosh (2013), it is clearly evident that social media is a very powerful means of exercising one's freedom of speech and expression. However, increasing abuse has given force to the Government's attempts at censoring social media. What is therefore desirable is regulation of social media through a specific legislation not its censorships. While Nigerians post their minds, some level of decency is required, and issues should be addressed rather than personality.

References

Bergström, A. (2008). *The Reluctant Audience: Online Participation in the Swedish Journalistic Context*. Westminster Papers in Communication and Culture 5 (2): 60–80.

Chung, D. S. (2007). Profits and Perils: Online News Producers' Perceptions of Interactivity and Uses of Interactive Features. Convergence: The Journal of Research into New Media Technologies 13 (1), 43–61.

Erjavec, K. and Kovačič M.P (2013). Abuse of Online Participatory Journalism in Slovenia: Offensive Comments under News Items. Medij. istraž 19 (2), 55-73

Fowler, R. (1991) *Language in the News*. London, New York: Routledge.

Jorgensen, M. & Phillips, L. (2002) Discourse analysis as theory and method. London: SAGE Publications Ltd.

Kaplan A. M. & Haenlein M. (2010). Users of the World, Unite! The Challenges and Opportunities of Social Media, Business Horizons 53 (2010), 59-68

Karlsson, M. (2008). *Increasingly interactive: Swedish online news 2005–2007*. International Communication Association. Montreal, Quebec.

Norman;F. and Holes, C (1995). Critical Discourse Analysis: The Critical Study of Language. Longman, London.

Paranjoy G. T. (2012). *Media Ethics*. New Delhi: Oxford University Press, p. 354.

Richardson, J. E. (2007) *Analysing Newspapers*. New York: Palgrave Macmillan.

Puddephatt, A. and Oesterlund P. (2012) *Freedom of expression, media and digital communications,* Berlin, The European Commission

Van Dijk, T. A. (1980) *Macrostructures*. Hillsdale: Lawrence Erlbaum

Documentation

Akingbolu R.(19 May, 2013) World Press Freedom Day: How Free is the
Nigerian Press?, *ThisDay Newspaper.* Retreived 8/2/2014 from
http://www.thisdaylive.com/articles/world-press-freedom-day-how-
free-is-the-nigerian-press-/147821/

Article 19.org, (2014) Freedom of expression · What we do . article19.org.
Retrieved 8/2/2014 from http://www.article19.org/pages/en/freedom-
of-expression.html

CP-AFRICA.COM (2013) Over 11 million Nigerians on Facebook; becomes
Facebook's largest user base in Sub Saharan Africa Retrieved 8/2/2014 from
http://www.cp-africa.com/2013/09/08/facebook-nigeria/

Elebeke, E(18 January, 2012) Nigeria climbs up in Facebook ranking,
Vanguard   Newspaper,   Retrieved   8/2/2014   from
http://www.vanguardngr.com/2012/01/nigeria-climbs-up-in-facebook-
ranking/

Federal Government of Nigeria (1999). Constitution of Nigeria, Abuja, Federal
Government of Nigeria

Office of the High Commission on Human Rights (OHCHR) (2011) "Freedom
of Expression Everywhere", (2011) Freedom of expression everywhere,
including in cyberspace , OHCHR, Retrieved 16/2/2014 from

http://www.ohchr.org/EN/NewsEvents/Pages/Freedomofexpressioneverywher e.aspx .

Grahl, T (2014) The 6 types of social media, Out:think, Retrieved, 16/02/2014 from www.ouththinkgroup.com/tips/the6-types-of-social-media

Premium Times (2014, February 2) BREAKING: Jonathan drops corrupt Aviation Minister, Stella Oduah, 3 others. Retrieved 16/2/2014 from http://premiumtimesng.com/news/155031-breaking-jonathan-drops-corrupt-aviation-minister-stella-oduah-3-others.html

Sahara Reporters (2013, October 16) Nigeria's Minister of Aviation Armored BMW Car Scandal: Car Sells For Only $170K In Europe And America, *Sahara Reporter*a. Retrieved 16/2/2014 from http://saharareporters.com/news-page/nigerias-minister-aviation-armored-bmw-car-scandal-car-sells-only-170k-europe-and-america

TechLoy (2012). Nigeria Crosses 6 Million Facebook Users, Overtakes South Africa [STATS] Retrieved 16/2/2014 from http://techloy.com/2012/10/21/nigeria-crosses-6-million-facebook-users-overtakes-south-africa-stats/

Tiwari, S. and Gosh, G. (2013). Social Media and Freedom of Speech and Expression: Challenges before the Indian law, Retreived 8/02/2014 from

www.academia.edu/4117408/Social_Media_and_Freedom_of_Speech_

and_Expression_Challenges_before_the_Indian_law

UNESCO (2013). *Freedom Of Expression Toolkit: A Guide Students*,

UNESCO, Retrieved 16/2/2014 from

http://unesdoc.unesco.org/images/0021/002186/218618e.pdf .

Wakawa A. S. Daily Trust (3 July 2013) Press freedom and Nigerian

journalists, *Daily Trust Newspaper. Retreived 16/2/2014 from*

http://weeklytrust.com.ng/index.php/opinion/13209-press-freedom-and-

nigerian-journalists

Citizen Journalism Practice in Nigeria: Trends, Concerns, and Believability

Joseph Wilson, Fancis Iloani Arinze

Abstract

Journalism practice globally in the last two decades has experienced some obvious changes. For instance, it is no longer the case that the business of gathering, processing and distribution of information which for several decades was supposedly a preserve of practitioners that have acquired some form of training in the field of journalism and are guided by journalism ethos or ethics. With societal development and technological advancement, individuals have delved into exercising the functions of journalists which has led to the emergence of concepts such as "Citizen Journalism" among others. The emergence of citizen journalism obviously has its plus in the rapid development of the information society, with the active participation of members of the society processing information. However, there are several concerns. Since journalism now seems to be an all-comers affair, obviously there are bound to be deficiencies in strictly upholding the tenets of Journalism profession such as truthfulness, accuracy, objectivity, impartiality, fairness, authentication of sources and public accountability. This chapter explores the nature of citizen journalism as practiced in Nigeria, the channels that propel citizen journalism practice in Nigeria, the concerns in respect to ethos or ethics and whether Nigerians believe the products of this new form of journalism (things posted online) and why.

Introduction

The media landscape has tremendously changed in recent times in ways that make it possible for a more engaged citizen participation in journalism. Citizens now exercise the functions of gathering, processing and dissemination of information; a phenomenon widely known as citizen Journalism.

The emergence of citizen journalism has obviously contributed to the rapid development of the information society, with the active participation of members of the society in processing information (Oak, 2011). In a country like Nigeria with a population of over 150 million, it would be of interest to know how Nigeria with its diversity fares in respect of citizens' participation in the information society. Since Journalism now seems an all comers affair irrespective of a participant's status, spurred on by the availability/affordability of new media technologies in Nigeria and bearing in mind that Nigeria due to its history of prolonged military leadership, which even though now in a democratic system, hitherto still exhibits the exclusivity and secrecy of the past military order plus speculative journalism , rumour and information fabrication taking a centre stage (Nnamani, 2003), what is the nature of this newly found form of Journalism (Citizen Journalism) in Nigeria? What are the concerns in citizen journalism in Nigeria? What is the status of the ethical principles of truthfulness, accuracy, objectivity, impartiality, fairness, authentication of sources and public accountability, among others? Do Nigerians believe the "products" of this form of journalism and why?

This paper attempts to provide answers to these questions and looks at citizen journalism practice in Nigeria with the following objectives: to identify channels of this participatory journalism in Nigeria, to look at the trend or nature of practice, to identify concerns in citizen journalism practice in Nigeria as it relates to ethos and to identify whether people believe the things they see posted online and why.

Citizen Journalism is a concept that has generated argument in respect of its appropriateness of the use of the concept, its definition, its channels, and who are those involved, among others. According to Meyer (1995) one measure of the discomfort that journalists feel over the concept of participatory journalism is the great variety of names given it, e.g. civic journalism, citizen journalism, community journalism, or communitarian journalism. It is as though all who try some version of it want to distance themselves from the questionable practices of the others and that each sees in it the manifestation of his or her fondest hopes or worst fears (ibid).

It might seem difficult to have a clear cut definition of the citizen journalism concept at the moment and the argument may rage on, but what is important is the understanding that participatory form of journalism exist. A form of journalism that gives individual or groups in the society the opportunity to participate in reporting events, opinion and occurrences using various channels. Banda (2010) notes that, whilst there are various perspectives on what constitutes citizen journalism, the underlying concept of citizen engagement in news gathering, processing and distribution remain the central focus.

Table 1. Publishing platforms and technologies

Information factor	Description
Mail lists and forums,	made of diverse communities of interest;
Weblogs	a 'many to many, few to few' medium whose 'ecosystem' is 'expanding into the space between email and the Web,
Wikis,	server programmes that allow users to collaborate in forming the content of a Web site;
SMSs	, a service offered by network providers which allows customers to send text messages over the cell phones;

Mobile-connected cameras,	which include the every-day digital cameras that allow users to download, store, edit, and transmit pictures anytime, anywhere;
Internet 'broadcasting',	whereby ordinary people can record and upload anything on to the Internet, as well as distribute it;
Peer-to-peer (P2P)	sharing of files;
• RSS (Really Simple Syndication	which allows readers of blogs and other kinds of sites to have their computers and other devices automatically retrieve the content they care about.

Gillmor (2006) provides a broader clarification on the concept of citizen journalism based on the various technologies involved. Gillmor notes that citizen journalism has been spurred on by the growth in the availability of the new-media platforms of desk-top publishing and other technologies that have come to characterize citizen journalism, which include those in **Error! Reference source not found.**.

The practice which enables individuals participate in news reportage is what is today referred to as citizen journalism (Rogers, 2011). Gaulin (2007) notes that

Citizen journalism, also sometimes referred to broadly as user-generated content, is when anyone can participate in the gathering, writing, reporting, and even the publishing of news. Citizen journalism can be published on a site like associated content, on a blog, or any other avenue online. Citizen journalism is a way for everyone to be involved in the media, and of fulfilling what Rogers, (2011), describes as their freedom of expression.

Table 2. Types of media for citizen journalism

Type	Examples
Audience participation	User comments attached to news stories, personal blogs, photos or video footage captured from personal mobile cameras, or local news written by residents of a community.
Independent news and information Websites:	Consumer Reports, the Drudge Report
Full-fledged participatory news sites	Sahara reporters, NowPublic, OhmyNews, DigitalJournal.com, GroundReport)

Collaborative and contributory media sites:	Slashdot, Kuro5hin, Newsvine)
Other kinds of "thin media.":	Mailing lists, email newsletters
Personal broadcasting sites:	Video broadcast sites such as KenRadio.

Citizen journalism, also known as participatory journalism, is the act of citizens playing an active role in the process of collecting, reporting, analysing and disseminating news and information. It is the concept of members of the public playing an active role in the process of collecting, reporting, analysing and disseminating news and information. The intent of this participation is to provide independent, wide-ranging and relevant information that a democracy requires (Bowman and Willis, 2003).

Rogers (2011) notes that citizen journalism is when private individuals do essentially what professional journalists or reporters do – source and report information which takes many forms, from a podcast editorial to a report about a city council meeting on a blog. It can include text, pictures, audio and video. But it is about communicating information of some kind. This practice was largely enhanced by the emergence of the Internet, mobile phone and other ICT - with blogs, podcasts, streaming video and other Web-related innovations - that have made citizen journalism possible. Similarly, Flew (2008) states that there are three elements critical to the rise of citizen journalism and citizen media: open publishing, collaborative editing and distributed content. Lasica (2003) classified media for citizen journalism into various types shown in **Error! Reference source not found.**.

"One mobile phone to many" Citizen Journalism

Another common form of citizen journalism is "one mobile phone to many". This classification of citizen journalism entails an individual using mobile phone to disseminate text messages, multimedia messages to as many contacts available to the sender.

Rogers (2011) further categorized citizen journalism into two forms: Semi-independent citizen journalism and Independent citizen journalism.

Semi-Independent Citizen Journalism

This has to do with citizens contributing, in one form or another, to existing professional news sites. In this case readers post their comments alongside news stories written by professional reporters – what Rogers (2011) described as essentially a 21st-century version of the letter to the editor. A growing number of news websites such as *Sahara Reporters*, *Premium Times*, *Next* and all Nigerian online newspapers allow readers to post comments and sometimes give updates and opinion about a news item or report. In most cases many websites require users to register to make such posts. In this regard, Rogers (2011) notes that, it is an effort to prevent obscene or objectionable messages, many websites require that readers register in order to post comments.

There are several news stories on issues of national interest have attracted a lot of posts from Nigerians, using various platforms. For example, post-election violence in Kaduna State of Nigeria in 2011. When the story appeared online, readers posted information about the post-election violence in areas not covered in the breaking news. The posts/comment also provided details on the role of the police during the post-election incidence. Another example is the recent abduction of over 200 school girls in Chibok-Nigeria. Citizens have often sent contributions to main stream media organizations on developments on the abduction. Such information is sometimes incorporated into the final news story that is sent out to the audience by such media organizations.

Independent Citizen Journalism

This involves citizen journalists working in ways that are fully independent of traditional, professional news outlets. For example blogs in which individuals can report on events in their communities or offer commentary on current issues. Franklin Avenue, Nairaland, Nigeroiabloggers.com are some examples independent citizen journalism. There are also hybrid sites such as Bluffton Today Ohmynews, in which professional and citizen journalists work together.

The independent citizen journalism also includes websites operated by an individual or a group of people that report on news events in the local community. Some have editors and screen content, others do not. Some even have print editions. Examples: *Sahara Reporters, Daily Heights, iBrattleboro.*

Glaser (2006) points out that the idea behind citizen journalism is "that people without professional journalism training can use the tools of modern technology and the global distribution of the Internet to create, augment or fact-check media on their own or in collaboration with others," adding that one "might snap a digital photo of a newsworthy event happening in your town and post it online," finally suggesting that one "might videotape a similar event and post it on a site such as YouTube."

For the purpose of conceptual clarification this paper adopts the definition of citizen Journalism as journalism practice that involves individual or group participation in gathering, processing dissemination information through several channels.

It is common in recent times to watch video footages, pictures, read and listen to reports of news event on several web pages, blogs and social media such as the Facebook, YouTube, twitter, and the websites of international mainstream media stations such as British Broadcasting Corporation (BBC), Voice of America (VOA), Cable News Network (CNN), Radio France International (RFI) Deutche Welle Radio, etc sent by amateurs or eye witnesses and are disseminated worldwide. For example, in August 2006, CNN launched CNN EXCHANGE, a page that encourages visitors to submit their stories, pictures and videos in order to enrich the professional 24/7 news coverage provided by CNN. Recent conflicts in the Middle East brought about a massive submission of stories, pictures and videos on blogs, online picture and video repositories around the web. In line with this, CNN and other international media decided to open their doors to such submissions to enrich their own news coverage and keep their audience on their pages.

Edmonds (2011) notes that citizens armed with cell phones or other digital-cameras, can be counted on to enhanced coverage of news worthy events. For example events like the tsunami, Hurricane Katrina, the New York twin tower tragedy, the Arab Spring, Nigeria 2011 general election and the post election violence, the occupy Nigeria removal of petrol subsidy street protest etc, got various forms of coverage from members of the public through still photos and streaming videos which in some cases were used by media giants such as BBC and CNN . Blog reports also provide an unmediated, ground-level view on huge stories like September 11 world trade centre tragedy, and most recently the Middle East uprising, the Nigeria post election violence May 2011 and the occupy Nigeria January 2012 fuel subsidy removal protest. Edmonds further notes that traditional media are now indulging in getting urgent about bringing blogs or citizen-written sites into their mix.

In line with Edmond's position, Rogers (2011) also points out, that the Egyptian uprising that led to the resignation of president Hosni Mubarak besides being historic in the politics of the Middle East, it was also a story about journalism – how citizens among other journalistic efforts, played a role in spreading word of the revolution and sent video footages to conventional media establishments.

Emergence and Development of Citizen Journalism

The notion of citizens' participation in the act of journalism has a long history in the developed countries like the United States. Glaser (2006), notes that the earliest form of citizen journalism is traced to the founding of the United States in the 18th century, when pamphleteers such as Thomas Paine and the anonymous authors of the Federalist Papers gained prominence by printing their own publications. In the modern era, video footage of the assassination of President John F. Kennedy in the '60s and footage of police beating Rodney King in Los Angeles in the '80s were both captured by citizens on the scene of the event, the rise of talk radio and the styling of cable access television gave people the opportunity to share their views and news stories with a much larger audience.

In newspapers, there were letters to the editor submitted by citizens, while pirate radio stations hit the airwaves without the permission of the regulation agencies, for example in Nigeria stations like Radio NADECO, Radio Kudirat, Voice of free Nigeria and Radio Voice of Biafra International were used during the military administrations in Nigeria by those opposed to military regimes. The advent of desktop publishing in the late 1980s allowed a lot of people to design and print out their own publications, but distribution was still limited. The unprecedented rise and penetration of the World Wide Web technology in the 1990s, made it possible for several people to set up a personal home page to share their thoughts with the world.

An important milestone in the history of citizen journalism was when journalists themselves began to question the predictability of their coverage of such events as the 1988 U.S. presidential election. Those journalists became part of the public, or civic, journalism movement, a countermeasure against the eroding trust in the news media and widespread public disillusionment with politics and civic affairs (Meyer , 1995, Merritt, 2004, Dvorkin , 2005,). Others include eyewitness bloggers in Iraq such as Salam Pax giving stunningly detailed early accounts of the war. The 2004 U.S. political conventions, bloggers were given press passes for the first time. In 2005, the earliest photos on the scene of the London bombings on July 7 were taken by ordinary citizens with their camera phones. The pictures and videos of 2011 post election violence in some parts of Northern Nigeria uploaded by individuals on

YouTube, facebook and other social networking sites. Mainstream media sites run by the BBC accepted photos, video and text reports -- a practice that continues to this day among many major broadcast organizations (Gaser , 2006).

What became known as citizen journalism is the result of the digital era's democratization of media - wide access to powerful, inexpensive tools of media creation; and wide access to what people created, via digital networks - after a long stretch when manufacturing-like mass media prevailed. Blogging was one of the first major tools in this genre (Gillmor, 2008).

Observably, Citizen Journalism began to develop, spurred by emerging internet and networking technologies, such as, chat rooms and weblogs. Then came the use of convergent polls, allowing editorials and opinions to be submitted and voted on. Gillmor (2008) notes that as to whom citizen journalism concept was first affiliated to in its current digital-age meaning is Oh Yeon Ho, founder of Korea's OhmyNews, who said that "Every citizen is a reporter. The South Korea based, OhmyNews started in year 2000 and became popular and commercially successful with the motto, "Every Citizen is a Reporter. It operates with about 40 traditional reporters and editors who write about 20% of its content, with the rest coming from other freelance contributors who are mostly ordinary citizens. OhmyNews now has an estimated 50,000 contributors, and has been credited with transforming South Korea's conservative political environment. Today the concept is used globally and the practice is everywhere.

Nigerian Context

Citizen journalism in Nigeria like other countries of the world is an old practice, in the sense that audience long before the penetration of new communication technologies had ways of interacting with the conventional media. However, the unprecedented involvement of citizen in reporting events and disseminating information have been greatly enhanced by the development in ICT. When Nigeria opened up its shores to information technologies and even came up with information technology policy to enhance and promote the use of technology for development generally in the late 1990 and the beginning of the new millennium, the country witnessed an unprecedented ICT penetration which has today placed it among the leading subscribers of technology like the mobile phone. The rise of internet cafes across the country and the floating of several telecommunication networks and services afforded Nigerians the opportunity to engage in massive gathering and dissemination of all sorts of information through the internet and mobile phones.

Banda (2010) adds that in Nigeria, citizen journalism is a growing phenomenon and this growth is being supported by traditional media organizations as well as individuals and non-governmental organizations. Olubunmi et al(2011) note that recent national and international developments are demonstrating the power of technology to transform communication channels, media sources, events, and the fundamental nature of journalism. Technological advances now allow citizens to record and instantly publicize information and images for immediate distribution on ubiquitous communication networks using social media such as Twitter, Facebook, and Youtube. These technologies are enabling non-journalists to become "citizen reporters" (also known as "citizen journalists"), who record and report information over informal networks or via traditional mass media channels

According to Kperogi (2011), two momentous developments have occurred in the Nigerian journalistic landscape in the last ten years which include the migration of all major Nigerian newspapers to the Internet and the robust growth and flowering of diasporan online news outlets that have actively sought and captured the attention and participation of readers.

With these developments, the trend and channels of citizen journalism in Nigeria now became obvious. Weblogs, made in or by Nigerian began to emerge and the international media like the BBC, VOA, Radio France International, Deutsche Welle Radio also provided avenues for Nigerians to post, and make calls and report event during broadcast hours. Popular news sites like the Sahara Reporters,Nairaland.com, Nigerian Plus, Nigeria village Squire, Point blank news, Huhuonline.com, Nigeria Plus Nigerian Best Forum, Webtrends Nigeria, Nigeria Plus , citizen journalism association of Nigeria, etc are some indigenous sites that give Nigerians opportunity to practice the form(s) of citizen journalism as categorized earlier.

These sites enable citizens send reports, comments and views on various issues affecting Nigeria and beyond. Nigerian newspapers if not all, almost all have online versions which also avails citizens the opportunity to make comments on issues covered by the online newspapers. Observation has shown that one of the widely patronized channels are the international radio stations that promote some form of citizen journalism by allowing citizens to phone in during broadcast and report on issues. For example the 2011 Nigeria general election witnessed a display of citizens' contribution to the broadcast items by the international media. The Social media are also not left out especially among the Information technology literates. The popular networking site, the Facebook, YouTube, Twitter, MySpace, also provide another popular avenue for Nigerians to post information as a form of citizen journalism practice.

A recent trend in citizen journalism is the emergence of online news sites inviting contributions from local residents of their subscription areas, who often report on topics that conventional newspapers tend to ignore. According to Glaser (2004), citizen participation in journalism has changed the conventional journalism practice .Instead of being the gatekeeper, telling people what is important to them, the public now serving as the eyes and ears for the Voice, rather than having everything filtered through the views of a small group of reporters and editors.

Theoretical Discussion

Patterson (2008) notes that since the days of ancient Greek, philosophers have tried to draft series of guidelines concerning ethical issues. There are contributions by scholars in the area of media ethics, some of which appear suitable to explaining ethos in citizen journalism. Some of these contributors include Aristotle's Golden Mean theory; Immanuel Kant's categorical imperative theory; Jeremy Banthem and John Staurt Mill's Utilitarianism; Pluralistic theory of value; and communitarianism. There is also the Media Ethics theory widely referred to as the four normative media ethics theory. This paper touches on a few of these theories as framework to further explain ethos in citizen journalism. The paper adopts Aristotle Golden theory, categorical imperative theory, communitarianism and the social responsibility theories as framework.

The Aristotle Golden Mean theory from the Nichmachean Ethics stipulates that one way to learn ethics is to select heroes and to try to model your individual acts and ultimately your professional character on what you believe they would do. That means this theory is about the proper emotional response to situation, rather than the proper action. That virtue come from character and character make one do the right thing (Murdarasi, 2008). This explains the need for a citizen journalist to model their practice after experts or professional in the field of journalism to ensure that contributions or reports should be ethos based.

The Immanuel Kent categorical imperatives asserts that an individual should act on the premise that choices one make for oneself could become universal law therefore one should act so that humanity is treated always as an end never as a means only. Kent asserts that there are certain things one always had a duty to always do irrespective of consequences of doing them. For example he believes people should always tell the truth and it is important to find out what ones moral duties are, achieved through reasoning (Patterson, 2008 and Guthrie 1994). Based on this theory, Patterson (2008) notes that, for instance an ethical person drive at a speed and in a manner that is appropriate to everyone else on the same highway. Patterson further notes that journalist can claim few special privileges, such as the right to lie or invade privacy in order to get a story, Kent view however remind one of what one gives up : truth and privacy. Citizen journalist may not have code of ethics but reasoning along Kent theory would help practitioners avoid ethical blunders.

Communitarianism theory places its dominant intellectual emphasis on individual and individual acts by emphasizing concepts such as character, choice, liberty and duty. Communitarian thinking allows ethical discussions to include value such as altruism. According to Turner (2006) Communitarianism emerged in the 1980s as a response by Charles Taylor, Michael Sandel, and

Michael Walze to the limits of liberal theory and practice. Its dominant themes are that individual rights need to be balanced with social responsibilities, and that autonomous selves do not exist in isolation, but are shaped by the values and culture of communities. Ethos in Citizen Journalism could fit in this context when citizen understand that certain responsibilities are expected of them based on community value.

Another theory relevant to this paper is Social Responsibility theory or media typology which McQuail (2000) postulates as: (1) media has obligation to society, (2) media ownership is a public trust, (3) news media should be should be truthful, accurate, fair , objective and relevant (4) media should be free but self-regulated, (5) media should follow agreed codes of ethics and professional conduct, (6) Under some circumstance, government may need to intervene to safeguard the public.

MCQuail further notes that the right of the people to have an adequate press and their rights taking precedence are fundamental bases for the demand for responsibility. Citizen journalism is a platform for individuals and groups to own or freely access means and freely disseminate information of their choices to the society. This freedom however requires certain level of responsibility and some touch of ethical standard, which Mgulwa (2008) points out that it should set guidelines, rules, norms, codes and principles that will lead journalists and all other media workers to make moral decisions. They should not be forced to do so because ethics is applied voluntarily. The emergence of new media such as the internet and mobile phone have transformed the conventional journalism, making it open for non-professionals which is creating challenges such as non-adherence to ethos of the profession

Trend and Channels of Citizen Journalism in Nigeria

In the wake of emerging technologies and new digital tools, the Nigeria journalism landscape is changing rapidly especially with the online presence of most media organization: both electronic and print. Making them more interactive and dynamic and in some cases provide pictorial and video support. Online editions of newspapers now offer readers the option to comment on their content and share links on various social networks. They also feature embedded videos, blogs and the concept of mobile applications including SMS alerts of breaking news on mobile phones which is now a common phenomenon in Nigeria Journalism business.

The digital transformation is gradual but an obvious trend in Nigeria Citizen journalism is the utilization of social media and foreign conventional media channels (radio and television stations) to carry out their citizen journalism practice. For example activities like webcasting - broadcasting live audio or video online – are popular channels in modern citizen journalism but observation has shown that the trend in Nigeria citizen journalism is the reliance on social media and foreign media channels to enjoy most of these services. For example the Facebook, Twitter, YouTube, British Broadcasting Corporation (BBC) World Service especially the Hausa service, Voice of America (VOA), Radio France International, Deutsche Welle Radio, Aljazera TV etc are channels utilized by Nigerians to post and report news stories.

The disturbing trend as regards these channels is the often uncensored and unedited reports which have little or no regards for media ethos or ethics and neither do such reports and videos display any sense of social responsibility. For example the spate of violence that trailed the Presidential polls in Nigeria in April 2011 and the current security challenges the country is facing. Nigerian citizens from various parts of the country covered the crises and still share information on the current security situation. For example, on facebook a Nigerian resident in the United States posted a picture of a young man lying dead in pool of blood with machete wounds and it was tagged "body of a Youth Corps member murdered in Bauchi" (Bauchi is one of Nigeria's Northern States) A disturbing video was uploaded on YouTube, of a man set ablaze and it was tagged "post-election violence in Jos". The Social media are readily available channels for citizens and thus it comes handy for spreading distorted information. The insurgence and the recent abduction of school girls in Chibok, Nigeria is constantly reported on various social media and other online platforms.

Social Media

Social media has an obvious place in citizen journalism practice in Nigeria. These media and other technologies shape the concept of citizen journalism. They make it easier and enable more people to participate in citizen journalism. The internet, mobile phones and affordable digital cameras have made the promotion of citizen journalism practice possible. Tools such as Twitter, Facebook and YouTube are widely used in citizen journalism practice in Nigeria. Banda (2010) notes that these technologies and media have in some instances determine shape of citizen journalism in Nigeria. Citizen journalists use social media platforms to disseminate news, comment and views on issues of national and international issues.

Nigerians have witnessed the power of the social media, with the presence of myriads of platform to share information gathered. Social sites like Facebook and Twitter and youtube, present a platform for individuals to share information and expression of ideas (Samson, 2011)

For example during the 2011 general elections, Nigerians went out ready to vote and monitor the process. They freely took pictures and shared them with friends and strangers alike. Samson (2011) notes that Daily Trust which has a wide followership on social sites became like a sub platform for the expression of opinion and the sharing of news with ordinary citizens sending in reports and photos from their various localities. Samson (2011) identified some of the messages sent via mobile phones, Facebook and Twitter, which can be seen below.

With respect to mobile phones:

"Accreditation has finished and voters have started queeing for voting. We have witness a serious low turnout in almost all the poling units in my home town Gashu'a" Adamu Kaku Gashu'a (+2348066014###).

"At kpansia 7 here in Yenagoa peoples cast as many as they like a friend of mind said he votes six times", Usman Adamu Yenagoa (+2348034011###).

On Facebook, many posted regular updates the crisis:

Sanusi Altine, "I have just been disenfranchised by INEC in my poling unit together with tens of other people."

Somson (2011) further notes that with news travelling so fast with no gatekeeper, especially with the protection of anonymity, it then poses a potential risk as people with ulterior motives can abuse it to ferment trouble. "People just disseminate whatever comes to their mind without consideration of implication, supporting them with damning pictures in some cases," they said. "This is no little matter as a single malicious tweet of Facebook can make the rounds and reach hundreds of thousands in a short time, creating a storm in its wake," they concluded.

Otufodunrin (2012) posits that, the social media provide an opportunity for non-journalists to report events from their own perspective. Keita (2012) points out that in the race for relevancy, big players in the print media used Twitter to invite citizen reporters to contribute reporting. For example, Nigeria *Vanguard* newspaper on 10 January 2012 tweeted in respect of a national strike in Nigeria thus.

"As Labour strike begins... report protest in your area!".

According to Olakitan (2012), the Internet has "given room to a new form of media freedom in information dissemination that has not been seen some few years ago." They argued that Nigerians are able to post information faster than an average journalist could send an article for production. "*The recent mass protests of the oil subsidy removal in Nigeria had many users of twitters sharing pictures of dead or dying protesters*," they said. "*Many Nigerians entered into meaningful discussions on the subjects of corruption, police brutality, comparing figures and statistics on Facebook and posting comments*," they concluded.

Many Nigerians covered the protests themselves through social media tools. Nigerians rarely rely on government owned media such as the National Television Authority, NTA and federal radio corporation that often broadcasts content in favour of the government. It is common scenario, in recent times for Nigerians to post their own videos on You Tube and inform friends on

Facebook, Twitter or Skype. When incidences happen such as police or security agencies brutality are denied by offenders, eye witnesses do not hesitate to post pictures of such incidences or, pictures of the horror were posted on You Tube for all to see.

"The beauty of social media is that I control the information I want people to hear. I won't let people listen to lies from government," twitted @ekekeee. However Adebanjo a professional journalist, points out that citizen reporting should be carried out with caution "Please use Social Media responsibly and only broadcast what you have confirmed,".

Idowu (2012) notes that "Social media have been helpful in mobilising public opinion against an unpopular public policy. But it is also a threat to responsible information dissemination. Unverified claims, outright lies have been dished almost in equal measure in the determination to coaltar the government and its officials."

The use of SMS is another trend though unconventional but has a wide reach and often disturbing. As millions of Nigeria mobile phone subscribers can beached in matter of minutes. Report whether false news, fact distorted or truth, gets to the mobile phone of Nigerians at the fastest possible time. It is considered faster than the widely used social media and radio channels, recent text message that that circulated all over Nigeria by an unknown source drew the attention of the Nigerian Police to assure Nigerians that the text was baseless and untrue. The text was a warning to Christians living in the North to leave as there was Jihad planned to eliminate Christians house to house. A similar text was circulated among Mulsims living in the North sometimes in 2011 that Muslims living in the south would be attacked. Another one was the text informing people living in Northern Nigerians to avoid the consumption of Palm oil that it has been poisoned. It took the intervention of Consumer Protection Agency to debase the text. There are several such text messages touching on all issues and it is a disturbing trend of unconventional form of citizen journalism.

Concerns

Banda (2010) notes that Journalism practice is often underpinned by a shared sense of values. This is translated into a set of ethos or ethics, represented in codes of ethical principles. These may be an appropriation of internationally agreed ethical standards and contextualised to guide the practices and routines in a given media institution.

Journalism ethos centres on the principle of good practice as applicable to the specific challenges faced by journalists. It is widely known to journalists as their professional code of ethics which is usually statements drafted by both professional journalism associations and individual print, broadcast, and online news organizations to guide the professional conducts of journalists.

Niles (2007), notes that journalism code of ethics are principles that help separate the good writers and publishers from the frauds and con artists. That, ethics of online journalism are, ultimately, not different from the ethics of mainstream journalism. Singar (2010) notes that the online platform has present varying enthusiasm for users. It also involves some ethical issues that require reconsideration.

Table 3. Factors affecting journalism

Factor	Expectation
Differentiate	Differentiate between facts and opinions.
Accuracy	Check your facts before you publish.
Originality	Do not plagiarize and do link to all references.
Preservation	Don't make digital modifications that change the meaning or context of pictures or video footage
Authenticity	Don't submit "posed" pictures as true news.
Safety	Don't put yourself in danger in order to get that "great" story or picture.
Honesty	Be honest

Authenticating Sources	Make personal contact with the person(s) you are writing about and link to their online material (eg blog) if they have any.
Transparency	Be sure to disclose any personal relationship you may have to the story you publish

The Society of Professional Journalists has articulated a comprehensive policy of journalism ethics that can help guide any conscientious online writer. Besides the popular codes, such as objectivity, fairness, confidentiality of sources, protection of children and minors, Niles (2007), identified some widely accepted ethical factors that affect journalism and the ethical expectations (see Table 3).

These ethical elements are often not strictly adhered to in citizen journalism practice. There are ethical disregards in reports, videos, audio and pictures sent or posted by citizens. Leach (2009) in line with this development notes that what appears on Web sites and on blogs is not generally regarded as adhering to standards that govern news organizations. There exist areas of disconnect between the practices of journalists and the emerging conventions of digital/social media which demonstrate the need for ethical guidelines. He identified some areas of ethical issues. These included: (1) Authenticating sources of information, especially when they are provided by an anonymous source, (2) assuring the reliability of information on linked sites, (3) dealing with conflicts of interest, and (4) concerns involving lack of oversight or accountability.

Citizen journalism is obviously a transformation in the practice of Journalism, but it has also drawn some criticism as it relates to ethical conduct. Maher, (2005) points out that it has drawn criticism from traditional media like the New York Times, which have accused proponents of public journalism of abandoning the traditional goal of 'objectivity'. Many traditional journalists view citizen journalism with some scepticism, believing that only trained journalists can understand the exactitude and ethos involved in reporting news.

One of the challenges of citizen journalism is regulating its operation. Heald (2010) posits that regulation and professionalization of online journalism news sites and blogs have continued to pose a major challenge to journalism practice, That, lapses often emerge in areas such as building consumer awareness of websites, asking why many sites do not provide adequate information on what the site is, who funds it, what the sources are and who the author is. Another issue is how to authenticate online commenting. Some news organizations or journalists use pseudonyms to comment on and hence promoted their own articles. All these fall short of ethical standards.

A critical look at other areas of journalism ethos, such as authenticating sources, obviously shows that there are lapses. For example on 30th May 2011, VOA Hausa service carried a report on the Mammy Market bomb blast in Bauchi State, Nigeria. The VOA correspondent reported and aired the voice of someone who claimed to be medical doctor and that he saw 10 corpses of the bomb blast victim, which was an unconfirmed figure from an unknown source. The current security challenge (insurgence) in Nigeria is characterised by exaggerated figures of the numbers of deaths as a result of insurgents' attacks. Most times eye witness reports exaggerate figures. For example, a recent attack on Gamboru Ngala by the insurgents on May 7 2014 the breaking news from various online sites reported that ovr 300 people were killed some eye witnesses reported that over 600 people, CNN reported that "*at least 150 people dead...*". Another example is the number of the abducted school girls in Chibok, Nigeria by the insurgents, has still not been ascertained, which among other reason has compelled the Federal government to set up a committee to look into the abduction saga. The main worry is the inability of the citizen journalists to concede to others the right to publish or broadcast what they consider good enough.

Otufodunrin (2012) notes that there are too many unverified reports posted by people using various platforms. People send comments or reports on websites and don't want to be moderated even when the words used are unduly abusive, "Freedom without responsibility is very dangerous". Frommer (2009) commented on the issue of false citizen journalism practice. *"CNN's iReport citizen journalism site was vandalized again with a false report claiming that AT&T CEO Randall Stephenson was 'found dead in his multimillion dollar beachfront mansion' after a coke binge with 'male dancers everywhere,'"* he said. *"[I]n 2010 an 18-year-old iReport prankster reported falsely that Apple CEO Steve Jobs had died of an apparent heart attack."* Frommer (2009) commented further. *"This highlights the risk of high-profile news organizations like CNN running citizen journalism sites,"* he said. *"While CNN includes a disclaimer on all of its pages that stories have not been vetted or fact-checked, it's still going to offer an added air of credibility over a random, blank site,"* he continued. *"And while it's good that CNN is able to take fraudulent posts like this one down so quickly, it's still going to be hard to ever achieve credibility when your platform is also being used for malice,"* he continued.

Gahran (2005) notes that all forms of journalism especially citizen journalism, face ethical quandaries. Three of the thorniest issues in journalism ethos are independence, objectivity, and transparency. Too many open Citizen Journalism (citJ) sites (especially those sponsored by news organizations) don't require or even facilitate transparency. That is, they generally don't require the people who post content to clarify how they are related to or involved in the story. These make it difficult for the audience to put citJ and other contributed content into perspective (Gahran, 2005). He adds that unfortunately, the idea of transparency is all too frequently violated. Journalism fails to say anything about methods, motives, and sources. These are challenges on ethos for citizen journalism practice which also pose a great threat for a credible journalism practice.

Bugeja (2008) notes that increasingly with the advent of interactivity wireless and portable technologies, a reporter or freelancer must guard against issues in respect of posts on the internet because it is an ethical issue that touches on such matters as credibility, conflict of interest, fairness and discretion. Some of the challenges as it relates to ethos in respect of citizen journalism in Nigeria include; accuracy, challenge, transparency, authenticating sources, assuring the reliability of information, accountability/social responsibility, issues of opinion and fact.

Accuracy

Accuracy still counts in online or citizen journalism even if it's now known as content generation (In-Went capacity Buidling International, 2009).   It is common to see post on blog sites with report that is far from the truth or the truth tilted to suit the citizen journalist's purpose. Such reports usually not accompanied by links to substantiate such posts. For example, Samson (2011), identifies some post on various networking sites during the violence that followed the presidential election in 2011 in Nigeria on Facebook, Twitter, YouTube etc, many posted regular update on the crisis:

Shaheed Maikudi tweeted:

"there is no killing of anybody in kaduna, there's serious protest,

infact protesters are been executed by military men and men of the

Nigerian Police. In fact even the burning of tyres has stoped. ....t".

Kels (@kelemukah) tweeted:

"Fitin in sme prts of northern Nigeria + d Wuse market area of Abuja

as a result of d outcome of d presidential election.warn pple u knw"

These tweets were distortion of the fact as they did not reflect the true situation. Recently, most main stream media organizations and several blog posted a news story accompanied by picture, that the American Marines that arrived Nigeria as part of US assistance to Nigeria to trace the abducted Chibok school girls have made their first arrest of two suspected Boko Haram members in Benue State (North Central Nigeria). The headline read *"US Marines carry out first arrests of two Boko Haram members in Benue State"* The military spokesman of Nigeria refuted the report. As no American Marine had been deployed to any part of Nigeria when the report was released by the media.

Other widely tweeted and reported issues on the abducted school girls in Chibok Nigeria that were false or unauthenticated include:

"Abducted Chibok Girls Seen In Central Africa"; "Breaking news:

kidnapped girls raped 15 times daily — escaped girl confessed";

"Breaking News: Abducted Girls Reported seen around Gwoza"; "US

Marin Loate Kidnaped School Girls in Sambisa Forest Using Surveillance Equipment".

It could be argued that citizen journalism is not the widely known conventional Journalism and thus the issue of ethos can be downplayed especially considering the difficulty in enforcing ethos or ethics on citizens. According to Hanson (2008) in journalism, informing people must come first and a responsible practitioner leans towards disseminating information but he or she has a responsibility not to kill a disturbing story or photo but to present it in a way that minimizes pain without holding back what the public needs to know. These channels used by Nigeria undoubtedly have policies that shield them from taking responsibility of inaccurate reports or manipulated videos and pictures but Hanson (2008) notes that there are cases when news organizations must withhold information. This is to guard against chaos in a peaceful society. Citizen Journalism might be an all-comers affair but the managers of channels through which practitioners information are disseminated have a responsibility of serving as gate keepers to check the reports that negates journalistic ethical provisions or ethos.

Authenticating Sources

This is also a common ethical issue in Nigeria Citizen journalism practice. This trend is inherent with the text and calls made by citizen to international radio station. People also send tweets and post to other social networking sites without concrete identification of such sources.

Assuring the reliability of information, accountability, social responsibility, issues of opinion and fact. Samson (2011) further identified some of such posts:

The following tweet by a mischievous fellow regarding Monday's post-election violence is one of such. Adam Sani (@abuabdallah92), who refused to put up a profile picture, tweeted,

> *"what we vote is not what we will be given, so we cant stay at home,*
>
> *we must come out and slaught every xtian in kaduna."*

In less than 5 minutes, the tweet generated an outcry and was circulated round generating differing opinions with most condemning the malicious tweet:

> *Ify Diani (@Taki_Liverbird): "But this @abuabdallah92 dude is a big*
>
> *fool. He wants christians slaughtered. Blame hin and his ilk for these riots,*
>
> *not Buhari. #ThinkPeople"s*

Still on the ethical issue on authenticating sources and responsible journalism, on 25 February 2011, Nairaland published a post that reads:

> *"Military Coup In Nigeria: This is my very first post on nairaland. I*
>
> *am still trying to figure things out but i would go straight to the point. A*
>
> *military coup is being plotted right now. I cannot disclose my real identity*

becos i fear for my safety. I was trying to create a blog site but i came across this website and i registered. There has been heavy military presence in places that we presume might give us problems. I pity Mr. jonathan."

There were several such posts by Nigerians that fall short of nearly all standards of journalism ethos. It is worrisome that this development observably is fostering division among Nigerians especially along ethnic and religious lines, as these sites and radio stations have wide followership, participation and their online posts/comments are believable by Nigerians.

Believability of Citizens Online Posts

It is obvious from the discussion above that there are ethical concerns in citizen journalism practice in Nigeria. However, what is of interest is that, it is observable that people, believe the ubiquitous information they see posted online even when sometimes things posted are not true or the truth distorted. It is also observable that people who read such online posts or text messages either start circulating it or send comments that seem to confirm their acceptance or believability without really verifying the truth from other available sources. The questions that readily come to mind are why do people believe these citizens online posts? How can people sift through the ubiquitous citizens' information and know what to trust?

Kiousis (2001) and Johnson and Kaye (2009) point out that when individual users rely more on a specific medium for information, they consider it to be more credible than other media; and that individual blog readers who rely on blogs for information are likely to consider blogs as more credible sources than other media (Kang, 2010). For example, Seipp (2002) points out that blog users relied considerably more on blog than other information sources for information and knowledge of and interest on issues which often becomes the strongest predication for visiting and believing such blogs.

The socio-cultural diversity of the Nigerian State plays a vital role in shaping or influencing array of issues such as governance, education, employment, media etc. It is observable that media credibility and believability is sometimes influenced by audience socio -cultural affiliation and trust in whether government or a political or regional affiliation. Tremayne (2007) examined the blog use for information in the context of the America/Iraq War and notes that trust in government positively predicted reliance on blog for war information despite relatively low political trust among blog users. Tremayne further notes that Conservative group of blog users trust the Conservative Bush Administration which translated into visiting blog sites supporting the war effort. These socio-cultural affiliations are identified by Names, religion, geopolitical origin etc. For example, a media organization owned by individual(s) from Northern Nigeria may enjoy higher credibility and believability rating among the Northerners than a media organization owned by individual(s) from the Southern part of Nigeria and vice-versa. Looking at citizen online posts in Nigeria, it is observable that the believability and credibility is high when it is posted by an individual(s) who have the same religious affiliation and geopolitical origin with the audience. In this case sifting of citizen online post and believability is often determined by religious and geopolitical affiliation. Similarly, Taylor (2006) notes that, individual's judge credibility based on level of believability and community affiliation. Believability is a subjective measure of fairness, accuracy and bias which matters to audience of media platform that stays involved in their communities to build local relationship and close association with audience. The closer a citizen journalism source to the community the more believable (Taylor, 2006).

A stereotype held by Nigerians about the traditional media (radio, television and newspapers) is another reason why Nigerians believe online citizen posts. It is observable that Nigerians hold stereotype about the traditional media as a result of media ownership and prolonged military leadership. Nigerians are of the opinion that Media owners influence media reports and that media pursue subjective consideration against the pursuit of truth and so have become compartmentalized to suit group of interests which in most cases are the proprietor's interests. These have compelled Nigerians to crave for other sources of information and the online posts have come handy. Kenya serves as an excellent example following the contested elections there in December 2007, around 600 blogs appeared in the web, many debating issues concealed by the established Kenyan media. Citizen posts are believed by Nigerian because sometimes they uncover issues concealed by mainstream Nigerian media.

Until recently when the Nigerian state underwent a measure of stability, with the advent of democracy, the socio-political environment had been marked by periodical political and social instability which kept the military in power for a long time. The military dictatorship created a scenario of secrecy and high handedness on the media. These affected media performance that Nnamani (2003) points out that hitherto one easy claim of the Nigerian press is that even though the country is in a democracy, it appears slightly difficult to pick valid information since according to them, much of the system still carries the exclusivity and secrecy of the past military order. Nnamani (2003) further notes that "speculative journalism took centre stage. 'Rumour' or 'concoction' became substitutes for information flow and the governed became easy preys of such concocted news items".

Credibility ratings or ranking of media organizations among Nigerians is another factor responsible for believing online posts. For example in Erdos and Morgan (2008) survey on American opinion leaders ranked BBC News one of the most objective and credible U.S. news sources (BBC, 2008). There exist such credibility rankings among media audience in Nigeria. For example it is observable that an average Northern Nigerian listener of the Hausa Services of the British Broadcasting Corporation ranks BBC Hausa Service high in terms of credibility content. It is common to hear a Nigerian refer to BBC news, Aljazeera, Sahara Reporters, Premium News etc as their sources of latest information. Hence whatever report is posted and accessed online via these media have high believability standing among Nigerians except proven otherwise by other media with the same credibility ranking.

Opinion leaders also play a role in the believability of online posts. Opinion leaders could range from religious leaders, heads of peer and social groups, head of family etc. This factor reflects the 1940 study of social influence that states that media effect are indirectly established through the personal influence of opinion leaders. Majority of people receive much of their information and are influenced by the media second hand through the personal influence of opinion leader. These opinion leaders gain their influence through more elite media such as online posts, news websites as opposed to mainstream media. In this process social influence is created and they then begin to disseminate these opinions through the public who become opinion followers (Baran, 2002). Nigerians have several social for a where individual exercise certain influence either as a result the person's social standing or appointment. These opinion leaders disseminate information from online post and followers believe these posts with little or no confirmation from other sources. For example, a religious cleric reads an online post and tells followers about it who in turn believe and spread same information.

Another reason Nigerians believe online posts is the opportunity of accessing several similar or related online posts on several news websites which serves as a sort of verification. This reason also serves as an avenue for sifting which post is true and which one is not. The verification opportunity made available through related links increases the level of believability of online posts and sifting true from false post. For example, if a citizen sends posts on Twitter or Facebook, Nigerians take another step of connecting to other sites to verify the stories or send text messages friends or relation who lives in an area an incidence occurred. For example, all National newspapers in Nigeria are online, hence, citizen verify reports from the sites of these dailies and other sites. Another example is the news of the plane crash of 2 June 2012 in Nigeria that claimed the lives of over 150 passengers started as a rumour but within 2 hours, several citizens had posted about the events in various online channels and online media organization had given a breaking news. The posts on several websites as a sort of verification make online posts believable.

Conclusion

Citizen Journalism obviously has given individual opportunity to disseminate information and essentially, it has profound implications for the flourishing of society in areas such as democracy (Salawu, 2011). Banda (2010) adds that the overall importance of citizen journalism would seem to lie in its ability to engender some action on the part of authorities and other interested groups in response to perceived citizens' felt needs. Change is imperative as Zachary, (2006) notes that it is already clear that a new journalism ethos is required; a new way of thinking and acting that acknowledges the criticisms and doubt that citizen journalists/ authors may never adopt journalistic standard from the parties involved.

Although a new way of thinking and acting that acknowledges the criticisms and doubt that citizen journalists/ authors may never adopt journalistic standard from the parties involved (Zachary, 2006), it is still imperative to consider the issue of ethos in this open source journalism, and how to regulate activities of the great number of participants, just to ensure the health of the society. No doubt, Citizen Journalism has brought forth an unprecedented flowering of news and information to an array of audience. But, it has also destabilized the old business models that have supported quality journalism for decades.

The growing concern in respect to non-adherence consideration of journalistic ethos in citizen journalism in Nigeria is observably propelled by the medium or channels citizens' use. The international broadcast organizations like the BBC Hausa service, VOA Hausa Service, Radio France International Deutch Wella Radio that have wide listenership especially in Northern Nigeria give listeners the opportunity to make phone calls and send text messages to live news programmes. These contributions from audience are usually characterized by issues that fall short of journalism ethos.

Social networks such as Facebook and twitter are some of the widely used platforms by Nigerians for posting matters bothering on nearly everything (health, music, governance, politics, economy, etc. and in some cases provide links to some news stories. The phone-to-phone form of citizen journalism, although it is an informal kind of citizen journalism, but it is one of the effective form of citizen journalism that is totally devoid of any elements of ethos. People receive and spread text and multimedia messages which often have no authenticated source. Citizen may seem not to be organized like the conventional journalism, but efforts can be made to inject some sanity to citizens postss. For example, Lewenstein (2008) points out that subscribers to online service such as the ComNet which offers a wide range of interactivity services agreed to abide by services rules of behaviour which include prohibitions against objectionable or lewd language, and use only their true names.

Regulating activities of citizen journalists is an important step in addressing the challenges in respect of disregard for journalistic ethos, especially the citizen journalism version promoted by international media which has in recent times fueled unpleasant situation such as inciting Nigerians. It might be difficult to regulate phone to phone (text) information dissemination but other forms can be checked or facilitated by agencies like the Nigeria Broadcasting Commission and Nigeria Union of Journalists should work towards regulating other forms of practice .For example British National Union of Journalists (BNUJ) has published its new "code of practice" for what it calls "witness contributors".

Regulation can start somewhere, particularly with those who play gatekeepers roles in media organizations and other channels. For example, Kiss (2011) notes that in respect BNUJ, that the code is intended "for publishers of citizen journalism designed to encourage responsible and ethical use of user-generated material". The online media or host sites could also adopt strict measures on the kind of information citizen upload on websites. Creating awareness on issues of ethos is important so that citizens can imbibe ethos that makes for meaningful participation.

Blogs and online posts are and would remain sources of information to the global internet public (In-Went Capacity Building International, 2009). Worldwide blogging and other forms of citizen journalism have increased in Nigeria in recent years. Observably, Nigerians believe and will continue to believe these online posts. Thus as audience continue to sift online posts to authenticate reports, it is worthy of note that Journalistic ethos cannot be neglected because of the assumption that citizen journalists would not adhere. Ethos is still valid in the era of digital media.

References

Banda, F.(2010) Citizen Journalism & Democracy in Africa: An Exploratory Study; South Africa, Highway Africa

Baran, S. (2002) Theories of Mass Communication Introduction to Mass Communication McGraw-Hill.

Bryan S. Turner (2006*) "Communitarianism." The Cambridge Dictionary of Socioloy.* Cambridge , Cambridge University Press,

Bugeja, M. (2008) "To post or not to post: the question for writers in the digital age" *Media Ehtics: Issues and Cases* 6th Ed.New York, McGraw-Hil Coy

Gillmore, D. (2006) We the media: grassroots journalism by the people, for the people. Cambridge, O'Reilly.

 Flew, T. (2008) *New media: An introduction,* , Melbourne, Oxford University Press

Hanson, C. (2008). Informing the Public Must Come First In: *Media Ehtics: Issues and Cases* (6th ed).New York, McGraw-Hil Coy

Johnson, T. J., & Kaye, B. K. (2009). In blog we trust? Deciphering credibility of components of the internet among politically interested internet users. *Computers in Human Behavior, 25*, 175-182.

Kang, M. (2010). Measuring social media credibility: A study on a measure of blog credibility. Submitted to the Institute for Public Relations for the 2009 Ketchum Excellence in Public Relations Research Award

Kiousis, S. (2001). Public trust or mistrust? Perceptions of media credibility in the information age. *Mass Communication and Society, 4*(4), 381-403.

Maher, V. (2005) Citizen journalism is dead. <u>*New media lab*</u>, School of Journalism & Media Studies, Rhodes University, South Africa.

McQuail, D. (2000) *McQaiul's Communication Theory*, (4th ed) , London, Sage Publication.

Olubunmi P. A., Caroline H.,Debra, B, Richard L. (2011) How technology transforms journalism business through citizen-reporters in Nigeria. *International Journal of Strategic Information Technology and Applications.* 2(2). 1-11

Patterson, P. (2008) An introduction to ethical decisions making. *Media Ethics: Issues and cases* (6th ed) .New York, McGraw-Hil Coy

Salawu, A. (2011) Citizen Journalism Off-Line: The (Nigerian) Punch Model, *Estudos em Comunicao* No. 9. 185-196

Seipp, C. (2002) Online uprising. *American Journalism Review.* 24(13) ,42-47

Singer, B.J. (2010) Norms and the network: Journalism ethics in a shared media space. In Meyers C. (ed) *Journalism ethics: A philosophical approach.* Oxford, Oxford University Press

Taylor, H.S. (2006) The executive blog as a communications tool. Califonia, ProQuest

Tremayne, M. (2007) Blogging, Citizenship, and the Future of Media. London Routledge

Wilson Joseph (2012) Ethical issues in citizen journalism practice in Nigeria.
In Wilson D. (ed.). Media, Terrorism, political communication and
multicultural environment, Nigeria, African Council for
Communication Education, pp.123-140

Documentation

BBC Press Office (2008, November, 11) *BBC news U.S. ranking.* Retrieved
4/6/2012 from
http://www.bbc.co.uk/pressoffice/bbcworldeide/worldwidestoriies/press
releases/2008/11_november/bbc_news_us_ranking.shtml

Bowman, S. and Willis, C. (2003). We media: How audiences are shaping the
future of news and information., The Media Center, American Press
Institute. http://www.hypergene.net/wemedia/weblog.php

CNN. (2014, July 5). http://www.cnn.com/../nigeria-abducted-girls/ or
http://www.edition.cnn.com/2014/05/07/world/Africa/Nigeria-
abducted-girls/

Frommer, D. (2009, July, 27), CNN's iReport vandalized again with false
report claiming ceo's death, coke binge. *Business Insider SAI,*
Retreived 12/9/2013 from http://www.businessinsider.com/cnns-
ireport-vandalized-again-with-false-report-claiming-ceos-death-2009-7

Dvorkin, J. A. (2005, January 27) Media matters: Can public radio journalism be re-invented?, *National Public Radio*, http://www.npr.org/yourturn/ombudsman/010705.html

Edmonds R (2011) As blogs and citizen journalism grow, where's the news? *Poynter*, http://www.poynter.org/uncategorized/71962/as-blogs-and-citizen-journalism-grow-wheres-the-news/

Gillmor D.(2008, Jul 14th) Where did citizen journalist come from? Retrieved 12/6/2013 from http://citmedia.org/blog/2008/07/14/where-did-citizen-journalist-come-from/

Gahran, A. (2006, January 26) UK: New code of practice for witness contributors *IReport*. Retrieved http://www.ireporter.org/ethics/

Gahran, A. (2005, June 27). Objectivity, independence, and transparency: Three-legged stool? *IReport,* Retrieved 12/6/2014 http://www.ireporter.org/2005/06/objectivity_ind.html#more

Gahran, A. (2005, November 4) Open CitJ Sites: Why not require transparency?. *IReport*, http://www.ireporter.org/ethics/

Gaulin, P. (2007, April 27) Are ethics missing in citizen journalism? *Yahoo Contributor Network*, http://contributor.yahoo.com/user/14067/pam_gaulin.html

Glasor, M. (2004, November 17). The new voices: Hyperlocal citizen media sites want you *Online Journalism Review*

Idowu, L. (2012). Occupynigeria-Protesters-Take-On-News-Media-Covera: Comment. Retreived 9/2/2013 from http://www.cpj.org/blog/2012/01/occupynigeria-protesters-take-on-news-media-covera.php#comment-129441

In-Went capacity Building International (2009). Online journalism: opportunities and challenges for press freedom, *IIJ Alumni Review*, January 2009 - 2.02-0001-2009, Retrieved from http://www.inwent.org/iij

Keita, M. (2012). Occupy Nigeria protesters take on news media coverage. Retrieved 12/02/2012 from http://www.cpj.org/blog/2012/01/occupynigeria-protesters-take-on-news-media-covera.php (Accessed)

Kperogi F. (2011). Webs of Resistance: The Citizen Online Journalism of the Nigerian Digital Diaspora, the Department of Communication at Digital Archive @ GSU Retrieved 12/10/2012 from http://digitalarchive.gsu.edu/cgi/viewcontent.cgi?article=1027&context =communication_diss

Lasica, J. D. (2003). What is Participatory Journalism? *Online Journalism Review,* August 7, Retrieved from http://www.ojr.org/ojr/workplace/1060217106.php

Leach, J. (2009). Creating ethical bridges from journalism to digital news, *Nieman Report*. Retrieved 23/7/2013 from http://www.nieman.harvard.edu/reports/article/101899/Creating-Ethical-Bridges-From-Journalism-to--Digital-News.aspx

Mark Glaser (2006, September 27). Your Guide to Citizen Journalism. Public Broadcasting Service. Retrieved 12/10/2011 from http://www.pbs.org/mediashift/2006/09/your-guide-to-citizen-journalism270.html

Meyer, P. (1995) paper presented at IRE conference on computer assisted reporting in Cleveland in September 1995. Retrieved 12/10/2011 from http://www.unc.edu/~pmeyer/ire95pj.htm

Merritt, D. (2004, September 29). News media must regain vigor, courage., *PJNet Today*. Retrieved from http://pjnet.org/post/318/

Murdarasi, K. (2008). Aristotle's golden mean ethics: classic moral theory from the Nichomachean ethics. Retrieved 12/10/2011from http://karenmurdarasi.suite101.com/aristotle-golden-mean

Nairaland (2014). http://www.nairaland.com/1736351/abducted-chibok-girls-seen-central

Niles, R. (2007) What are the ethics of online journalism? *ORJ Online Journalism Review* . Retrieved from http://www.ojr.org/ojr/wiki/ethics/

Nnamani, C (2003) The Press and the Nigerian Project, A public lecture of the Newspaper Proprietors Association of Nigeria (NPAN) Diamond Hall, Golden Gate Restaurant, Ikoyi, Lagos. Thursday, 23rd October, Retrieved 2/6/2012 from http://www.dawodu.com/nnamani12.htm

Oak, M., (2011) Positive effect of the Media. Retrieved 25/5/2012 from

http://www.buzzle.com/articles/positive-effect-of-the-media.html

Olakitan,Y (2012) How New Media is affecting Traditional Journalism in

Nigeria, Retrieved 12/02/2012 from

http://www.twitterjournalism.com/tag/marriage/

OS Under Fender (2014). http://www.osundefender.org/?p=162522 ;

http://www.nigerianwatch.com/news/4377-us-marines-carry-out-first-

arrests-of-two-boko-haram-members-in-benue-state

Otufodunrin L. (2012) Occupynigeria-Protesters-Take-on-news-media-cover:

comments. Retrieved 12/10/2011 from:

http://www.cpj.org/blog/2012/01/occupynigeria-protesters-take-on-

news-media-covera.php#comment-129202

Rogers, T. (2011) Journalism and the Egyptian Uprising , *About.com*

Journalism. Retrieved 12/10/2011from

http://journalism.about.com/od/citizenjournalism/a/whatiscitizen.htm

Punch NG (2014). http://www.punchng.com/news/abducted-chibok-girls-

seen-in-central-africa/?;utm_source=twitterfeed&utm_medium=twitter ;

www.informationng.com/2014/05/us-marines-locate-kidnapped-school-

girls-in-sambisa.forest.html

Samson, K. (22nd April, 2011) The New Media And The Nigerian Citizen

Journalist. *Naijastories.com*, Retrieved 12/10/2011from

http://www.naijastories.com/2011/04/the-new-media-and-the-nigerian-citizen-journalist/

Zachary P. G. (2006) Truth or Consequences: The Future of the Journalist in America, Retrieved 12/02/2012 from

http://www.dvorak.org/blog/essays/zachary1.htm

Afterword

Jonathan Bishop

This book, '*Perspectives on the Information Society*,' has brought together several chapters that cover the latest trends in how our society is changing – and needs to change – because of increased use of the Internet for good and bad. The book is divided into three sections, which I will discuss in the order they are presented.

The first section, 'The Information Society,' looked broadly at the organisational and other issues affecting the information society today, including the Cloud and Internet trolling. Samuel Sudhakar, Anna Y Ni and Jake Zhu discuss how public bodies can move to the cloud based on a case study of migrating information systems in a public university. Sabiiti Mulema discussed the influence of electronic banking on the performing of a bank, namely Ecobank Burundi.

The chapter explores the various forms of banking available, including automated teller machines (ATMs) and electronic banking. It is quite clear from his study that electronic banking is going to have to move away from password-based approaches to security as it is increasingly the case according to him that paper-based money is giving way to an increasing demand from consumers for electronic services.

In the second section on 'Information Management and Data Misuse', Shefali Virkar discussed the impact of the Internet on transnational civil society networks, including unmasking the Anonymous Movement. Ashu M.G. Solo looked at disinformation online, including by the toxic online community Kiwi Farms, and by a discredited academic, namely Bhanu Prasad. His recommendation of allowing defamation cases to be heard in the small claims court could make it easier for members of the public affected by online misinformation an effective means to achieve a small amount of compensation for damages. In the United Kingdom this can in some cases be done through the Protection from Harassment Act 1997, which has a civil remedy available.

The third section, 'A United Kingdom Perspective', looks at how the information society operates in the UK, including in relation to cybercrime and other legal issues such as technology liability.

The first chapter by Ivan Mugabi looks at microchips law in the UK and animal liability Post-2016. Also in this section is a republished chapter by me, entitled 'Transforming the UK Home Office into a Department for Homeland Security: Reflecting on an Interview with a Litigant Defending Against Online Retaliatory Feedback in the US.' This chapter was approved for publication by the Journal of Homeland Security and Emergency Management, but was retracted after junior Canadian academic, Filippo Salustri objected to the publication of a graphic of an email he posted to the PHD-Design group in which he furthered the defamation of an academic conference. He asked for the article to be retracted on copyright grounds making this perhaps one of the first occasions a person has claimed copyright breach because they did not want to be identified the author of a work, rather than the reverse. With only a few minor changes the chapter is reproduced in full. It has particular relevance at the time of going to press, where the United Kingdom was going through constitutional change by leaving the European Union.

If there were to be a homeland security department in the UK, then it would make sense for all members of the armed forces to be accountable to it as reservists while they are stationed in the UK. It would equally make sense for the armed forces to be accountable to the Ministry of Defence (MOD) as regulars while they are serving overseas. However, if the international development and international aid functions of the UK government were to be put into the defence budget, a Ministry of Overseas Development (MOD) could be created so that when the armed forces are overseas they are as focused on developing the countries they are serving in as ending whatever it is that is causing war in them.

Spending international aid on members of the armed forces to provide human and other resources may be more effective than giving it to potentially corrupt governments or wasteful charities. It may also make sense for the Foreign and Commonwealth Office to be responsible for international trade and immigration, with the exception of illegal immigration, which the Home Office should retain.

The fourth section, 'An African Perspective' looked at freedom of expression, social media and citizen journalism as it exists in Africa today.

The chapters make an important contribution to understanding how Africa operates today and how some of the stereotypes used by charities and NGOs to persuade the public to donate to them may not be as relevant today as previously.

Jonathan Bishop

Centre for Research into Online Communities, E-Learning and Socialnomics

Local councillor for Cam East & Nantgarw and formerly Lower Cam, Treforest and Llantwit Fardre

Former parliamentary candidate for Liverpool Walton, Exeter and Pontypridd

Index

www.ingramcontent.com/pod-product-compliance
Lightning Source LLC
Chambersburg PA
CBHW062036050326
40690CB00016B/2957